# IN THE CATSKILLS
### AND
## MY BOYHOOD

New York Classics

# IN THE CATSKILLS
## AND
# MY BOYHOOD

## JOHN BURROUGHS

WITH A NEW INTRODUCTION BY EDWARD RENEHAN

AN IMPRINT OF STATE UNIVERSITY OF NEW YORK PRESS

Cover Image: John Burroughs at his cabin, "Slabsides," in 1901. Library of Congress.

*In the Catskills* was originally published in 1910 by Houghton Mifflin Company.

*My Boyhood* was originally published in 1922 by Doubleday, Page & Co.; small changes to spelling have been made in this new version.

A selection of the original photographs taken by Clifton Johnson is reprinted courtesy of the Jones Library, Inc., Amherst, Massachusetts.

Published by State University of New York Press, Albany

Introduction © 2021 State University of New York Press

All rights reserved

Printed in the United States of America

No part of this book may be used or reproduced in any manner whatsoever without written permission. No part of this book may be stored in a retrieval system or transmitted in any form or by any means including electronic, electrostatic, magnetic tape, mechanical, photocopying, recording, or otherwise without the prior permission in writing of the publisher.

Excelsior Editions is an imprint of State University of New York Press

For information, contact State University of New York Press, Albany, NY
www.sunypress.edu

Library of Congress Cataloging-in-Publication Data

Names: Burroughs, John, 1837–1921, author.
Title: In the Catskills and my boyhood / John Burroughs ; introduction by Edward Renehan.
Description: Albany : State University of New York Press, [2021] | Series: New York classics | In the Catskills was originally published in 1910 by Houghton Mifflin Company.
Identifiers: LCCN 2021000446 | ISBN 9781438485690 (hardcover : alk. paper) | ISBN 9781438485706 (pbk. : alk.paper) ISBN 9781438485713 (ebook)
Subjects: LCSH: Natural history—New York (State)—Catskill Mountains—Outdoor books. | Mountain life—Literary collections. | Catskill Mountains Region (N.Y.)—Literary collections.
Classification: LCC QH81 .B9355 2021 | DDC 508.747/38—dc23
LC record available at https://lccn.loc.gov/2021000446

10 9 8 7 6 5 4 3 2 1

# CONTENTS

| | |
|---|---|
| NEW INTRODUCTION<br>*Edward Renehan* | vii |
| IN THE CATSKILLS | xiii |
|     ILLUSTRATIONS | xvii |
|     INTRODUCTION | xix |
|     I. THE SNOW-WALKERS | 1 |
|     II. A WHITE DAY AND A RED FOX | 21 |
|     III. PHASES OF FARM LIFE | 31 |
|     IV. IN THE HEMLOCKS | 53 |
|     V. BIRDS'-NESTS | 77 |
|     VI. THE HEART OF THE SOUTHERN CATSKILLS | 101 |
|     VII. SPECKLED TROUT | 121 |
|     VIII. A BED OF BOUGHS | 143 |
| MY BOYHOOD | 163 |

# NEW INTRODUCTION

JOHN Burroughs had a special affinity for his native Catskills where he'd been born in 1837, in the town of Roxbury, and where he'd been raised along with his boyhood friend and neighbor, the future mogul and "robber baron" Jay Gould. Although as an adult he made his primary residence on a fruit farm—"Riverby," in the Hudson Valley village of West Park (part of the town of Esopus)—he returned to the nearby Catskills again and again throughout his life.[1] He even summered there in his later years in a cottage he called "Woodchuck Lodge," which sat on the edge of the old Burroughs family farm in the lap of the mountain known as "Old Clump."[2]

When he died in the spring of 1921, he was buried nearby, on his eighty-forth birthday, within a mile of the farm where he'd been born, still owned at the time by family members. His grave sits at the foot of a huge boulder—his "Boyhood Rock," as he called it—upon which he'd sat when a young man and first read the words of his great spiritual mentor Ralph Waldo Emerson.

Throughout his long life, Burroughs's literary output was prodigious: everything from nature essays to philosophical ruminations

---

[1] Burroughs established his farm Riverby, on the banks of the Hudson River, in 1874, and made this his primary residence for the rest of his life. In 1895 he built himself a small cabin retreat and secondary residence, Slabsides, about one mile inland from Riverby. The farm, although not cultivated, is still owned and occupied by Burroughs's descendants. Slabsides, preserved very much as Burroughs left it, sits in the middle of the John Burroughs Nature Sanctuary in the village of West Park. To get to the Sanctuary, watch for the New York State Historical Marker on 9W in the middle of the village, and there turn onto Park Lane, headed west. Make a right onto Floyd Ackert Road, cross the railroad tracks, and then proceed up a steep hill until you see the sign for the Sanctuary and Burroughs Drive on your left. The sanctuary and cabin are owned by the nonprofit John Burroughs Association, with offices at the American Museum of Natural History in Manhattan.

[2] Woodchuck Lodge is today carefully preserved by the nonprofit Woodchuck Lodge, Inc. To reach the house, take Route 30 into Roxbury and turn onto Hardscrabble Road, headed west, then left onto Burroughs Memorial Road. The house will be on your right and is clearly marked. Just a bit further on you will come to the John Burroughs Memorial Field, in which one can find his grave. Beyond this is the original Burroughs family homestead, now a commercial guesthouse.

to one of the first in-depth studies of his hero and close friend Walt Whitman. Regularly published in such national magazines as *The Atlantic*, his essays were also collected in some twenty-seven volumes published first by Boston's Hurd & Houghton and, later, by that firm's successor company Houghton Mifflin. As his reputation and sales grew through the years, the Boston firm sought out ways to maximize its return on its star author. It did this by repackaging previously published writings. Special editions of his works were bundled as readers for grade-school students.

In the same spirit, the Houghton editors cherry-picked what they considered to be the best of Burroughs's Catskill Mountain writings from his various books and gathered them to create *In the Catskills* in 1910. Part of the rationale for the publication was the ever-increasing popularity of John Burroughs as a "name." But another rationale was the growing interest in the Catskills as a place for vacation and recreation during the early years of the twentieth century. At this time, the famed Catskill Mountain House in Palenville, standing atop the Catskill High Peaks, drew more guests than ever at any time since its opening in 1824. Scenic destinations such as Kaaterskill Falls, which had in the mid-nineteenth century attracted Thomas Cole and other painters of the Hudson River School, now drew hordes of tourists from Manhattan and elsewhere. Hudson River steamers did a brisk business bringing passengers up the river to the dock at Catskill, New York, from which they were then carried by coach and rail into the nether reaches of the Catskills peaks. The attraction was pure scenic beauty and fresh mountain air. The attraction, in other words, was *nature*. In this regard, Burroughs in his time was the region's greatest advocate and proselytizer. As one of Burroughs's acquaintances commented: "God made the Catskills; [Washington] Irving put them on the map; but it is John Burroughs who has brought them home to us."[3]

Burroughs had deep roots in the Catskills. Three generations of his family before him had worked the "home farm," as he always called it. His attachment to the place and its setting was profound. As he would write in an essay composed at Woodchuck Lodge:

> The boon is mine when I go to my little gray farmhouse on a broad hill slope on the home farm in the Catskills. Especially is it mine when, to get still nearer nature . . . I retreat to the big hay-barn, and on an improvised table in front of the big open barn doors, looking out into the sunlit fields where I hoed corn or made hay as a boy, I write this and other papers.

---

[3] T. Morris Longstreth, *The Catskills* (New York: Century, 1918), 238.

# IN THE CATSKILLS

The peace of the hills is about me and upon me, and the leisure of the summer clouds, whose shadows I see slowly drifting across the face of the landscape, is mine. . . .

    In the circuit of the hills, the days take form and character as they do not in town, or in a country of low horizons. . . . This is especially true in hilly and mountainous country, where the eye has a great depth of perspective opened to it. . . . The deep, cradle-like valleys, and the long-flowing mountain lines, make a fit receptacle for the day's beauty; they hold and accumulate it, as it were.[4]

None other than Henry James once described Burroughs as "a more humorous, more available and more sociable Thoreau. The minuteness of Burroughs's observation, the keenness of his perception, give him a real originality, and his sketches have a delightful oddity, vivacity, and freshness."[5] This is particularly true with regard to Burroughs's memoirs of his rambles on Wittenberg and Slide Mountains (as recounted here in the essay "In The Heart of Southern Catskills"), his treks up Hardscrabble Creek and other such waters in various piscatorial adventures (as recorded in the essay "Speckled Trout"), as well as his sojourns around and about Peakamoose Mountain and the valley of the Rondout Creek, combining hiking with fishing (see the essay "A Bed of Boughs").

In these and other essays, Burroughs's prose is what I would call "participatory." He is not dryly informing his reader of sights seen and natural occurrences observed so much as he is inviting his reader to come along and walk with him on a hike across the ridge from Wittenberg to Slide, or on a quest for trout, after which the reader sits by the fire with Burroughs devouring the fresh-cooked catch of the day. One can smell the wood smoke, taste the fish, hear the summer cicadas. There is a freshness and levity to Burroughs's accounts of his adventures, along with an assumed comradeship and kinship with the reader. In other words, Burroughs's prose is an invitation to fully partake: to follow Burroughs into the mountains and woodlands, either literally or vicariously.

Burroughs's Catskills writings contain a great deal of nostalgia: for his boyhood, for family and friends long passed, and for a vanishing way of life. Burroughs wrote: "These hills fathered and mothered me. I am blood of their blood and bone of their bone."[6] He once told his longtime secretary and confidante Clara Barrus that he was afflicted

---

  [4] John Burroughs, *The Summit of the Years* (Boston: Houghton Mifflin, 1913), 25. Note: The hay barn no longer stands
  [5] Henry James, "A Note on John Burroughs," *The Nation*, January 1876, 66.
  [6] Clara Barrus, *The Life and Letters of John Burroughs*, vol. 2 (Boston: Houghton Mifflin, 1925), 159.

by a "homesickness which home cannot cure." His hunger, he said, was a "hunger of the imagination. Bring all my dead back to me, and place me amid them in the old home, and a vague longing and regret would still possess me."[7]

The one thing that remained constant for him was the landscape: the view across the valley to the blue mountains beyond, the woods and creeks and peaks he celebrated so eloquently. The terrain was the one thing he could hold onto, the one thing that never subsided or retreated or died. He was tethered to it. As he would write in his essay, "A Sharp Lookout": "One's own landscape comes in time to be a sort of outlying part of himself; he has sowed himself broadcast upon it; and it reflects his own moods and feelings; he is sensitive to the verge of the horizon; cut those trees, and he bleeds; mar those hills, and he suffers."[8]

Burroughs's nostalgia is especially present in the beautiful slice of writing newly added for this edition of *In the Catskills*. Burroughs wrote *My Boyhood* in 1913 as a personal memoir for his son Julian. It was not intended for publication. Nevertheless, Julian saw to its publication by Doubleday, Page & Co. in 1922, one year after his father's death. He paired it with an essay of his own entitled "My Father." In *My Boyhood*, Burroughs dives deep into his well of memory. Here he recounts his life growing up on the family's Catskills dairy farm, his adventures with other boys of the neighborhood (including Jay Gould), the work of maple sugaring in the springtime, and his first experience beyond the mountains—as a boy accompanying his father down to the distant river port of Catskill with a wagonload of cheese.

Today Burroughs's presence remains strong in the Catskills, not just at his grave or at his carefully preserved Woodchuck Lodge, but also elsewhere. His three favorite mountains for hiking and climbing—Wittenberg, Slide, and Cornell—are now called the "Burroughs Range" in his honor. On a ledge at the top of Slide, the highest peak of the Catskills, a plaque reads:

IN MEMORIAM

JOHN BURROUGHS

WHO IN HIS EARLY WRITING INTRODUCED SLIDE

MOUNTAIN TO THE WORLD. HE MADE MANY VISITS TO

THIS PEAK AND SLEPT SEVERAL NIGHTS BENEATH THIS

ROCK. THIS REGION IS THE SCENE OF MANY OF HIS ESSAYS.

"HERE THE WORKS OF MAN DWINDLE" IN THE

HEART OF THE SOUTHERN CATSKILLS.[9]

---

[7] Clara Barrus, *Our Friend John Burroughs* (Boston: Houghton Mifflin, 1914), 196.
[8] John Burroughs, *Signs and Seasons* (Boston: Houghton Mifflin, 1886), 3.
[9] This plaque was installed by the Winnisook Club not long after Burroughs's death.

## IN THE CATSKILLS

During the years I spent researching my book *John Burroughs: An American Naturalist*, I made a point of trekking all the trails that Burroughs had noted in his writings, walking in his footsteps, as it were.[10] I remember being astonished by the accuracy of his descriptions even seven decades after his death. Many of the trails upon which Burroughs trod still exist, including those upon which he walked during his ascents of Wittenberg and Slide. I recall taking an ancient and beat-up copy of *In the Catskills* with me up to the summit of Slide, and there sitting and reading Burroughs's narrative of his sojourn there. The bond I felt with him became more and more profound as I read his words while leaning against the ledge of which he'd written and taking in the view he'd sought to celebrate.

My hope is that readers of this edition will likewise consider Burroughs's words an invitation to explore and relish a region Burroughs rightly believed to be among the most beautiful on earth.

*Edward Renehan, Wickford, RI*

---

[10] Edward Renehan, *John Burroughs: An American Naturalist* (Hensonville, New York: Black Dome Press, 1998).

# IN THE CATSKILLS

SELECTIONS FROM THE WRITINGS OF

## JOHN BURROUGHS

WITH
ILLUSTRATIONS FROM PHOTOGRAPHS
BY CLIFTON JOHNSON

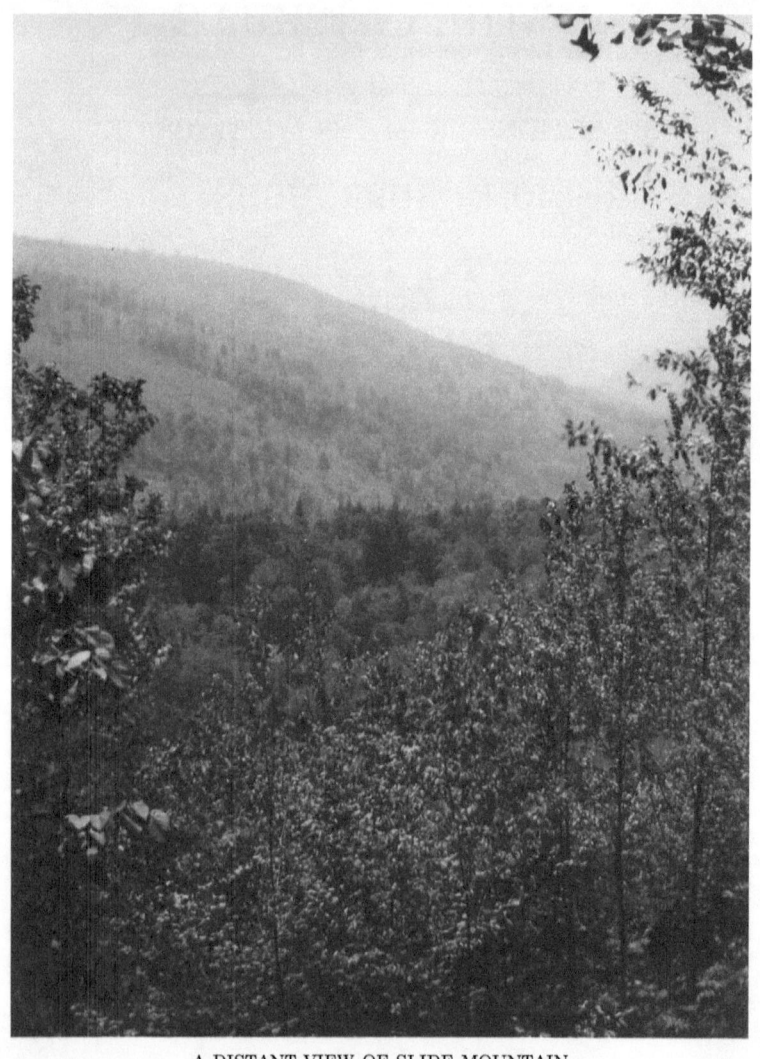

A DISTANT VIEW OF SLIDE MOUNTAIN
The highest of the Catskills

# CONTENTS

| | |
|---|---|
| ILLUSTRATIONS | xvii |
| INTRODUCTION | xix |
| I. THE SNOW-WALKERS | 3 |
| II. A WHITE DAY AND A RED FOX | 23 |
| III. PHASES OF FARM LIFE | 33 |
| IV. IN THE HEMLOCKS | 55 |
| V. BIRDS'-NESTS | 79 |
| VI. THE HEART OF THE SOUTHERN CATSKILLS | 103 |
| VII. SPECKLED TROUT | 123 |
| VIII. A BED OF BOUGHS | 145 |

# ILLUSTRATIONS

| | |
|---|---:|
| A Distant View Of Slide Mountain<br>    The highest of the Catskills | *Frontispiece* |
| The Stone Walls Buried by the Drifts<br>    Showing Mr. Burroughs's boyhood home | 5 |
| At the Edge of the Woods | 10 |
| The Chopper in the Woods | 15 |
| The Downlook from a High Hillside | 24 |
| The Fox-Hunter and his Hound | 28 |
| The Cows at the Pasture Bars | 34 |
| A Mower | 39 |
| Haying | 45 |
| Cattle at the Spring under the Hill | 47 |
| Waiting for the Cows | 51 |
| At the Headwaters of the Delaware<br>    Overlooking Mr. Burroughs's boyhood home | 57 |
| Hemlocks | 62 |
| A Trout Stream | 66 |
| Finding a Bird's-Nest | 80 |
| In a Sheep Pasture | 87 |
| One of Mr. Burroughs's Favorite Places of Observation | 93 |

## ILLUSTRATIONS

| | |
|---|---:|
| The Wittenberg from Woodland Valley | 105 |
| Larkins's Humble Dwelling | 117 |
| The Farm Boy | 125 |
| A Settler's House | 136 |
| The Beaverkill | 139 |
| Stopping for Food at the House of a Settler | 151 |
| Some People of the Catskills | 159 |

# INTRODUCTION

THE eight essays in this volume all deal with the home region of their author; for not only did Mr. Burroughs begin life in the Catskills, and dwell among them until early manhood, but, as he himself declares, he has never taken root anywhere else. Their delectable heights and valleys have engaged his deepest affections as far as locality is concerned, and however widely he journeys and whatever charms he discovers in nature elsewhere, still the loveliness of those pastoral boyhood uplands is unsurpassed.

The ancestral farm is in Roxbury among the western Catskills, where the mountains are comparatively gentle in type and always graceful in contour. Cultivated fields and sunny pastures cling to their mighty slopes far up toward the summits, there are patches of woodland including frequent groves of sugar maples, and there are apple orchards and winding roadways, and endless lines of rude stone fences, and scattered dwellings. In every hollow runs a clear trout brook, with its pools and swift shallows and silvery falls. Birds and other wild creatures abound; for the stony earth and the ledges that crop out along the hillsides, the thickets and forest patches, the sheltered glens and windy heights offer great variety in domicile to animal life. The creatures of the outdoor world are much in evidence, and at no time do their numbers impress one more than when in winter one sees the handwriting of their tracks on the snow.

The work on the farm and the workers are genuinely rustic, but not nearly so primitive as in the times that Mr. Burroughs most enjoys recalling. Oxen are of the past, the mowing-machine goes over the fields where formerly he labored with his scythe, stacks at which the cattle pull in the winter time are a rarity, and the gray old barns have given place to modern red ones. It is a dairy country, and on every farm is found a large herd of cows; but the milk goes to the creameries. The women, however, still share in the milking, and there is much of unaffected simplicity in the ways of the household. On days when work is not pushing, the men are likely to go hunting or fishing, and they are always alert to observe

# INTRODUCTION

chances to take advantage of those little gratuities which nature in the remoter rural regions is constantly offering, both in the matter of game and in that of herbs and roots, berries and nuts.

Mr. Burroughs's old home has continued in the family, and the house and its surroundings have in many ways continued essentially unaltered ever since he can remember. What is most important—the wide-reaching view down the vales and across to the ridges that rise height on height until they blend with the sky in the ethereal distance, is just what it always has been.

That the Catskills have proved an inspiration to Mr. Burroughs cannot be doubted. Possibly we should never have had him as a nature writer at all, had he spent his impressible youthful years in a less favored locality. It is, however, a curious fact that the town which produced this lover of nature also produced one other man of national fame, who was as different from him as could well be imagined. I refer to Jay Gould. He was born in the same town and in the same part of the town, went to the same school, saw the same scenes, was a farm boy like Burroughs, and had practically the same experiences. Indeed, the two were a good deal together. But how different their later lives! It seems easy to grant that environment helped make the one; but what effect, if any, did that beautiful Catskill country have on the other?

There are two seasons of the year when Mr. Burroughs is particularly fond of getting back to his old home. The first is in sap-time, when maple sugar is being made in the little shack on the borders of the rock-maple grove. The second is in midsummer, when haying is in progress. Both occasions have exceptional power for arousing pleasant memories of the past, though such memories have also their touch of sadness. In his early years he helped materially in the farm work while on these visits; but latterly he gives his time to rambling and contemplation. He once said to me, in speaking of a neighbor: "That man hasn't a lazy bone in his body. But I have lots of 'em—lots of 'em."

This affirmation is not to be interpreted too literally. He has made a business success in raising small fruits, and his literary output has been by no means meagre. I might also mention that in youth he was something of a champion at swinging the scythe, and few could mow as much in the course of a day. But certainly labor is no fetich of his, and he has a real genius for loafing. In another man his leisurely rambling with its pauses to rest on rock or grassy bank or fallen tree, his mind meanwhile absolutely free from the feeling that he ought to be up and doing, might be shiftlessness. But how else could he have acquired his delightful intimacy with the woods

## INTRODUCTION

and fields and streams, and with wild life in all its moods? Surely most of our hustling, untiring workers would be better off if they had some of this same ability to cast aside care and responsibility and get back to Nature—the good mother of us all.

CLIFTON JOHNSON.

*Hadley, Mass., 1910.*

NOTE.—The pictures in this volume were all made in the Catskills and are the results of several trips to the regions described in the essays.

# I
## THE SNOW-WALKERS

# IN THE CATSKILLS

## I

### THE SNOW-WALKERS

HE who marvels at the beauty of the world in summer will find equal cause for wonder and admiration in winter. It is true the pomp and the pageantry are swept away, but the essential elements remain,—the day and the night, the mountain and the valley, the elemental play and succession and the perpetual presence of the infinite sky. In winter the stars seem to have rekindled their fires, the moon achieves a fuller triumph, and the heavens wear a look of a more exalted simplicity. Summer is more wooing and seductive, more versatile and human, appeals to the affections and the sentiments, and fosters inquiry and the art impulse. Winter is of a more heroic cast, and addresses the intellect. The severe studies and disciplines come easier in winter. One imposes larger tasks upon himself, and is less tolerant of his own weaknesses.

The tendinous part of the mind, so to speak, is more developed in winter; the fleshy, in summer. I should say winter had given the bone and sinew to Literature, summer the tissues and blood.

The simplicity of winter has a deep moral. The return of nature, after such a career of splendor and prodigality, to habits so simple and austere, is not lost either upon the head or the heart. It is the philosopher coming back from the banquet and the wine to a cup of water and a crust of bread.

And then this beautiful masquerade of the elements,—the novel disguises our nearest friends put on! Here is another rain and another dew, water that will not flow, nor spill, nor receive the taint of an unclean vessel. And if we see truly, the same old beneficence and willingness to serve lurk beneath all.

Look up at the miracle of the falling snow,—the air a dizzy maze of whirling, eddying flakes, noiselessly transforming the world, the exquisite crystals dropping in ditch and gutter, and disguising in the same suit of spotless livery all objects upon which they fall. How novel and fine the first drifts! The old, dilapidated fence is suddenly set off with the most fantastic ruffles, scalloped and fluted after an unheard-of fashion! Looking down a long line of decrepit stone wall, in the trimming of which the wind had fairly run riot, I saw, as for the first time, what a severe yet master artist old Winter is. Ah, a severe artist! How stern the woods look, dark and cold and as rigid against the horizon as iron!

All life and action upon the snow have an added emphasis and significance. Every expression is underscored. Summer has few finer pictures than this winter one of the farmer foddering his cattle from a stack upon the clean snow,—the movement, the sharply defined figures, the great green flakes of hay, the long file of patient cows, the advance just arriving and pressing eagerly for the choicest morsels, and the bounty and providence it suggests. Or the chopper in the woods,—the prostrate tree, the white new chips scattered about, his easy triumph over the cold, his coat hanging to a limb, and the clear, sharp ring of his axe. The woods are rigid and tense, keyed up by the frost, and resound like a stringed instrument. Or the road-breakers, sallying forth with oxen and sleds in the still, white world, the day after the storm, to restore the lost track and demolish the beleaguering drifts.

All sounds are sharper in winter; the air transmits better. At night I hear more distinctly the steady roar of the North Mountain. In summer it is a sort of complacent purr, as the breezes stroke down its sides; but in winter always the same low, sullen growl.

A severe artist! No longer the canvas and the pigments, but the marble and the chisel. When the nights are calm and the moon full, I go out to gaze upon the wonderful purity of the moonlight and the snow. The air is full of latent fire, and the cold warms me—after a different fashion from that of the kitchen stove. The world lies about me in a "trance of snow." The clouds are pearly and iridescent, and seem the farthest possible remove from the condition of a storm,—the ghosts of clouds, the indwelling beauty freed from all dross. I see the hills, bulging with great drifts, lift themselves up cold and white against the sky, the black lines of fences here and there obliterated by the depth of the snow. Presently a fox barks away up next the mountain, and I imagine I can almost see him sitting there, in his furs, upon the illuminated surface, and looking down in my direction. As I listen, one answers him from behind the woods in the valley. What a wild winter sound, wild and weird, up among the ghostly hills! Since the wolf has ceased to howl upon these mountains, and the panther to scream, there is nothing to be compared with it. So wild! I get up in the middle of the night to

THE STONE WALLS BURIED BY THE DRIFTS
Showing Mr. Burroughs's boyhood home

hear it. It is refreshing to the ear, and one delights to know that such wild creatures are among us. At this season Nature makes the most of every throb of life that can withstand her severity. How heartily she indorses this fox! In what bold relief stand out the lives of all walkers of the snow! The snow is a great tell-tale, and blabs as effectually as it obliterates. I go into the woods, and know all that has happened. I cross the fields, and if only a mouse has visited his neighbor, the fact is chronicled.

The red fox is the only species that abounds in my locality; the little gray fox seems to prefer a more rocky and precipitous country, and a less rigorous climate; the cross fox is occasionally seen, and there are traditions of the silver gray among the oldest hunters. But the red fox is the sportsman's prize, and the only fur-bearer worthy of note in these mountains.[1] I go out in the morning, after a fresh fall of snow, and see at all points where he has crossed the road. Here he has leisurely passed within rifle-range of the house, evidently reconnoitring the premises with an eye to the hen-roost. That clear, sharp track,—there is no mistaking it for the clumsy footprint of a little dog. All his wildness and agility are photographed in it. Here he has taken fright, or suddenly recollected an engagement, and in long, graceful leaps, barely touching the fence, has gone careering up the hill as fleet as the wind.

The wild, buoyant creature, how beautiful he is! I had often seen his dead carcass, and at a distance had witnessed the hounds drive him across the upper fields; but the thrill and excitement of meeting him in his wild freedom in the woods were unknown to me till, one cold winter day, drawn thither by the baying of a hound, I stood near the summit of the mountain, waiting a renewal of the sound, that I might determine the course of the dog and choose my position,—stimulated by the ambition of all young Nimrods to bag some notable game. Long I waited, and patiently, till, chilled and benumbed, I was about to turn back, when, hearing a slight noise, I looked up and beheld a most superb fox, loping along with inimitable grace and ease, evidently disturbed, but not pursued by the hound, and so absorbed in his private meditations that he failed to see me, though I stood transfixed with amazement and admiration, not ten yards distant. I took his measure at a glance,—a large male, with dark legs, and massive tail tipped with white,—a most magnificent creature; but so astonished and fascinated was I by this sudden appearance and matchless beauty, that not till I had caught the last glimpse of him, as he disappeared over a knoll, did I awake to my duty as a sportsman, and realize what an opportunity to distinguish

---

[1] A spur of the Catskills.

myself I had unconsciously let slip. I clutched my gun, half angrily, as if it was to blame, and went home out of humor with myself and all fox-kind. But I have since thought better of the experience, and concluded that I bagged the game after all, the best part of it, and fleeced Reynard of something more valuable than his fur, without his knowledge.

This is thoroughly a winter sound,—this voice of the hound upon the mountain,—and one that is music to many ears. The long trumpet-like bay, heard for a mile or more,—now faintly back in the deep recesses of the mountain,—now distinct, but still faint, as the hound comes over some prominent point and the wind favors,—anon entirely lost in the gully,—then breaking out again much nearer, and growing more and more pronounced as the dog approaches, till, when he comes around the brow of the mountain, directly above you, the barking is loud and sharp. On he goes along the northern spur, his voice rising and sinking as the wind and the lay of the ground modify it, till lost to hearing.

The fox usually keeps half a mile ahead, regulating his speed by that of the hound, occasionally pausing a moment to divert himself with a mouse, or to contemplate the landscape, or to listen for his pursuer. If the hound press him too closely, he leads off from mountain to mountain, and so generally escapes the hunter; but if the pursuit be slow, he plays about some ridge or peak, and falls a prey, though not an easy one, to the experienced sportsman.

A most spirited and exciting chase occurs when the farm-dog gets close upon one in the open field, as sometimes happens in the early morning. The fox relies so confidently upon his superior speed, that I imagine he half tempts the dog to the race. But if the dog be a smart one, and their course lies down-hill, over smooth ground, Reynard must put his best foot forward, and then sometimes suffer the ignominy of being run over by his pursuer, who, however, is quite unable to pick him up, owing to the speed. But when they mount the hill, or enter the woods, the superior nimbleness and agility of the fox tell at once, and he easily leaves the dog far in his rear. For a cur less than his own size he manifests little fear, especially if the two meet alone, remote from the house. In such cases, I have seen first one turn tail, then the other.

A novel spectacle often occurs in summer, when the female has young. You are rambling on the mountain, accompanied by your dog, when you are startled by that wild, half-threatening squall, and in a moment perceive your dog, with inverted tail, and shame and confusion in his looks, sneaking toward you, the old fox but a few rods in his rear. You speak to him sharply, when he bristles up, turns about, and, barking, starts off vigorously, as if to wipe out the dishonor; but in a moment comes sneaking back more abashed than ever, and owns himself unworthy to be called a dog. The fox fairly shames him out of the woods. The secret of the matter is her sex, though her conduct, for the honor of the fox be it said, seems to be prompted only by solicitude for the safety of her young.

One of the most notable features of the fox is his large and massive tail. Seen running on the snow at a distance, his tail is quite as conspicuous as his body; and, so far from appearing a burden, seems to contribute to his lightness and buoyancy. It softens the outline of his movements, and repeats or continues to the eye the ease and poise of his carriage. But, pursued by the hound on a wet, thawy day, it often becomes so heavy and bedraggled as to prove a serious inconvenience, and compels him to take refuge in his den. He is very loath to do this; both his pride and the traditions of his race stimulate him to run it out, and win by fair superiority of wind and speed; and only a wound or a heavy and moppish tail will drive him to avoid the issue in this manner.

To learn his surpassing shrewdness and cunning, attempt to take him with a trap. Rogue that he is, he always suspects some trick, and one must be more of a fox than he is himself to overreach him. At first sight it would appear easy enough. With apparent indifference he crosses your path, or walks in your footsteps in the field, or travels along the beaten highway, or lingers in the vicinity of stacks and remote barns. Carry the carcass of a pig, or a fowl, or a dog, to a distant field in midwinter, and in a few nights his tracks cover the snow about it.

The inexperienced country youth, misled by this seeming carelessness of Reynard, suddenly conceives a project to enrich himself with fur, and wonders that the idea has not occurred to him before, and to others. I knew a youthful yeoman of this kind, who imagined he had found a mine of wealth on discovering on a remote side-hill, between two woods, a dead porker, upon which it appeared all the foxes of the neighborhood had nightly banqueted. The clouds were burdened with snow; and as the first flakes commenced to eddy down, he set out, trap and broom in hand, already counting over in imagination the silver quarters he would receive for his first fox-skin. With the utmost care, and with a palpitating heart, he removed enough of the trodden snow to allow the trap to sink below the surface. Then, carefully sifting the light element over it and sweeping his tracks full, he quickly withdrew, laughing exultingly over the little surprise he had prepared for the cunning rogue. The elements conspired to aid him, and the falling snow rapidly obliterated all vestiges of his work. The next morning at dawn he was on his way to bring in his fur. The snow had done its work effectually, and, he believed, had kept his secret well. Arrived in sight of the locality, he strained his vision to make out his prize lodged against the fence at the foot of the hill. Approaching nearer, the surface was unbroken, and doubt usurped the place of certainty in his mind. A slight mound marked the site of the porker, but there was no footprint near it. Looking up the hill, he saw where Reynard had walked leisurely down toward his wonted bacon till within a few yards of it, when he had wheeled, and with prodigious strides disappeared in the woods. The young trapper saw at a glance what a comment this was upon his skill in the art, and, indignantly exhuming the iron, he walked home with it, the stream of silver quarters suddenly setting in another direction.

The successful trapper commences in the fall, or before the first deep snow. In a field not too remote, with an old axe he cuts a small place, say ten inches by fourteen, in the frozen ground, and removes the earth to the depth of three or four inches, then fills the cavity with dry ashes, in which are placed bits of roasted cheese. Reynard is very suspicious at first, and gives the place a wide berth. It looks like design, and he will see how the thing behaves before he approaches too near. But the cheese is savory and the cold severe. He ventures a little closer every night, until he can reach and pick a piece from the surface. Emboldened by success, like other mortals, he presently digs freely among the ashes, and, finding a fresh supply of the delectable morsels every night, is soon thrown off his guard and his suspicions quite lulled. After a week of baiting in this manner, and on the eve of a light fall of snow, the trapper carefully conceals his trap in the bed, first smoking it thoroughly with hemlock boughs to kill or neutralize the smell of the iron. If the weather favors and the proper precautions have been taken, he may succeed, though the chances are still greatly against him.

Reynard is usually caught very lightly, seldom more than the ends of his toes being between the jaws. He sometimes works so cautiously as to spring the trap without injury even to his toes, or may remove the cheese night after night without even springing it. I knew an old trapper who, on finding himself outwitted in this manner, tied a bit of cheese to the pan, and next morning had poor Reynard by the jaw. The trap is not fastened, but only encumbered with a clog, and is all the more sure in its hold by yielding to every effort of the animal to extricate himself.

When Reynard sees his captor approaching, he would fain drop into a mouse-hole to render himself invisible. He crouches to the ground and remains perfectly motionless until he perceives himself discovered, when he makes one desperate and final effort to escape, but ceases all struggling as you come up, and behaves in a manner

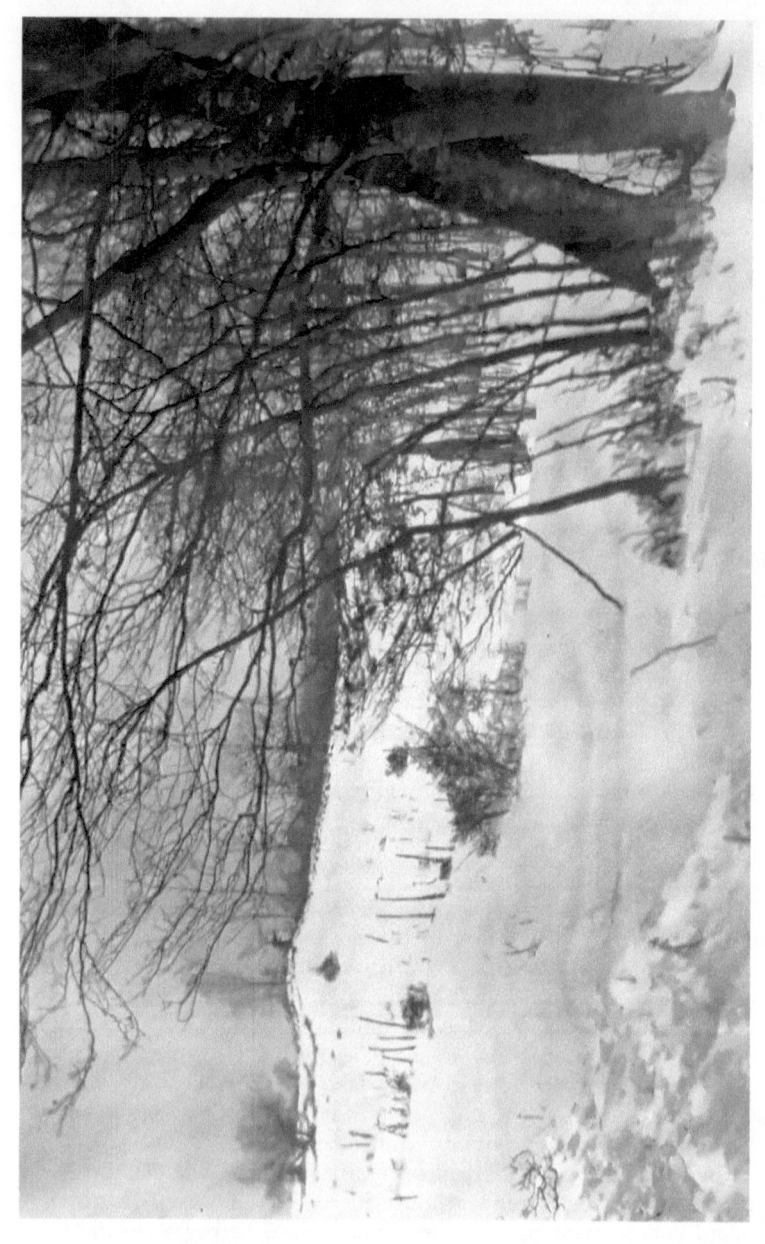

AT THE EDGE OF THE WOODS

## THE SNOW-WALKERS

that stamps him a very timid warrior,—cowering to the earth with a mingled look of shame, guilt, and abject fear. A young farmer told me of tracing one with his trap to the border of a wood, where he discovered the cunning rogue trying to hide by embracing a small tree. Most animals, when taken in a trap, show fight; but Reynard has more faith in the nimbleness of his feet than in the terror of his teeth.

Entering the woods, the number and variety of the tracks contrast strongly with the rigid, frozen aspect of things. Warm jets of life still shoot and play amid this snowy desolation. Fox-tracks are far less numerous than in the fields; but those of hares, skunks, partridges, squirrels, and mice abound. The mice tracks are very pretty, and look like a sort of fantastic stitching on the coverlid of the snow. One is curious to know what brings these tiny creatures from their retreats; they do not seem to be in quest of food, but rather to be traveling about for pleasure or sociability, though always going post-haste, and linking stump with stump and tree with tree by fine, hurried strides. That is when they travel openly; but they have hidden passages and winding galleries under the snow, which undoubtedly are their main avenues of communication. Here and there these passages rise so near the surface as to be covered by only a frail arch of snow, and a slight ridge betrays their course to the eye. I know him well. He is known to the farmer as the "deer mouse," to the naturalist as the white-footed mouse,—a very beautiful creature, nocturnal in his habits, with large ears, and large, fine eyes, full of a wild, harmless look. He is daintily marked, with white feet and a white belly. When disturbed by day he is very easily captured, having none of the cunning or viciousness of the common Old World mouse.

It is he who, high in the hollow trunk of some tree, lays by a store of beechnuts for winter use. Every nut is carefully shelled, and the cavity that serves as storehouse lined with grass and leaves. The wood-chopper frequently squanders this precious store. I have seen half a peck taken from one tree, as clean and white as if put up by the most delicate hands,—as they were. How long it must have taken the little creature to collect this quantity, to hull them one by one, and convey them up to his fifth-story chamber! He is not confined to the woods, but is quite as common in the fields, particularly in the fall, amid the corn and potatoes. When routed by the plow, I have seen the old one take flight with half a dozen young hanging to her teats, and with such reckless speed that some of the young would lose their hold and fly off amid the weeds. Taking refuge in a stump with the rest of her family, the anxious mother would presently come back and hunt up the missing ones.

The snow-walkers are mostly night-walkers also, and the record they leave upon the snow is the main clew one has to their life and doings. The hare is nocturnal in its habits, and though a very lively creature at night, with regular courses and run-ways through the wood, is entirely quiet by day. Timid as he is, he makes little effort to conceal himself, usually squatting beside a log, stump, or tree, and seeming to avoid rocks and ledges where he might be partially housed from the cold and the snow, but where also—and this consideration undoubtedly determines his choice—he would be more apt to fall a prey to his enemies. In this, as well as in many other respects, he differs from the rabbit proper: he never burrows in the ground, or takes refuge in a den or hole, when pursued. If caught in the open fields, he is much confused and easily overtaken by the dog; but in the woods, he leaves him at a bound. In summer, when first disturbed, he beats the ground violently with his feet, by which means he would express to you his surprise or displeasure; it is a dumb way he has of scolding. After leaping a few yards, he pauses an instant, as if to determine the degree of danger, and then hurries away with a much lighter tread.

His feet are like great pads, and his track has little of the sharp, articulated expression of Reynard's, or of animals that climb or dig. Yet it is very pretty like all the rest, and tells its own tale. There is nothing bold or vicious or vulpine in it, and his timid, harmless character is published at every leap. He abounds in dense woods, preferring localities filled with a small undergrowth of beech and birch, upon the bark of which he feeds. Nature is rather partial to him, and matches his extreme local habits and character with a suit that corresponds with his surroundings,—reddish gray in summer and white in winter.

The sharp-rayed track of the partridge adds another figure to this fantastic embroidery upon the winter snow. Her course is a clear, strong line, sometimes quite wayward, but generally very direct, steering for the densest, most impenetrable places,—leading you over logs and through brush, alert and expectant, till, suddenly, she bursts up a few yards from you, and goes humming through the trees,—the complete triumph of endurance and vigor. Hardy native bird, may your tracks never be fewer, or your visits to the birch-tree less frequent!

The squirrel tracks—sharp, nervous, and wiry—have their histories also. But how rarely we see squirrels in winter! The naturalists say they are mostly torpid; yet evidently that little pocket-faced depredator, the chipmunk, was not carrying buckwheat for so many

## THE SNOW-WALKERS

days to his hole for nothing: was he anticipating a state of torpidity, or providing against the demands of a very active appetite? Red and gray squirrels are more or less active all winter, though very shy, and, I am inclined to think, partially nocturnal in their habits. Here a gray one has just passed,—came down that tree and went up this; there he dug for a beechnut, and left the burr on the snow. How did he know where to dig? During an unusually severe winter I have known him to make long journeys to a barn, in a remote field, where wheat was stored. How did he know there was wheat there? In attempting to return, the adventurous creature was frequently run down and caught in the deep snow.

His home is in the trunk of some old birch or maple, with an entrance far up amid the branches. In the spring he builds himself a summer-house of small leafy twigs in the top of a neighboring beech, where the young are reared and much of the time is passed. But the safer retreat in the maple is not abandoned, and both old and young resort thither in the fall, or when danger threatens. Whether this temporary residence amid the branches is for elegance or pleasure, or for sanitary reasons or domestic convenience, the naturalist has forgotten to mention.

The elegant creature, so cleanly in its habits, so graceful in its carriage, so nimble and daring in its movements, excites feelings of admiration akin to those awakened by the birds and the fairer forms of nature. His passage through the trees is almost a flight. Indeed, the flying squirrel has little or no advantage over him, and in speed and nimbleness cannot compare with him at all. If he miss his footing and fall, he is sure to catch on the next branch; if the connection be broken, he leaps recklessly for the nearest spray or limb, and secures his hold, even if it be by the aid of his teeth.

His career of frolic and festivity begins in the fall, after the birds have left us and the holiday spirit of nature has commenced to subside. How absorbing the pastime of the sportsman who goes to the woods in the still October morning in quest of him! You step lightly across the threshold of the forest, and sit down upon the first log or rock to await the signals. It is so still that the ear suddenly seems to have acquired new powers, and there is no movement to confuse the eye. Presently you hear the rustling of a branch, and see it sway or spring as the squirrel leaps from or to it; or else you hear a disturbance in the dry leaves, and mark one running upon the ground. He has probably seen the intruder, and, not liking his stealthy movements, desires to avoid a nearer acquaintance. Now he mounts a stump to see if the way is clear, then pauses a moment at the foot of a tree to take his bearings, his tail, as he skims along, undulating behind him, and adding to the easy grace and dignity of his movements. Or else you are first advised of his proximity by the dropping of a false nut, or the fragments of the shucks rattling upon the leaves. Or, again, after contemplating you awhile unobserved, and making up his mind that you are not dangerous, he strikes an attitude on a branch, and commences to quack and bark, with an accompanying movement of his tail. Late in the afternoon, when the same stillness reigns, the same scenes are repeated. There is a black variety, quite rare, but mating freely with the gray, from which he seems to be distinguished only in color.

The track of the red squirrel may be known by its smaller size. He is more common and less dignified than the gray, and oftener guilty of petty larceny about the barns and grain-fields. He is most abundant in old barkpeelings, and low, dilapidated hemlocks, from which he makes excursions to the fields and orchards, spinning along the tops of the fences, which afford not only convenient lines of communication, but a safe retreat if danger threatens. He loves to linger about the orchard; and, sitting upright on the topmost stone in the wall, or on the tallest stake in the fence, chipping up an apple for the seeds, his tail conforming to the curve of his back, his paws shifting and turning the apple, he is a pretty sight, and his bright, pert appearance atones for all the mischief he does. At home, in the woods, he is the most frolicsome and loquacious. The appearance of anything unusual, if, after contemplating it a moment, he concludes it not dangerous, excites his unbounded mirth and ridicule, and he snickers and chatters, hardly able to contain himself; now darting up the trunk of a tree and squealing in derision, then hopping into position on a limb and dancing to the music of his own cackle, and all for your special benefit.

There is something very human in this apparent mirth and mockery of the squirrels. It seems to be a sort of ironical laughter, and implies self-conscious pride and exultation in the laugher. "What a ridiculous thing you are, to be sure!" he seems to say; "how clumsy and awkward, and what a poor show for a tail! Look at me, look at me!"—and he capers about in his best style. Again, he would seem to tease you and provoke your attention; then suddenly assumes a tone of good-natured, childlike defiance and derision. That pretty little imp, the chipmunk, will sit on the stone above his den and defy you, as plainly as if he said so, to catch him before he can get into his hole if you can. You hurl a stone at him, and "No you didn't!" comes up from the depth of his retreat.

In February another track appears upon the snow, slender and delicate, about a third larger than that of the gray squirrel, indicating no haste or speed, but, on the contrary, denoting the most

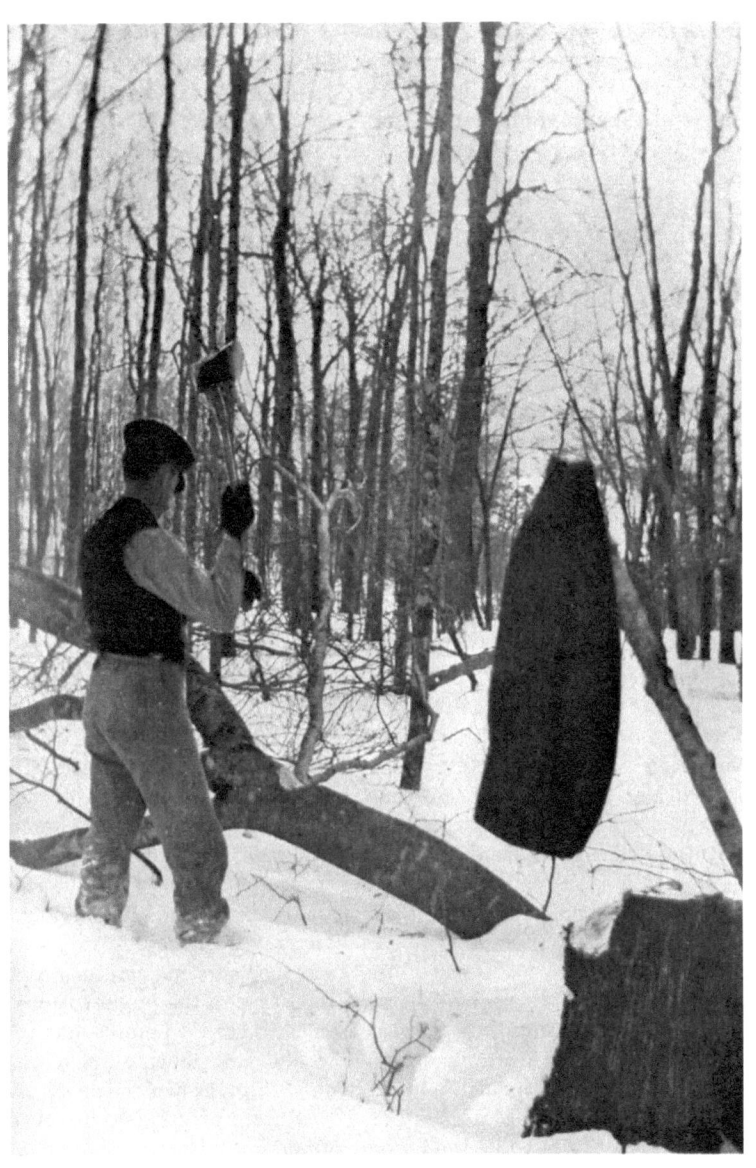

THE CHOPPER IN THE WOODS

imperturbable ease and leisure, the footprints so close together that the trail appears like a chain of curiously carved links. Sir *Mephitis mephitica*, or, in plain English, the skunk, has awakened from his six weeks' nap, and come out into society again. He is a nocturnal traveler, very bold and impudent, coming quite up to the barn and outbuildings, and sometimes taking up his quarters for the season under the haymow. There is no such word as hurry in his dictionary, as you may see by his path upon the snow. He has a very sneaking, insinuating way, and goes creeping about the fields and woods, never once in a perceptible degree altering his gait, and, if a fence crosses his course, steers for a break or opening to avoid climbing. He is too indolent even to dig his own hole, but appropriates that of a woodchuck, or hunts out a crevice in the rocks, from which he extends his rambling in all directions, preferring damp, thawy weather. He has very little discretion or cunning, and holds a trap in utter contempt, stepping into it as soon as beside it, relying implicitly for defense against all forms of danger upon the unsavory punishment he is capable of inflicting. He is quite indifferent to both man and beast, and will not hurry himself to get out of the way of either. Walking through the summer fields at twilight, I have come near stepping upon him, and was much the more disturbed of the two. When attacked in the open field he confounds the plans of his enemies by the unheard-of tactics of exposing his rear rather than his front. "Come if you dare," he says, and his attitude makes even the farm-dog pause. After a few encounters of this kind, and if you entertain the usual hostility towards him, your mode of attack will speedily resolve itself into moving about him in a circle, the radius of which will be the exact distance at which you can hurl a stone with accuracy and effect.

He has a secret to keep and knows it, and is careful not to betray himself until he can do so with the most telling effect. I have known him to preserve his serenity even when caught in a steel trap, and look the very picture of injured innocence, manœuvring carefully and deliberately to extricate his foot from the grasp of the naughty jaws. Do not by any means take pity on him, and lend a helping hand!

How pretty his face and head! How fine and delicate his teeth, like a weasel's or a cat's! When about a third grown, he looks so well that one covets him for a pet. He is quite precocious, however and capable, even at this tender age, of making a very strong appeal to your sense of smell.

No animal is more cleanly in his habits than he. He is not an awkward boy who cuts his own face with his whip; and neither his flesh nor his fur hints the weapon with which he is armed. The most silent creature known to me, he makes no sound, so far as I

## THE SNOW-WALKERS

have observed, save a diffuse, impatient noise, like that produced by beating your hand with a whisk-broom, when the farm-dog has discovered his retreat in the stone fence. He renders himself obnoxious to the farmer by his partiality for hens' eggs and young poultry. He is a confirmed epicure, and at plundering hen-roosts an expert. Not the full-grown fowls are his victims, but the youngest and most tender. At night Mother Hen receives under her maternal wings a dozen newly hatched chickens, and with much pride and satisfaction feels them all safely tucked away in her feathers. In the morning she is walking about disconsolately, attended by only two or three of all that pretty brood. What has happened? Where are they gone? That pickpocket, Sir Mephitis, could solve the mystery. Quietly has he approached, under cover of darkness, and one by one relieved her of her precious charge. Look closely and you will see their little yellow legs and beaks, or part of a mangled form, lying about on the ground. Or, before the hen has hatched, he may find her out, and, by the same sleight of hand, remove every egg, leaving only the empty blood-stained shells to witness against him. The birds, especially the ground-builders, suffer in like manner from his plundering propensities.

The secretion upon which he relies for defense, and which is the chief source of his unpopularity, while it affords good reasons against cultivating him as a pet, and mars his attractiveness as game, is by no means the greatest indignity that can be offered to a nose. It is a rank, living smell, and has none of the sickening qualities of disease or putrefaction. Indeed, I think a good smeller will enjoy its most refined intensity. It approaches the sublime, and makes the nose tingle. It is tonic and bracing, and, I can readily believe, has rare medicinal qualities. I do not recommend its use as eyewater, though an old farmer assures me it has undoubted virtues when thus applied. Hearing, one night, a disturbance among his hens, he rushed suddenly out to catch the thief, when Sir Mephitis, taken by surprise, and no doubt much annoyed at being interrupted, discharged the vials of his wrath full in the farmer's face, and with such admirable effect that, for a few moments, he was completely blinded, and powerless to revenge himself upon the rogue, who embraced the opportunity to make good his escape; but he declared that afterwards his eyes felt as if purged by fire, and his sight was much clearer.

In March that brief summary of a bear, the raccoon, comes out of his den in the ledges, and leaves his sharp digitigrade track upon the snow,—traveling not unfrequently in pairs,—a lean, hungry couple, bent on pillage and plunder. They have an unenviable time of it,—feasting in the summer and fall, hibernating in winter, and starving in spring. In April I have found the young of the previous year creeping about the fields, so reduced by starvation as to be quite helpless, and offering no resistance to my taking them up by the tail and carrying them home.

The old ones also become very much emaciated, and come boldly up to the barn or other outbuildings in quest of food. I remember, one morning in early spring, of hearing old Cuff, the farm-dog, barking vociferously before it was yet light. When we got up we discovered him, at the foot of an ash-tree standing about thirty rods from the house, looking up at some gray object in the leafless branches, and by his manners and his voice evincing great impatience that we were so tardy in coming to his assistance. Arrived on the spot, we saw in the tree a coon of unusual size. One bold climber proposed to go up and shake him down. This was what old Cuff wanted, and he fairly bounded with delight as he saw his young master shinning up the tree. Approaching within eight or ten feet of the coon, he seized the branch to which it clung and shook long and fiercely. But the coon was in no danger of losing its hold, and, when the climber paused to renew his hold, it turned toward him with a growl, and showed very clearly a purpose to advance to the attack. This caused his pursuer to descend to the ground with all speed. When the coon was finally brought down with a gun, he fought the dog, which was a large, powerful animal, with great fury, returning bite for bite for some moments; and after a quarter of an hour had elapsed and his unequal antagonist had shaken him as a terrier does a rat, making his teeth meet through the small of his back, the coon still showed fight.

They are very tenacious of life, and like the badger will always whip a dog of their own size and weight. A woodchuck can bite severely, having teeth that cut like chisels, but a coon has agility and power of limb as well.

They are considered game only in the fall, or towards the close of summer, when they become fat and their flesh sweet. At this time, cooning in the remote interior is a famous pastime. As this animal is entirely nocturnal in its habits, it is hunted only at night. A piece of corn on some remote side-hill near the mountain, or between two pieces of woods, is most apt to be frequented by them. While the corn is yet green they pull the ears down like hogs, and, tearing open the sheathing of husks, eat the tender, succulent kernels, bruising and destroying much more than they devour. Sometimes their ravages are a matter of serious concern to the farmer. But every such neighborhood has its coon-dog, and the boys and young men dearly love the sport. The party sets out about eight or nine o'clock of a dark, moonless night, and stealthily approaches the cornfield. The dog knows his business, and when he is put into a patch of corn and told to "hunt them up" he makes a thorough search, and will not be misled by any other scent. You hear him rattling through the corn, hither and yon, with great speed. The coons prick up their ears, and leave on the opposite side of the field. In the stillness you may sometimes hear a single stone rattle on the wall as they hurry toward the woods. If the dog finds nothing, he comes back to his master in a short time, and says in his dumb way, "No coon there." But if he strikes a trail, you presently hear a louder rattling on the stone wall, and then a hurried bark as he enters the woods, followed in a few minutes by loud and repeated barking as he reaches the foot of the tree in which the coon has taken refuge. Then follows a pellmell rush of the cooning party up the hill, into the woods, through the brush and the darkness, falling over prostrate trees, pitching into gullies and hollows, losing hats and tearing clothes, till finally, guided by the baying of the faithful dog, the tree is reached. The first thing now in order is to kindle a fire, and, if its light reveals the coon, to shoot him; if not, to fell the tree with an axe. If this happens to be too great a sacrifice of timber and of strength, to sit down at the foot of the tree till morning.

But with March our interest in these phases of animal life, which winter has so emphasized and brought out, begins to decline. Vague rumors are afloat in the air of a great and coming change. We are eager for Winter to be gone, since he, too, is fugitive and cannot keep his place. Invisible hands deface his icy statuary; his chisel has lost its cunning. The drifts, so pure and exquisite, are now earth-stained and weather-worn,—the flutes and scallops, and fine, firm lines, all gone; and what was a grace and an ornament to the hills is now a disfiguration. Like worn and unwashed linen appear the remains of that spotless robe with which he clothed the world as his bride.

But he will not abdicate without a struggle. Day after day he rallies his scattered forces, and night after night pitches his white tents on the hills, and would fain regain his lost ground; but the young prince in every encounter prevails. Slowly and reluctantly the gray old hero retreats up the mountain, till finally the south rain comes in earnest, and in a night he is dead.

# II

A WHITE DAY AND A RED FOX

## II

## A WHITE DAY AND A RED FOX

THE day was indeed white, as white as three feet of snow and a cloudless St. Valentine's sun could make it. The eye could not look forth without blinking, or veiling itself with tears. The patch of plowed ground on the top of the hill, where the wind had blown the snow away, was as welcome to it as water to a parched tongue. It was the one refreshing oasis in this desert of dazzling light. I sat down upon it to let the eye bathe and revel in it. It took away the smart like a poultice. For so gentle and on the whole so beneficent an element, the snow asserts itself very proudly. It takes the world quickly and entirely to itself. It makes no concessions or compromises, but rules despotically. It baffles and bewilders the eye, and it returns the sun glare for glare. Its coming in our winter climate is the hand of mercy to the earth and to everything in its bosom, but it is a barrier and an embargo to everything that moves above.

We toiled up the long steep hill, where only an occasional mulleinstalk or other tall weed stood above the snow. Near the top the hill was girded with a bank of snow that blotted out the stone wall and every vestige of the earth beneath. These hills wear this belt till May, and sometimes the plow pauses beside them. From the top of the ridge an immense landscape in immaculate white stretches before us. Miles upon miles of farms, smoothed and padded by the stainless element, hang upon the sides of the mountains, or repose across the long sloping hills. The fences or stone walls show like halfobliterated black lines. I turn my back to the sun, or shade my eyes with my hand. Every object or movement in the landscape is sharply revealed; one could see a fox half a league. The farmer foddering his cattle, or drawing manure afield, or leading his horse to water; the pedestrian crossing the hill below; the children wending their way toward the distant schoolhouse,—the eye cannot help but note them: they are black specks upon square miles of luminous white. What a multitude of sins this unstinted charity of the snow covers!

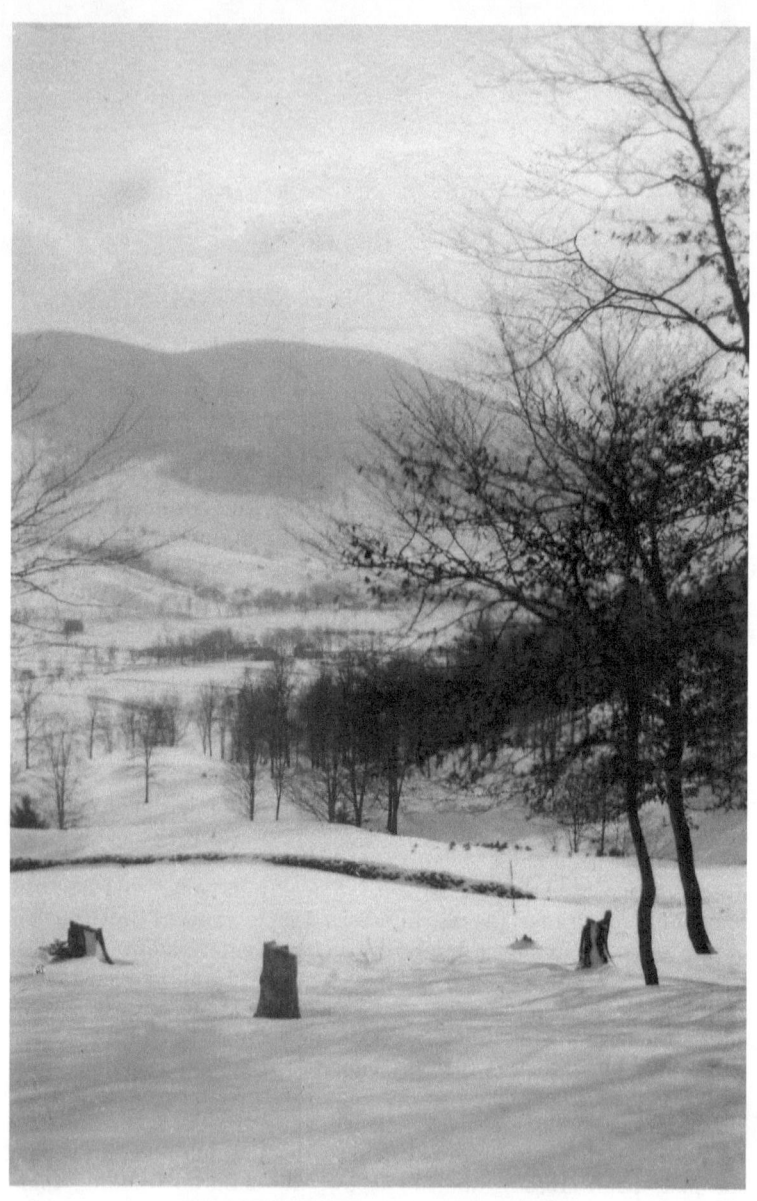

THE DOWNLOOK FROM A HIGH HILLSIDE

## A WHITE DAY AND A RED FOX

How it flatters the ground! Yonder sterile field might be a garden, and you would never suspect that that gentle slope with its pretty dimples and curves was not the smoothest of meadows, yet it is paved with rocks and stone.

But what is that black speck creeping across that cleared field near the top of the mountain at the head of the valley, three quarters of a mile away? It is like a fly moving across an illuminated surface. A distant mellow bay floats to us, and we know it is the hound. He picked up the trail of the fox half an hour since, where he had crossed the ridge early in the morning, and now he has routed him and Reynard is steering for the Big Mountain. We press on and attain the shoulder of the range, where we strike a trail two or three days old of some former hunters, which leads us into the woods along the side of the mountain. We are on the first plateau before the summit; the snow partly supports us, but when it gives way and we sound it with our legs, we find it up to our hips. Here we enter a white world indeed. It is like some conjurer's trick. The very trees have turned to snow. The smallest branch is like a cluster of great white antlers. The eye is bewildered by the soft fleecy labyrinth before it. On the lower ranges the forests were entirely bare, but now we perceive the summit of every mountain about us runs up into a kind of arctic region where the trees are loaded with snow. The beginning of this colder zone is sharply marked all around the horizon; the line runs as level as the shore line of a lake or sea; indeed, a warmer aerial sea fills all the valleys, sub-merging the lower peaks, and making white islands of all the higher ones. The branches bend with the rime. The winds have not shaken it down. It adheres to them like a growth. On examination I find the branches coated with ice, from which shoot slender spikes and needles that penetrate and hold the cord of snow. It is a new kind of foliage wrought by the frost and the clouds, and it obscures the sky, and fills the vistas of the woods nearly as much as the myriad leaves of summer. The sun blazes, the sky is without a cloud or a film, yet we walk in a soft white shade. A gentle breeze was blowing on the open crest of the mountain, but one could carry a lighted candle through these snow-curtained and snow-canopied chambers. How shall we see the fox if the hound drives him through this white obscurity? But we listen in vain for the voice of the dog and press on. Hares' tracks were numerous. Their great soft pads had left their imprint everywhere, sometimes showing a clear leap of ten feet. They had regular circuits which we crossed at intervals. The woods were well suited to them, low and dense, and, as we saw, liable at times to wear a livery whiter than their own.

## IN THE CATSKILLS

The mice, too, how thick their tracks were, that of the white-footed mouse being most abundant; but occasionally there was a much finer track, with strides or leaps scarcely more than an inch apart. This is perhaps the little shrew-mouse of the woods, the body not more than an inch and a half long, the smallest mole or mouse kind known to me. Once, while encamping in the woods, one of these tiny shrews got into an empty pail standing in camp, and died before morning, either from the cold, or in despair of ever getting out of the pail.

At one point, around a small sugar maple, the mice-tracks are unusually thick. It is doubtless their granary; they have beech-nuts stored there, I'll warrant. There are two entrances to the cavity of the tree,—one at the base, and one seven or eight feet up. At the upper one, which is only just the size of a mouse, a squirrel has been trying to break in. He has cut and chiseled the solid wood to the depth of nearly an inch, and his chips strew the snow all about. He knows what is in there, and the mice know that he knows; hence their apparent consternation. They have rushed wildly about over the snow, and, I doubt not, have given the piratical red squirrel a piece of their minds. A few yards away the mice have a hole down into the snow, which perhaps leads to some snug den under the ground. Hither they may have been slyly removing their stores while the squirrel was at work with his back turned. One more night and he will effect an entrance: what a good joke upon him if he finds the cavity empty! These native mice are very provident, and, I imagine, have to take many precautions to prevent their winter stores being plundered by the squirrels, who live, as it were, from hand to mouth.

We see several fresh fox-tracks, and wish for the hound, but there are no tidings of him. After half an hour's floundering and cautiously picking our way through the woods, we emerge into a cleared field that stretches up from the valley below, and just laps over the back of the mountain. It is a broad belt of white that drops down and down till it joins other fields that sweep along the base of the mountain, a mile away. To the east, through a deep defile in the mountains, a landscape in an adjoining county lifts itself up, like a bank of white and gray clouds.

When the experienced fox-hunter comes out upon such an eminence as this, he always scrutinizes the fields closely that lie beneath him, and it many times happens that his sharp eye detects Reynard asleep upon a rock or a stone wall, in which case, if he be armed with a rifle and his dog be not near, the poor creature never wakens from his slumber. The fox nearly always takes his nap in the open fields, along the sides of the ridges, or under the mountain, where he can look down upon the busy farms beneath and hear

## A WHITE DAY AND A RED FOX

their many sounds, the barking of dogs, the lowing of cattle, the cackling of hens, the voices of men and boys, or the sound of travel upon the highway. It is on that side, too, that he keeps the sharpest lookout, and the appearance of the hunter above and behind him is always a surprise.

We pause here, and, with alert ears turned toward the Big Mountain in front of us, listen for the dog. But not a sound is heard. A flock of snow buntings pass high above us, uttering their contented twitter, and their white forms seen against the intense blue give the impression of large snowflakes drifting across the sky. I hear a purple finch, too, and the feeble lisp of the redpoll. A shrike (the first I have seen this season) finds occasion to come this way also. He alights on the tip of a dry limb, and from his perch can see into the valley on both sides of the mountain. He is prowling about for chickadees, no doubt, a troop of which I saw coming through the wood. When pursued by the shrike, the chickadee has been seen to take refuge in a squirrel-hole in a tree. Hark! Is that the hound, or doth expectation mock the eager ear? With open mouths and bated breaths we listen. Yes, it is old "Singer;" he is bringing the fox over the top of the range toward Butt End, the *Ultima Thule* of the hunters' tramps in this section. In a moment or two the dog is lost to hearing again. We wait for his second turn; then for his third.

"He is playing about the summit," says my companion.

"Let us go there," say I, and we are off.

More dense snow-hung woods beyond the clearing where we begin our ascent of the Big Mountain,—a chief that carries the range up several hundred feet higher than the part we have thus far traversed. We are occasionally to our hips in the snow, but for the most part the older stratum, a foot or so down, bears us; up and up we go into the dim, muffled solitudes, our hats and coats powdered like millers'. A half-hour's heavy tramping brings us to the broad, level summit, and to where the fox and hound have crossed and recrossed many times. As we are walking along discussing the matter, we suddenly hear the dog coming straight on to us. The woods are so choked with snow that we do not hear him till he breaks up from under the mountain within a hundred yards of us.

"We have turned the fox!" we both exclaim, much put out.

Sure enough, we have. The dog appears in sight, is puzzled a moment, then turns sharply to the left, and is lost to eye and to ear as quickly as if he had plunged into a cave. The woods are, indeed, a kind of cave,—a cave of alabaster, with the sun shining upon it. We take up positions and wait. These old hunters know exactly where to stand.

THE FOX-HUNTER AND HIS HOUND

## A WHITE DAY AND A RED FOX

"If the fox comes back," said my companion, "he will cross up there or down here," indicating two points not twenty rods asunder. We stood so that each commanded one of the runways indicated. How light it was, though the sun was hidden! Every branch and twig beamed in the sun like a lamp. A downy woodpecker below me kept up a great fuss and clatter,—all for my benefit, I suspected. All about me were great, soft mounds, where the rocks lay buried. It was a cemetery of drift boulders. There! that is the hound. Does his voice come across the valley from the spur off against us, or is it on our side down under the mountain? After an interval, just as I am thinking the dog is going away from us along the opposite range, his voice comes up astonishingly near. A mass of snow falls from a branch, and makes one start; but it is not the fox. Then through the white vista below me I catch a glimpse of something red or yellow, yellowish red or reddish yellow; it emerges from the lower ground, and, with an easy, jaunty air, draws near. I am ready and just in the mood to make a good shot. The fox stops just out of range and listens for the hound. He looks as bright as an autumn leaf upon the spotless surface. Then he starts on, but he is not coming to me, he is going to the other man. Oh, foolish fox, you are going straight into the jaws of death! My comrade stands just there beside that tree. I would gladly have given Reynard the wink, or signaled to him, if I could. It did seem a pity to shoot him, now he was out of my reach. I cringe for him, when crack goes the gun! The fox squalls, picks himself up, and plunges over the brink of the mountain. The hunter has not missed his aim, but the oil in his gun, he says, has weakened the strength of his powder. The hound, hearing the report, comes like a whirlwind and is off in hot pursuit. Both fox and dog now bleed,—the dog at his heels, the fox from his wounds.

In a few minutes there came up from under the mountain that long, peculiar bark which the hound always makes when he has run the fox in, or when something new and extraordinary has happened. In this instance he said plainly enough, "The race is up, the coward has taken to his hole, ho-o-o-le." Plunging down in the direction of the sound, the snow literally to our waists, we were soon at the spot, a great ledge thatched over with three or four feet of snow. The dog was alternately licking his heels and whining and berating the fox. The opening into which the latter had fled was partially closed, and, as I scraped out and cleared away the snow, I thought of the familiar saying, that so far as the sun shines in, the snow will blow in. The fox, I suspect, has always his house of refuge, or knows at once where to flee to if hard pressed. This place proved to be a large vertical seam in the rock, into which the dog, on a little encouragement from his master, made his way. I thrust my head into the ledge's mouth, and in the dim light watched the dog. He progressed slowly and cautiously till only his bleeding heels were visible. Here some obstacle impeded him a few moments, when he entirely disappeared and was presently face to face with the fox and engaged in mortal combat with him. It is a fierce encounter there beneath the rocks, the fox silent, the dog very vociferous. But after a time the superior weight and strength of the latter prevails and the fox is brought to light nearly dead. Reynard winks and eyes me suspiciously, as I stroke his head and praise his heroic defense; but the hunter quickly and mercifully puts an end to his fast-ebbing life. His canine teeth seem unusually large and formidable, and the dog bears the marks of them in many deep gashes upon his face and nose. His pelt is quickly stripped off, revealing his lean, sinewy form.

The fox was not as poor in flesh as I expected to see him, though I'll warrant he had tasted very little food for days, perhaps for weeks. How his great activity and endurance can be kept up, on the spare diet he must of necessity be confined to, is a mystery. Snow, snow everywhere, for weeks and for months, and intense cold, and no henroost accessible, and no carcass of sheep or pig in the neighborhood! The hunter, tramping miles and leagues through his haunts, rarely sees any sign of his having caught anything. Rarely, though, in the course of many winters, he may have seen evidence of his having surprised a rabbit or a partridge in the woods. He no doubt at this season lives largely upon the memory (or the fat) of the many good dinners he had in the plentiful summer and fall.

As we crossed the mountain on our return, we saw at one point blood-stains upon the snow, and, as the fox-tracks were very thick on and about it, we concluded that a couple of males had had an encounter there, and a pretty sharp one. Reynard goes a-wooing in February, and it is to be presumed that, like other dogs, he is a jealous lover. A crow had alighted and examined the blood-stains, and now, if he will look a little farther along, upon a flat rock he will find the flesh he was looking for. Our hound's nose was so blunted now, speaking without metaphor, that he would not look at another trail, but hurried home to rest upon his laurels.

# III

PHASES OF FARM LIFE

## III

## PHASES OF FARM LIFE

I have thought that a good test of civilization, perhaps one of the best, is country life. Where country life is safe and enjoyable, where many of the conveniences and appliances of the town are joined to the large freedom and large benefits of the country, a high state of civilization prevails. Is there any proper country life in Spain, in Mexico, in the South American States? Man has always dwelt in cities, but he has not always in the same sense been a dweller in the country. Rude and barbarous people build cities. Hence, paradoxical as it may seem, the city is older than the country. Truly, man made the city, and after he became sufficiently civilized, not afraid of solitude, and knew on what terms to live with nature, God promoted him to life in the country. The necessities of defense, the fear of enemies, built the first city, built Athens, Rome, Carthage, Paris. The weaker the law, the stronger the city. After Cain slew Abel he went out and built a city, and murder or the fear of murder, robbery or the fear of robbery, have built most of the cities since. Penetrate into the heart of Africa, and you will find the people, or tribes, all living in villages or little cities. You step from the jungle or the forest into the town; there is no country. The best and most hopeful feature in any people is undoubtedly the instinct that leads them to the country and to take root there, and not that which sends them flocking to the town and its distractions.

The lighter the snow, the more it drifts; and the more frivolous the people, the more they are blown by one wind or another into towns and cities.

The only notable exception I recall to city life preceding country life is furnished by the ancient Germans, of whom Tacitus says that they had no cities or contiguous settlements. "They dwell scattered and separate, as a spring, a meadow, or a grove may chance to invite them. Their villages are laid out, not like ours [the Romans] in rows of adjoining buildings, but every one surrounds his house with a vacant space, either by way of security, or against fire, or through ignorance of the art of building."

THE COWS AT THE PASTURE BARS

## PHASES OF FARM LIFE

These ancient Germans were indeed true countrymen. Little wonder that they overran the empire of the city-loving Romans, and finally sacked Rome itself. How hairy and hardy and virile they were! In the same way is the more fresh and vigorous blood of the country always making eruptions into the city. The Goths and Vandals from the woods and the farms,—what would Rome do without them, after all? The city rapidly uses men up; families run out, man becomes sophisticated and feeble. A fresh stream of humanity is always setting from the country into the city; a stream not so fresh flows back again into the country, a stream for the most part of jaded and pale humanity. It is arterial blood when it flows in, and venous blood when it comes back.

A nation always begins to rot first in its great cities, is indeed perhaps always rotting there, and is saved only by the antiseptic virtues of fresh supplies of country blood.

But it is not of country life in general that I am to speak, but of some phases of farm life, and of farm life in my native State.

Many of the early settlers of New York were from New England, Connecticut perhaps sending out the most. My own ancestors were from the latter State. The Connecticut emigrant usually made his first stop in our river counties, Putnam, Dutchess, or Columbia. If he failed to find his place there, he made another flight to Orange, to Delaware, or to Schoharie County, where he generally stuck. But the State early had one element introduced into its rural and farm life not found farther east, namely, the Holland Dutch. These gave features more or less picturesque to the country that are not observable in New England. The Dutch took root at various points along the Hudson, and about Albany and in the Mohawk valley, and remnants of their rural and domestic architecture may still be seen in these sections of the State. A Dutch barn became proverbial. "As broad as a Dutch barn" was a phrase that, when applied to the person of a man or woman, left room for little more to be said. The main feature of these barns was their enormous expansion of roof. It was a comfort to look at them, they suggested such shelter and protection. The eaves were very low and the ridge-pole very high. Long rafters and short posts gave them a quaint, short-waisted, grandmotherly look. They were nearly square, and stood very broad upon the ground. Their form was doubtless suggested by the damper climate of the Old World, where the grain and hay, instead of being packed in deep solid mows, used to be spread upon poles and exposed to the currents of air under the roof. Surface and not cubic capacity is more important in these matters in Holland than in this country. Our farmers have found that, in a climate where there is so much weather as with us, the less roof you have the better. Roofs will leak, and cured hay will keep sweet in a mow of any depth and size in our dry atmosphere.

The Dutch barn was the most picturesque barn that has been built, especially when thatched with straw, as they nearly all were, and forming one side of an inclosure of lower roofs or sheds also covered with straw, beneath which the cattle took refuge from the winter storms. Its immense, unpainted gable, cut with holes for the swallows, was like a section of a respectable-sized hill, and its roof like its slope. Its great doors always had a hood projecting over them, and the doors themselves were divided horizontally into upper and lower halves; the upper halves very frequently being left open, through which you caught a glimpse of the mows of hay, or the twinkle of flails when the grain was being threshed.

The old Dutch farmhouses, too, were always pleasing to look upon. They were low, often made of stone, with deep window-jambs and great family fireplaces. The outside door, like that of the barn, was always divided into upper and lower halves. When the weather permitted, the upper half could stand open, giving light and air without the cold draught over the floor where the children were playing that our wide-swung doors admit. This feature of the Dutch house and barn certainly merits preservation in our modern buildings.

The large, unpainted timber barns that succeeded the first Yankee settlers' log stables were also picturesque, especially when a lean-to for the cow-stable was added, and the roof carried down with a long sweep over it; or when the barn was flanked by an open shed with a hayloft above it, where the hens cackled and hid their nests, and from the open window of which the hay was always hanging.

Then the great timbers of these barns and the Dutch barn, hewn from maple or birch or oak trees from the primitive woods, and put in place by the combined strength of all the brawny arms in the neighborhood when the barn was raised,—timbers strong enough and heavy enough for docks and quays, and that have absorbed the odors of the hay and grain until they look ripe and mellow and full of the pleasing sentiment of the great, sturdy, bountiful interior! The "big beam" has become smooth and polished from the hay that has been pitched over it, and the sweaty, sturdy forms that have crossed it. One feels that he would like a piece of furniture—a chair, or a table, or a writing-desk, a bedstead, or a wainscoting—made from these long-seasoned, long-tried, richly toned timbers of the old barn. But the smart-painted, natty barn that follows the humbler

## PHASES OF FARM LIFE

structure, with its glazed windows, its ornamented ventilator and gilded weather vane,—who cares to contemplate it? The wise human eye loves modesty and humility; loves plain, simple structures; loves the unpainted barn that took no thought of itself, or the dwelling that looks inward and not outward; is offended when the farm-buildings get above their business and aspire to be something on their own account, suggesting, not cattle and crops and plain living, but the vanities of the town and the pride of dress and equipage.

Indeed, the picturesque in human affairs and occupations is always born of love and humility, as it is in art or literature; and it quickly takes to itself wings and flies away at the advent of pride, or any selfish or unworthy motive. The more directly the farm savors of the farmer, the more the fields and buildings are redolent of human care and toil, without any thought of the passer-by, the more we delight in the contemplation of it.

It is unquestionably true that farm life and farm scenes in this country are less picturesque than they were fifty or one hundred years ago. This is owing partly to the advent of machinery, which enables the farmer to do so much of his work by proxy, and hence removes him farther from the soil, and partly to the growing distaste for the occupation among our people. The old settlers—our fathers and grandfathers—loved the farm, and had no thoughts above it; but the later generations are looking to the town and its fashions, and only waiting for a chance to flee thither. Then pioneer life is always more or less picturesque; there is no room for vain and foolish thoughts; it is a hard battle, and the people have no time to think about appearances. When my grandfather and grandmother came into the country where they reared their family and passed their days, they cut a road through the woods and brought all their worldly gear on a sled drawn by a yoke of oxen. Their neighbors helped them build a house of logs, with a roof of black-ash bark and a floor of hewn white-ash plank. A great stone chimney and fireplace—the mortar of red clay—gave light and warmth, and cooked the meat and baked the bread, when there was any to cook or to bake. Here they lived and reared their family, and found life sweet. Their unworthy descendant, yielding to the inherited love of the soil, flees the city and its artificial ways, and gets a few acres in the country, where he proposes to engage in the pursuit supposed to be free to every American citizen,—the pursuit of happiness. The humble old farmhouse is discarded, and a smart, modern country-house put up. Walks and roads are made and graveled; trees and hedges are planted; the rustic old barn is rehabilitated; and, after it is all fixed, the uneasy proprietor stands off and looks, and calculates by how much he has missed the picturesque, at which he aimed. Our new houses undoubtedly have greater comforts and conveniences than the old; and, if we could keep our pride and vanity in abeyance and forget that all the world is looking on, they might have beauty also.

The man that forgets himself, he is the man we like; and the dwelling that forgets itself, in its purpose to shelter and protect its inmates and make them feel at home in it, is the dwelling that fills the eye. When you see one of the great cathedrals, you know that it was not pride that animated these builders, but fear and worship; but when you see the house of the rich farmer, or of the millionaire from the city, you see the pride of money and the insolence of social power.

Machinery, I say, has taken away some of the picturesque features of farm life. How much soever we may admire machinery and the faculty of mechanical invention, there is no machine like a man; and the work done directly by his hands, the things made or fashioned by them, have a virtue and a quality that cannot be imparted by machinery. The line of mowers in the meadows, with the straight swaths behind them, is more picturesque than the "Clipper" or "Buckeye" mower, with its team and driver. So are the flails of the threshers, chasing each other through the air, more pleasing to the eye and the ear than the machine, with its uproar, its choking clouds of dust, and its general hurly-burly.

Sometimes the threshing was done in the open air, upon a broad rock, or a smooth, dry plat of greensward; and it is occasionally done there yet, especially the threshing of the buckwheat crop, by a farmer who has not a good barn floor, or who cannot afford to hire the machine. The flail makes a louder *thud* in the fields than you would imagine; and in the splendid October weather it is a pleasing spectacle to behold the gathering of the ruddy crop, and three or four lithe figures beating out the grain with their flails in some sheltered nook, or some grassy lane lined with cedars. When there are three flails beating together, it makes lively music; and when there are four, they follow each other so fast that it is a continuous roll of sound, and it requires a very steady stroke not to hit or get hit by the others. There is just room and time to get your blow in, and that is all. When one flail is upon the straw, another has just left it, another is halfway down, and the fourth is high and straight in the air. It is like a swiftly revolving wheel that delivers four blows at each revolution. Threshing, like mowing, goes much easier in company than when alone; yet many a farmer or laborer spends nearly all the late fall and winter days shut in the barn, pounding doggedly upon the endless sheaves of oats and rye.

A MOWER

When the farmers made "bees," as they did a generation or two ago much more than they do now, a picturesque element was added. There was the stone bee, the husking bee, the "raising," the "moving," etc. When the carpenters had got the timbers of the house or the barn ready, and the foundation was prepared, then the neighbors for miles about were invited to come to the "raisin'." The afternoon was the time chosen. The forenoon was occupied by the carpenter and the farm hands in putting the sills and "sleepers" in place ("sleepers," what a good name for those rude hewn timbers that lie under the floor in the darkness and silence!). When the hands arrived, the great beams and posts and joists and braces were carried to their place on the platform, and the first "bent," as it was called, was put together and pinned by oak pins that the boys brought. Then pike poles were distributed, the men, fifteen or twenty of them, arranged in a line abreast of the bent; the boss carpenter steadied and guided the corner post and gave the word of command,—"Take holt, boys!" "Now, set her up!" "Up with her!" "Up she goes!" When it gets shoulder high, it becomes heavy, and there is a pause. The pikes are brought into requisition; every man gets a good hold and braces himself, and waits for the words. "All together now!" shouts the captain; "Heave her up!" "He-o-he!" (heave-all,—heave), "he-o-he," at the top of his voice, every man doing his best. Slowly the great timbers go up; louder grows the word of command, till the bent is up. Then it is plumbed and stay-lathed, and another is put together and raised in the same way, till they are all up. Then comes the putting on the great plates,—timbers that run lengthwise of the building and match the sills below. Then, if there is time, the putting up of the rafters.

In every neighborhood there was always some man who was especially useful at "raisin's." He was bold and strong and quick. He helped guide and superintend the work. He was the first one up on the bent, catching a pin or a brace and putting it in place. He walked the lofty and perilous plate with the great beetle in hand, put the pins in the holes, and, swinging the heavy instrument through the air, drove the pins home. He was as much at home up there as a squirrel.

Now that balloon frames are mainly used for houses, and lighter sawed timbers for barns, the old-fashioned raising is rarely witnessed.

Then the moving was an event, too. A farmer had a barn to move, or wanted to build a new house on the site of the old one, and the latter must be drawn to one side. Now this work is done with pulleys and rollers by a few men and a horse; then the building was drawn by sheer bovine strength. Every man that had a yoke of cattle in the country round about was invited to assist. The barn or house was pried up and great runners, cut in the woods, placed under it, and under the runners were placed skids. To these runners it was securely chained and pinned; then the cattle—stags, steers, and oxen, in two long lines, one at each runner—were hitched fast, and, while men and boys aided with great levers, the word to go was given. Slowly the two lines of bulky cattle straightened and settled into their bows; the big chains that wrapped the runners tightened, a dozen or more "gads" were flourished, a dozen or more lusty throats urged their teams at the top of their voices, when there was a creak or a groan as the building stirred. Then the drivers redoubled their efforts; there was a perfect Babel of discordant sounds; the oxen bent to the work, their eyes bulged, their nostrils distended; the lookers-on cheered, and away went the old house or barn as nimbly as a boy on a hand-sled. Not always, however; sometimes the chains would break, or one runner strike a rock, or bury itself in the earth. There were generally enough mishaps or delays to make it interesting.

In the section of the State of which I write, flax used to be grown, and cloth for shirts and trousers, and towels and sheets, woven from it. It was no laughing matter for the farm-boy to break in his shirt or trousers, those days. The hair shirts in which the old monks used to mortify the flesh could not have been much before them in this mortifying particular. But after the bits of shives and sticks were subdued, and the knots humbled by use and the washboard, they were good garments. If you lost your hold in a tree and your shirt caught on a knot or limb, it would save you.

But when has any one seen a crackle, or a swingling-knife, or a hetchel, or a distaff, and where can one get some tow for strings or for gun-wadding, or some swingling-tow for a bonfire? The quill-wheel, and the spinning-wheel, and the loom are heard no more among us. The last I knew of a certain hetchel, it was nailed up behind the old sheep that did the churning; and when he was disposed to shirk or hang back and stop the machine, it was always ready to spur him up in no uncertain manner. The old loom became a hen-roost in an outbuilding; and the crackle upon which the flax was broken,—where, oh, where is it?

When the produce of the farm was taken a long distance to market,—that was an event, too; the carrying away of the butter in the fall, for instance, to the river, a journey that occupied both ways four days. Then the family marketing was done in a few groceries. Some cloth, new caps and boots for the boys, and a dress, or a shawl, or a cloak for the girls were brought back, besides news and adventure, and strange tidings of the distant world. The farmer was

# IN THE CATSKILLS

days in getting ready to start; food was prepared and put in a box to stand him on the journey, so as to lessen the hotel expenses, and oats were put up for the horses. The butter was loaded up overnight, and in the cold November morning, long before it was light, he was up and off. I seem to hear the wagon yet, its slow rattle over the frozen ground diminishing in the distance. On the fourth day toward night all grew expectant of his return, but it was usually dark before his wagon was heard coming down the hill, or his voice from before the door summoning a light. When the boys got big enough, one after the other accompanied him each year, until all had made the famous journey and seen the great river and the steamboats, and the thousand and one marvels of the far-away town. When it came my turn to go, I was in a great state of excitement for a week beforehand, for fear my clothes would not be ready, or else that it would be too cold, or else that the world would come to an end before the time fixed for starting. The day previous I roamed the woods in quest of game to supply my bill of fare on the way, and was lucky enough to shoot a partridge and an owl, though the latter I did not take. Perched high on a "spring-board" I made the journey, and saw more sights and wonders than I have ever seen on a journey since, or ever expect to again.

But now all this is changed. The railroad has found its way through or near every settlement, and marvels and wonders are cheap. Still, the essential charm of the farm remains and always will remain: the care of crops, and of cattle, and of orchards, bees, and fowls; the clearing and improving of the ground; the building of barns and houses; the direct contact with the soil and with the elements; the watching of the clouds and of the weather; the privacies with nature, with bird, beast, and plant; and the close acquaintance with the heart and virtue of the world. The farmer should be the true naturalist; the book in which it is all written is open before him night and day, and how sweet and wholesome all his knowledge is!

The predominant feature of farm life in New York, as in other States, is always given by some local industry of one kind or another. In many of the high, cold counties in the eastern centre of the State, this ruling industry is hop-growing; in the western, it is grain and fruit growing; in sections along the Hudson, it is small-fruit growing, as berries, currants, grapes; in other counties, it is milk and butter; in others, quarrying flagging-stone. I recently visited a section of Ulster County, where everybody seemed getting out hoop-poles and making hoops. The only talk was of hoops, hoops! Every team that went by had a load or was going for a load of hoops. The principal fuel was hoop-shavings or discarded hoop-poles. No

## PHASES OF FARM LIFE

man had any money until he sold his hoops. When a farmer went to town to get some grain, or a pair of boots, or a dress for his wife, he took a load of hoops. People stole hoops and poached for hoops, and bought, and sold, and speculated in hoops. If there was a corner, it was in hoops; big hoops, little hoops, hoops for kegs, and firkins, and barrels, and hogsheads, and pipes; hickory hoops, birch hoops, ash hoops, chestnut hoops, hoops enough to go around the world. Another place it was shingle, shingle; everybody was shaving hemlock shingle.

In most of the eastern counties of the State, the interest and profit of the farm revolve about the cow. The dairy is the one great matter,—for milk, when milk can be shipped to the New York market, and for butter when it cannot. Great barns and stables and milking-sheds, and immense meadows and cattle on a thousand hills, are the prominent agricultural features of these sections of the country. Good grass and good water are the two indispensables to successful dairying. And the two generally go together. Where there are plenty of copious cold springs, there is no dearth of grass. When the cattle are compelled to browse upon weeds and various wild growths, the milk and butter will betray it in the flavor. Tender, juicy grass, the ruddy blossoming clover, or the fragrant, well-cured hay, make the delicious milk and the sweet butter. Then there is a charm about a natural pastoral country that belongs to no other. Go through Orange County in May and see the vivid emerald of the smooth fields and hills. It is a new experience of the beauty and effectiveness of simple grass. And this grass has rare virtues, too, and imparts a flavor to the milk and butter that has made them famous.

Along all the sources of the Delaware the land flows with milk, if not with honey. The grass is excellent, except in times of protracted drought, and then the browsings in the beech and birch woods are a good substitute. Butter is the staple product. Every housewife is or wants to be a famous butter-maker, and Delaware County butter rivals that of Orange in market. Delaware is a high, cool grazing country. The farms lie tilted up against the sides of the mountain or lapping over the hills, striped or checked with stone walls, and presenting to the eye long stretches of pasture and meadow land, alternating with plowed fields and patches of waving grain. Few of their features are picturesque; they are bare, broad, and simple. The farmhouse gets itself a coat of white paint, and green blinds to the windows, and the barn and wagon-house a coat of red paint with white trimmings, as soon as possible. A penstock flows by the doorway, rows of tin pans sun themselves in the yard, and the great wheel of the churning-machine flanks the milk-house, or rattles behind it. The winters are severe, the snow deep. The principal fuel is still wood,—beech, birch, and maple. It is hauled off the mountain in great logs when the first November or December snows come, and cut up and piled in the wood-houses and under a shed. Here the axe still rules the winter, and it may be heard all day and every day upon the wood-pile, or echoing through the frost-bound wood, the coat of the chopper hanging to a limb, and his white chips strewing the snow.

Many cattle need much hay; hence in dairy sections haying is the period of "storm and stress" in the farmer's year. To get the hay in, in good condition, and before the grass gets too ripe, is a great matter. All the energies and resources of the farm are bent to this purpose. It is a thirty or forty days' war, in which the farmer and his "hands" are pitted against the heat and the rain and the legions of timothy and clover. Everything about it has the urge, the hurry, the excitement of a battle. Outside help is procured; men flock in from adjoining counties, where the ruling industry is something else and is less imperative; coopers, blacksmiths, and laborers of various kinds drop their tools, and take down their scythes and go in quest of a job in haying. Every man is expected to pitch his endeavors in a little higher key than at any other kind of work. The wages are extra, and the work must correspond. The men are in the meadow by half-past four or five in the morning, and mow an hour or two before breakfast. A good mower is proud of his skill. He does not "lop in," and his "pointing out" is perfect, and you can hardly see the ribs of his swath. He stands up to his grass and strikes level and sure. He will turn a double down through the stoutest grass, and when the hay is raked away you will not find a spear left standing. The Americans are—or were—the best mowers. A foreigner could never quite give the masterly touch. The hayfield has its code. One man must not take another's swath unless he expects to be crowded. Each expects to take his turn leading the band. The scythe may be so whetted as to ring out a saucy challenge to the rest. It is not good manners to mow up too close to your neighbor, unless you are trying to keep out of the way of the man behind you. Many a race has been brought on by some one being a little indiscreet in this respect. Two men may mow all day together under the impression that each is trying to put the other through. The one that leads strikes out briskly, and the other, not to be outdone, follows close. Thus the blood of each is soon up; a little heat begets more heat, and it is fairly a race before long. It is a great ignomiy to be mowed out of your swath. Hay-gathering is clean, manly work all through. Young fellows work in haying who do not do another stroke on the

HAYING

farm the whole year. It is a gymnasium in the meadows and under the summer sky. How full of pictures, too!—the smooth slopes dotted with cocks with lengthening shadows; the great, broad-backed, soft-cheeked loads, moving along the lanes and brushing under the trees; the unfinished stacks with forkfuls of hay being handed up its sides to the builder, and when finished the shape of a great pear, with a pole in the top for the stem. Maybe in the fall and winter the calves and yearlings will hover around it and gnaw its base until it overhangs them and shelters them from the storm. Or the farmer will "fodder" his cows there,—one of the most picturesque scenes to be witnessed on the farm,—twenty or thirty or forty milchers filing along toward the stack in the field, or clustered about it, waiting the promised bite. In great, green flakes the hay is rolled off, and distributed about in small heaps upon the unspotted snow. After the cattle have eaten, the birds—snow buntings and red-polls—come and pick up the crumbs, the seeds of the grasses and weeds. At night the fox and the owl come for mice.

What a beautiful path the cows make through the snow to the stack or to the spring under the hill!—always more or less wayward, but broad and firm, and carved and indented by a multitude of rounded hoofs.

In fact, the cow is the true pathfinder and pathmaker. She has the leisurely, deliberate movement that insures an easy and a safe way. Follow her trail through the woods, and you have the best, if not the shortest, course. How she beats down the brush and briers and wears away even the roots of the trees! A herd of cows left to themselves fall naturally into single file, and a hundred or more hoofs are not long in smoothing and compacting almost any surface.

Indeed, all the ways and doings of cattle are pleasant to look upon, whether grazing in the pasture, or browsing in the woods, or ruminating under the trees, or feeding in the stall, or reposing upon the knolls. There is virtue in the cow; she is full of goodness; a wholesome odor exhales from her; the whole landscape looks out of her soft eyes; the quality and the aroma of miles of meadow and pasture lands are in her presence and products. I had rather have the care of cattle than be the keeper of the great seal of the nation. Where the cow is, there is Arcadia; so far as her influence prevails, there is contentment, humility, and sweet, homely life.

Blessed is he whose youth was passed upon the farm, and if it was a dairy farm, his memories will be all the more fragrant. The driving of the cows to and from the pasture, every day and every season for years,—how much of summer and of nature he got into him on these journeys! What rambles and excursions did this errand

CATTLE AT THE SPRING UNDER THE HILL

furnish the excuse for! The birds and birds'-nests, the berries, the squirrels, the woodchucks, the beech woods with their treasures into which the cows loved so to wander and to browse, the fragrant wintergreens and a hundred nameless adventures, all strung upon that brief journey of half a mile to and from the remote pastures. Sometimes a cow or two will be missing when the herd is brought home at night; then to hunt them up is another adventure. My grandfather went out one night to look up an absentee from the yard, when he heard something in the brush, and out stepped a bear into the path before him.

Every Sunday morning the cows were salted. The farm-boy would take a pail with three or four quarts of coarse salt, and, followed by the eager herd, go to the field and deposit the salt in handfuls upon smooth stones and rocks and upon clean places on the turf. If you want to know how good salt is, see a cow eat it. She gives the true saline smack. How she dwells upon it, and gnaws the sward and licks the stones where it has been deposited! The cow is the most delightful feeder among animals. It makes one's mouth water to see her eat pumpkins, and to see her at a pile of apples is distracting. How she sweeps off the delectable grass! The sound of her grazing is appetizing; the grass betrays all its sweetness and succulency in parting under her sickle.

The region of which I write abounds in sheep also. Sheep love high, cool, breezy lands. Their range is generally much above that of cattle. Their sharp noses will find picking where a cow would fare poorly indeed. Hence most farmers utilize their high, wild, and mountain lands by keeping a small flock of sheep. But they are the outlaws of the farm and are seldom within bounds. They make many lively expeditions for the farm-boy,—driving them out of mischief, hunting them up in the mountains, or salting them on the breezy hills. Then there is the annual sheep-washing, when on a warm day in May or early June the whole herd is driven a mile or more to a suitable pool in the creek, and one by one doused and washed and rinsed in the water. We used to wash below an old grist-mill, and it was a pleasing spectacle,—the mill, the dam, the overhanging rocks and trees, the round, deep pool, and the huddled and frightened sheep.

One of the features of farm life peculiar to this country, and one of the most picturesque of them all, is sugar-making in the maple woods in spring. This is the first work of the season, and to the boys is more play than work. In the Old World, and in more simple and imaginative times, how such an occupation as this would have got into literature, and how many legends and associations would have clustered around it! It is woodsy, and savors of the trees; it is an

## PHASES OF FARM LIFE

encampment among the maples. Before the bud swells, before the grass springs, before the plow is started, comes the sugar harvest. It is the sequel of the bitter frost; a sap-run is the sweet good-by of winter. It denotes a certain equipoise of the season; the heat of the day fully balances the frost of the night. In New York and New England, the time of the sap hovers about the vernal equinox, beginning a week or ten days before, and continuing a week or ten days after. As the days and nights get equal, the heat and cold get equal, and the sap mounts. A day that brings the bees out of the hive will bring the sap out of the maple-tree. It is the fruit of the equal marriage of the sun and the frost. When the frost is all out of the ground, and all the snow gone from its surface, the flow stops. The thermometer must not rise above 38° or 40° by day, or sink below 24° or 25° at night, with wind in the northwest; a relaxing south wind, and the run is over for the present. Sugar weather is crisp weather. How the tin buckets glisten in the gray woods; how the robins laugh; how the nuthatches call; how lightly the thin blue smoke rises among the trees! The squirrels are out of their dens; the migrating water-fowls are streaming northward; the sheep and cattle look wistfully toward the bare fields; the tide of the season, in fact, is just beginning to rise.

Sap-letting does not seem to be an exhaustive process to the trees, as the trees of a sugar-bush appear to be as thrifty and as long-lived as other trees. They come to have a maternal, large-waisted look, from the wounds of the axe or the auger, and that is about all.

In my sugar-making days, the sap was carried to the boiling-place in pails by the aid of a neck-yoke and stored in hogsheads, and boiled or evaporated in immense kettles or caldrons set in huge stone arches; now, the hogshead goes to the trees hauled upon a sled by a team, and the sap is evaporated in broad, shallow, sheet-iron pans,—a great saving of fuel and of labor.

Many a farmer sits up all night boiling his sap, when the run has been an extra good one, and a lonely vigil he has of it amid the silent trees and beside his wild hearth. If he has a sap-house, as is now so common, he may make himself fairly comfortable; and if a companion, he may have a good time or a glorious wake.

Maple sugar in its perfection is rarely seen, perhaps never seen, in the market. When made in large quantities and indifferently, it is dark and coarse; but when made in small quantities—that is, quickly from the first run of sap and properly treated—it has a wild delicacy of flavor that no other sweet can match. What you smell in freshly cut maple-wood, or taste in the blossom of the tree, is in it. It is then, indeed, the distilled essence of the tree. Made into syrup, it is white and clear as clover-honey; and crystallized into sugar, it is as pure as the wax. The way to attain this result is to evaporate the sap under cover in an enameled kettle; when reduced about twelve times, allow it to settle half a day or more; then clarify with milk or the white of an egg. The product is virgin syrup, or sugar worthy the table of the gods.

Perhaps the most heavy and laborious work of the farm in the section of the State of which I write is fence-building. But it is not unproductive labor, as in the South or West, for the fence is of stone, and the capacity of the soil for grass or grain is, of course, increased by its construction. It is killing two birds with one stone: a fence is had, the best in the world, while the available area of the field is enlarged. In fact, if there are ever sermons in stones, it is when they are built into a stone wall,—turning your hindrances into helps, shielding your crops behind the obstacles to your husbandry, making the enemies of the plow stand guard over its products. This is the kind of farming worth imitating. A stone wall with a good rock bottom will stand as long as a man lasts. Its only enemy is the frost, and it works so gently that it is not till after many years that its effect is perceptible. An old farmer will walk with you through his fields and say, "This wall I built at such and such a time, or the first year I came on the farm, or when I owned such and such a span of horses," indicating a period thirty, forty, or fifty years back. "This other, we built the summer so and so worked for me," and he relates some incident, or mishap, or comical adventures that the memory calls up. Every line of fence has a history; the mark of his plow or his crowbar is upon the stones; the sweat of his early manhood put them in place; in fact, the long black line covered with lichens and in places tottering to the fall revives long-gone scenes and events in the life of the farm.

The time for fence-building is usually between seed-time and harvest, May and June; or in the fall after the crops are gathered. The work has its picturesque features,—the prying of rocks; supple forms climbing or swinging from the end of the great levers; or the blasting of the rocks with powder, the hauling of them into position with oxen or horses, or with both; the picking of the stone from the greensward; the bending, athletic forms of the wall-layers; the snug new fence creeping slowly up the hill or across the field, absorbing the wind-row of loose stones; and, when the work is done, much ground reclaimed to the plow and the grass, and a strong barrier erected.

It is a common complaint that the farm and farm life are not appreciated by our people. We long for the more elegant pursuits, or the ways and fashions of the town. But the farmer has the most

WAITING FOR THE COWS

sane and natural occupation, and ought to find life sweeter, if less highly seasoned, than any other. He alone, strictly speaking, has a home. How can a man take root and thrive without land? He writes his history upon his field. How many ties, how many resources, he has,—his friendships with his cattle, his team, his dog, his trees, the satisfaction in his growing crops, in his improved fields; his intimacy with nature, with bird and beast, and with the quickening elemental forces; his coöperations with the clouds, the sun, the seasons, heat, wind, rain, frost! Nothing will take the various social distempers which the city and artificial life breed out of a man like farming, like direct and loving contact with the soil. It draws out the poison. It humbles him, teaches him patience and reverence, and restores the proper tone to his system.

Cling to the farm, make much of it, put yourself into it, bestow your heart and your brain upon it, so that it shall savor of you and radiate your virtue after your day's work is done!

"Be thou diligent to know the state of thy flocks, and look well to thy herds.

"For riches are not forever; and doth the crown endure to every generation?

"The hay appeareth, and the tender grass showeth itself, and herbs of the mountains are gathered.

"The lambs are for thy clothing, and the goats are the price of the field.

"And thou shalt have goat's milk enough for thy food, for the food of thy household, and for the maintenance for thy maidens."

# IV

IN THE HEMLOCKS

## IV

## IN THE HEMLOCKS

MOST people receive with incredulity a statement of the number of birds that annually visit our climate. Very few even are aware of half the number that spend the summer in their own immediate vicinity. We little suspect, when we walk in the woods, whose privacy we are intruding upon,—what rare and elegant visitants from Mexico, from Central and South America, and from the islands of the sea, are holding their reunions in the branches over our heads, or pursuing their pleasure on the ground before us.

I recall the altogether admirable and shining family which Thoreau dreamed he saw in the upper chambers of Spaulding's woods, which Spaulding did not know lived there, and which were not put out when Spaulding, whistling, drove his team through their lower halls. They did not go into society in the village; they were quite well; they had sons and daughters; they neither wove nor spun; there was a sound as of suppressed hilarity.

I take it for granted that the forester was only saying a pretty thing of the birds, though I have observed that it does sometimes annoy them when Spaulding's cart rumbles through their house. Generally, however, they are as unconscious of Spaulding as Spaulding is of them.

Walking the other day in an old hemlock wood, I counted over forty varieties of these summer visitants, many of them common to other woods in the vicinity, but quite a number peculiar to these ancient solitudes, and not a few that are rare in any locality. It is quite unusual to find so large a number abiding in one forest,— and that not a large one,—most of them nesting and spending the summer there. Many of those I observed commonly pass this season much farther north. But the geographical distribution of birds is rather a climatical one. The same temperature, though under different parallels, usually attracts the same birds; difference in altitude being equivalent to the difference in latitude. A given height above the sea-level under the parallel of thirty degrees may have the same climate as places under that of thirty-five degrees, and similar flora and fauna. At the headwaters of the Delaware, where I write, the latitude is that of Boston, but the region has a much greater elevation, and hence a climate that compares better with the northern part of the State and of New England. Half a day's drive to the southeast brings me down into quite a different temperature, with an older geological formation, different forest timber, and different birds,—even with different mammals. Neither the little gray rabbit nor the little gray fox is found in my locality, but the great northern hare and the red fox are. In the last century a colony of beavers dwelt here, though the oldest inhabitant cannot now point to even the traditional site of their dams. The ancient hemlocks, whither I propose to take the reader, are rich in many things besides birds. Indeed, their wealth in this respect is owing mainly, no doubt, to their rank vegetable growths, their fruitful swamps, and their dark, sheltered retreats.

Their history is of an heroic cast. Ravished and torn by the tanner in his thirst for bark, preyed upon by the lumberman, assaulted and beaten back by the settler, still their spirit has never been broken, their energies never paralyzed. Not many years ago a public highway passed through them, but it was at no time a tolerable road; trees fell across it, mud and limbs choked it up, till finally travelers took the hint and went around; and now, walking along its deserted course, I see only the footprints of coons, foxes, and squirrels.

Nature loves such woods, and places her own seal upon them. Here she shows me what can be done with ferns and mosses and lichens. The soil is marrowy and full of innumerable forests. Standing in these fragrant aisles, I feel the strength of the vegetable kingdom, and am awed by the deep and inscrutable processes of life going on so silently about me.

No hostile forms with axe or spud now visit these solitudes. The cows have half-hidden ways through them, and know where the best browsing is to be had. In spring, the farmer repairs to their bordering of maples to make sugar; in July and August, women and boys from all the country about penetrate the old Barkpeelings for raspberries and blackberries; and I know a youth who wonderingly follows their languid stream casting for trout.

In like spirit, alert and buoyant, on this bright June morning go I also to reap my harvest,—pursuing a sweet more delectable than sugar, fruit more savory than berries, and game for another palate than that tickled by trout.

June, of all the months, the student of ornithology can least afford to lose. Most birds are nesting then, and in full song and plumage.

AT THE HEADWATERS OF THE DELAWARE
Overlooking Mr. Burroughs's boyhood home

And what is a bird without its song? Do we not wait for the stranger to speak? It seems to me that I do not know a bird till I have heard its voice; then I come nearer it at once, and it possesses a human interest to me. I have met the gray-cheeked thrush in the woods, and held him in my hand; still I do not know him. The silence of the cedar-bird throws a mystery about him which neither his good looks nor his petty larcenies in cherry time can dispel. A bird's song contains a clew to its life, and establishes a sympathy, an understanding, between itself and the listener.

I descend a steep hill, and approach the hemlocks through a large sugar-bush. When twenty rods distant, I hear all along the line of the forest the incessant warble of the red-eyed vireo, cheerful and happy as the merry whistle of a schoolboy. He is one of our most common and widely distributed birds. Approach any forest at any hour of the day, in any kind of weather, from May to August, in any of the Middle or Eastern districts, and the chances are that the first note you hear will be his. Rain or shine, before noon or after, in the deep forest or in the village grove,—when it is too hot for the thrushes or too cold and windy for the warblers,—it is never out of time or place for this little minstrel to indulge his cheerful strain. In the deep wilds of the Adirondacks, where few birds are seen and fewer heard, his note was almost constantly in my ear. Always busy, making it a point never to suspend for one moment his occupation to indulge his musical taste, his lay is that of industry and contentment. There is nothing plaintive or especially musical in his performance, but the sentiment expressed is eminently that of cheerfulness. Indeed, the songs of most birds have some human significance, which, I think, is the source of the delight we take in them. The song of the bobolink to me expresses hilarity; the song sparrow's, faith; the bluebird's, love; the catbird's, pride; the white-eyed flycatcher's, self-consciousness; that of the hermit thrush, spiritual serenity: while there is something military in the call of the robin.

The red-eye is classed among the flycatchers by some writers, but is much more of a worm-eater, and has few of the traits or habits of the *Muscicapa* or the true *Sylvia*. He resembles somewhat the warbling vireo, and the two birds are often confounded by careless observers. Both warble in the same cheerful strain, but the latter more continuously and rapidly. The red-eye is a larger, slimmer bird, with a faint bluish crown, and a light line over the eye. His movements are peculiar. You may see him hopping among the limbs, exploring the under side of the leaves, peering to the right and left, now flitting a few feet, now hopping as many, and warbling

## IN THE HEMLOCKS

incessantly, occasionally in a subdued tone, which sounds from a very indefinite distance. When he has found a worm to his liking, he turns lengthwise of the limb and bruises its head with his beak before devouring it.

As I enter the woods the slate-colored snowbird starts up before me and chirps sharply. His protest when thus disturbed is almost metallic in its sharpness. He breeds here, and is not esteemed a snowbird at all, as he disappears at the near approach of winter, and returns again in spring, like the song sparrow, and is not in any way associated with the cold and the snow. So different are the habits of birds in different localities. Even the crow does not winter here, and is seldom seen after December or before March.

The snowbird, or "black chipping-bird," as it is known among the farmers, is the finest architect of any of the ground-builders known to me. The site of its nest is usually some low bank by the roadside, near a wood. In a slight excavation, with a partially concealed entrance, the exquisite structure is placed. Horse and cow hair are plentifully used, imparting to the interior of the nest great symmetry and firmness as well as softness.

Passing down through the maple arches, barely pausing to observe the antics of a trio of squirrels,—two gray ones and a black one,—I cross an ancient brush fence and am fairly within the old hemlocks, and in one of the most primitive, undisturbed nooks. In the deep moss I tread as with muffled feet, and the pupils of my eyes dilate in the dim, almost religious light. The irreverent red squirrels, however, run and snicker at my approach, or mock the solitude with their ridiculous chattering and frisking.

This nook is the chosen haunt of the winter wren. This is the only place and these the only woods in which I find him in this vicinity. His voice fills these dim aisles, as if aided by some marvelous sounding-board. Indeed, his song is very strong for so small a bird, and unites in a remarkable degree brilliancy and plaintiveness. I think of a tremulous vibrating tongue of silver. You may know it is the song of a wren, from its gushing lyrical character; but you must needs look sharp to see the little minstrel, especially while in the act of singing. He is nearly the color of the ground and the leaves; he never ascends the tall trees, but keeps low, flitting from stump to stump and from root to root, dodging in and out of his hiding-places, and watching all intruders with a suspicious eye. He has a very pert, almost comical look. His tail stands more than perpendicular: it points straight toward his head. He is the least ostentatious singer I know of. He does not strike an attitude, and lift up his head in preparation, and, as it were, clear his throat; but sits there on a log and pours out his music, looking straight before him, or even down at the ground. As a songster, he has but few superiors. I do not hear him after the first week in July.

While sitting on this soft-cushioned log, tasting the pungent acidulous wood-sorrel, the blossoms of which, large and pink-veined, rise everywhere above the moss, a rufous-colored bird flies quickly past, and, alighting on a low limb a few rods off, salutes me with "Whew! Whew!" or "Whoit! Whoit!" almost as you would whistle for your dog. I see by his impulsive, graceful movements, and his dimly speckled breast, that it is a thrush. Presently he utters a few soft, mellow, flute-like notes, one of the most simple expressions of melody to be heard, and scuds away, and I see it is the veery, or Wilson's thrush. He is the least of the thrushes in size, being about that of the common bluebird, and he may be distinguished from his relatives by the dimness of the spots upon his breast. The wood thrush has very clear, distinct oval spots on a white ground; in the hermit, the spots run more into lines, on a ground of a faint bluish white; in the veery, the marks are almost obsolete, and a few rods off his breast presents only a dull yellowish appearance. To get a good view of him you have only to sit down in his haunts, as in such cases he seems equally anxious to get a good view of you.

From those tall hemlocks proceeds a very fine insect-like warble, and occasionally I see a spray tremble, or catch the flit of a wing. I watch and watch till my head grows dizzy and my neck is in danger of permanent displacement, and still do not get a good view. Presently the bird darts, or, as it seems, falls down a few feet in pursuit of a fly or a moth, and I see the whole of it, but in the dim light am undecided. It is for such emergencies that I have brought my gun. A bird in the hand is worth half a dozen in the bush, even for ornithological purposes; and no sure and rapid progress can be made in the study without taking life, without procuring specimens. This bird is a warbler, plainly enough, from his habits and manner; but what kind of warbler? Look on him and name him: a deep orange or flame-colored throat and breast; the same color showing also in a line over the eye and in his crown; back variegated black and white. The female is less marked and brilliant. The orange-throated warbler would seem to be his right name, his characteristic cognomen; but no, he is doomed to wear the name of some discoverer, perhaps the first who rifled his nest or robbed him of his mate,—Blackburn; hence Blackburnian warbler. The *burn* seems appropriate enough, for in these dark evergreens his throat and breast show like flame. He has a very fine warble, suggesting that of the redstart, but not especially musical. I find him in no other woods in this vicinity.

## IN THE HEMLOCKS

I am attracted by another warble in the same locality, and experience a like difficulty in getting a good view of the author of it. It is quite a noticeable strain, sharp and sibilant, and sounds well amid the old trees. In the upland woods of beech and maple it is a more familiar sound than in these solitudes. On taking the bird in hand, one cannot help exclaiming, "How beautiful!" So tiny and elegant, the smallest of the warblers; a delicate blue back, with a slight bronze-colored triangular spot between the shoulders; upper mandible black; lower mandible yellow as gold; throat yellow, becoming a dark bronze on the breast. Blue yellow-back he is called, though the yellow is much nearer a bronze. He is remarkably delicate and beautiful,—the handsomest as he is the smallest of the warblers known to me. It is never without surprise that I find amid these rugged, savage aspects of nature creatures so fairy and delicate. But such is the law. Go to the sea or climb the mountain, and with the ruggedest and the savagest you will find likewise the fairest and the most delicate. The greatness and the minuteness of nature pass all understanding.

Ever since I entered the woods, even while listening to the lesser songsters, or contemplating the silent forms about me, a strain has reached my ears from out the depths of the forest that to me is the finest sound in nature,—the song of the hermit thrush. I often hear him thus a long way off, sometimes over a quarter of a mile away, when only the stronger and more perfect parts of his music reach me; and through the general chorus of wrens and warblers I detect this sound rising pure and serene, as if a spirit from some remote height were slowly chanting a divine accompaniment. This song appeals to the sentiment of the beautiful in me, and suggests a serene religious beatitude as no other sound in nature does. It is perhaps more of an evening than a morning hymn, though I hear it at all hours of the day. It is very simple, and I can hardly tell the secret of its charm. "O spheral, spheral!" he seems to say; "O holy, holy! O clear away, clear away! O clear up, clear up!" interspersed with the finest trills and the most delicate preludes. It is not a proud, gorgeous strain, like the tanager's or the grosbeak's; suggests no passion or emotion,—nothing personal,—but seems to be the voice of that calm, sweet solemnity one attains to in his best moments. It realizes a peace and a deep, solemn joy that only the finest souls may know. A few nights ago I ascended a mountain to see the world by moonlight, and when near the summit the hermit commenced his evening hymn a few rods from me. Listening to this strain on the lone mountain, with the full moon just rounded from the horizon, the pomp of your cities and the pride of your civilization seemed trivial and cheap.

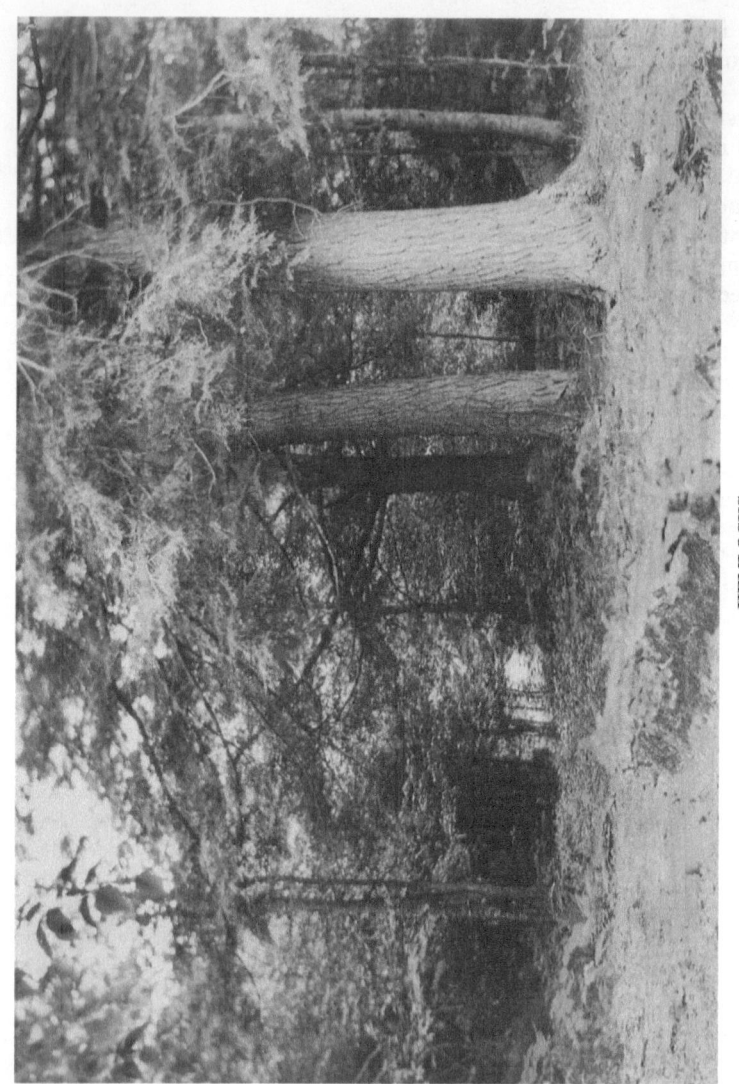

HEMLOCKS

## IN THE HEMLOCKS

I have seldom known two of these birds to be singing at the same time in the same locality, rivaling each other, like the wood thrush or the veery. Shooting one from a tree, I have observed another take up the strain from almost the identical perch in less than ten minutes afterward. Later in the day, when I had penetrated the heart of the old Barkpeeling, I came suddenly upon one singing from a low stump, and for a wonder he did not seem alarmed, but lifted up his divine voice as if his privacy was undisturbed. I open his beak and find the inside yellow as gold. I was prepared to find it inlaid with pearls and diamonds, or to see an angel issue from it.

He is not much in the books. Indeed, I am acquainted with scarcely any writer on ornithology whose head is not muddled on the subject of our three prevailing song-thrushes, confounding either their figures or their songs. A writer in the "Atlantic"[1] gravely tells us the wood thrush is sometimes called the hermit, and then, after describing the song of the hermit with great beauty and correctness, coolly ascribes it to the veery! The new Cyclopædia, fresh from the study of Audubon, says the hermit's song consists of a single plaintive note, and that the veery's resembles that of the wood thrush! The hermit thrush may be easily identified by his color; his back being a clear olive-brown becoming rufous on his rump and tail. A quill from his wing placed beside one from his tail on a dark ground presents quite a marked contrast.

I walk along the old road, and note the tracks in the thin layer of mud. When do these creatures travel here? I have never yet chanced to meet one. Here a partridge has set its foot; there, a woodcock; here, a squirrel or mink; there, a skunk; there, a fox. What a clear, nervous track reynard makes! how easy to distinguish it from that of a little dog,—it is so sharply cut and defined! A dog's track is coarse and clumsy beside it. There is as much wildness in the track of an animal as in its voice. Is a deer's track like a sheep's or a goat's? What winged-footed fleetness and agility may be inferred from the sharp, braided track of the gray squirrel upon the new snow! Ah! in nature is the best discipline. How wood-life sharpens the senses, giving a new power to the eye, the ear, the nose! And are not the rarest and most exquisite songsters wood-birds?

Everywhere in these solitudes I am greeted with the pensive, almost pathetic note of the wood pewee. The pewees are the true flycatchers, and are easily identified. They are very characteristic birds, have strong family traits and pugnacious dispositions. They are the least attractive or elegant birds of our fields or forests. Sharp-shouldered, big-headed, short-legged, of no particular color, of

---

[1] For December, 1858.

little elegance in flight or movement, with a disagreeable flirt of the tail, always quarreling with their neighbors and with one another, no birds are so little calculated to excite pleasurable emotions in the beholder, or to become objects of human interest and affection. The kingbird is the best dressed member of the family, but he is a braggart; and, though always snubbing his neighbors, is an arrant coward, and shows the white feather at the slightest display of pluck in his antagonist. I have seen him turn tail to a swallow, and have known the little pewee in question to whip him beautifully. From the great-crested to the little green flycatcher, their ways and general habits are the same. Slow in flying from point to point, they yet have a wonderful quickness, and snap up the fleetest insects with little apparent effort. There is a constant play of quick, nervous movements underneath their outer show of calmness and stolidity. They do not scour the limbs and trees like the warblers, but, perched upon the middle branches, wait, like true hunters, for the game to come along. There is often a very audible snap of the beak as they seize their prey.

The wood pewee, the prevailing species in this locality, arrests your attention by his sweet, pathetic cry. There is room for it also in the deep woods, as well as for the more prolonged and elevated strains.

Its relative, the phœbe-bird, builds an exquisite nest of moss on the side of some shelving cliff or overhanging rock. The other day, passing by a ledge near the top of a mountain in a singularly desolate locality, my eye rested upon one of these structures, looking precisely as if it grew there, so in keeping was it with the mossy character of the rock, and I have had a growing affection for the bird ever since. The rock seemed to love the nest and to claim it as its own. I said, what a lesson in architecture is here! Here is a house that was built, but with such loving care and such beautiful adaptation of the means to the end, that it looks like a product of nature. The same wise economy is noticeable in the nests of all birds. No bird could paint its house white or red, or add aught for show.

At one point in the grayest, most shaggy part of the woods, I come suddenly upon a brood of screech owls, full grown, sitting together upon a dry, moss-draped limb, but a few feet from the ground. I pause within four or five yards of them and am looking about me, when my eye lights upon these gray, motionless figures. They sit perfectly upright, some with their backs and some with their breasts toward me, but every head turned squarely in my direction. Their eyes are closed to a mere black line; through this crack they are watching me, evidently thinking themselves unobserved. The spectacle is weird and grotesque, and suggests something impish and uncanny. It is a new effect, the night side of the woods by daylight. After observing them a moment I take a single step toward them, when, quick as thought, their eyes fly wide open, their attitude is changed, they bend, some this way, some that, and, instinct with life and motion, stare wildly around them. Another step, and they all take flight but one, which stoops low on the branch, and with the look of a frightened cat regards me for a few seconds over its shoulder. They fly swiftly and softly, and disperse through the trees. I shoot one, which is of a tawny red tint, like that figured by Wilson. It is a singular fact that the plumage of these owls presents two totally distinct phases, which "have no relation to sex, age, or season," one being an ashen gray, the other a bright rufous.

Coming to a drier and less mossy place in the woods, I am amused with the golden-crowned thrush,—which, however, is no thrush at all, but a warbler. He walks on the ground ahead of me with such an easy, gliding motion, and with such an unconscious, preoccupied air, jerking his head like a hen or a partridge, now hurrying, now slackening his pace, that I pause to observe him. I sit down, he pauses to observe me, and extends his pretty ramblings on all sides, apparently very much engrossed with his own affairs, but never losing sight of me. But few of the birds are walkers, most being hoppers, like the robin.

Satisfied that I have no hostile intentions, the pretty pedestrian mounts a limb a few feet from the ground, and gives me the benefit of one of his musical performances, a sort of accelerating chant. Commencing in a very low key, which makes him seem at a very uncertain distance, he grows louder and louder till his body quakes and his chant runs into a shriek, ringing in my ear with a peculiar sharpness. This lay may be represented thus: "Teacher, *teacher*, TEACHER, TEACHER, *TEACHER!*"—the accent on the first syllable and each word uttered with increased force and shrillness. No writer with whom I am acquainted gives him credit for more musical ability than is displayed in this strain. Yet in this the half is not told. He has a far rarer song, which he reserves for some nymph whom he meets in the air. Mounting by easy flights to the top of the tallest tree, he launches into the air with a sort of suspended, hovering flight, like certain of the finches, and bursts into a perfect ecstasy of song,—clear, ringing, copious, rivaling the goldfinch's in vivacity, and the linnet's in melody. This strain is one of the rarest bits of bird melody to be heard, and is oftenest indulged in late in the afternoon or after sundown. Over the woods, hid from view, the ecstatic singer warbles his finest strain. In this song you instantly detect his relationship to the water-wagtail,—erroneously called water-thrush,—whose song is likewise a sudden burst, full and

A TROUT STREAM

## IN THE HEMLOCKS

ringing, and with a tone of youthful joyousness in it, as if the bird had just had some unexpected good fortune. For nearly two years this strain of the pretty walker was little more than a disembodied voice to me, and I was puzzled by it as Thoreau by his mysterious night-warbler, which, by the way, I suspect was no new bird at all, but one he was otherwise familiar with. The little bird himself seems disposed to keep the matter a secret, and improves every opportunity to repeat before you his shrill, accelerating lay, as if this were quite enough and all he laid claim to. Still, I trust I am betraying no confidence in making the matter public here. I think this is preëminently his love-song, as I hear it oftenest about the mating season. I have caught half-suppressed bursts of it from two males chasing each other with fearful speed through the forest.

Turning to the left from the old road, I wander over soft logs and gray yielding débris, across the little trout brook, until I emerge in the overgrown Barkpeeling,—pausing now and then on the way to admire a small, solitary white flower which rises above the moss, with radical, heart-shaped leaves, and a blossom precisely like the liverwort except in color, but which is not put down in my botany,— or to observe the ferns, of which I count six varieties, some gigantic ones nearly shoulder-high.

At the foot of a rough, scraggy yellow birch, on a bank of club-moss, so richly inlaid with partridge-berry and curious shining leaves—with here and there in the bordering a spire of the false wintergreen strung with faint pink flowers and exhaling the breath of a May orchard—that it looks too costly a couch for such an idler, I recline to note what transpires. The sun is just past the meridian, and the afternoon chorus is not yet in full tune. Most birds sing with the greatest spirit and vivacity in the forenoon, though there are occasional bursts later in the day in which nearly all voices join; while it is not till the twilight that the full power and solemnity of the thrush's hymn is felt.

My attention is soon arrested by a pair of hummingbirds, the ruby-throated, disporting themselves in a low bush a few yards from me. The female takes shelter amid the branches, and squeaks exultingly as the male, circling above, dives down as if to dislodge her. Seeing me, he drops like a feather on a slender twig, and in a moment both are gone. Then, as if by a preconcerted signal, the throats are all atune. I lie on my back with eyes half closed, and analyze the chorus of warblers, thrushes, finches, and flycatchers; while, soaring above all, a little withdrawn and alone rises the divine contralto of the hermit. That richly modulated warble proceeding from the top of yonder birch, and which unpracticed ears would mistake for the voice of the scarlet tanager, comes from that rare visitant, the rose-breasted grosbeak. It is a strong, vivacious strain, a bright noonday song, full of health and assurance, indicating fine talents in the performer, but not genius. As I come up under the tree he casts his eye down at me, but continues his song. This bird is said to be quite common in the Northwest, but he is rare in the Eastern districts. His beak is disproportionately large and heavy, like a huge nose, which slightly mars his good looks; but Nature has made it up to him in a blush rose upon his breast, and the most delicate of pink linings to the under side of his wings. His back is variegated black and white, and when flying low the white shows conspicuously. If he passed over your head, you would note the delicate flush under his wings.

That bit of bright scarlet on yonder dead hemlock, glowing like a live coal against the dark background, seeming almost too brilliant for the severe northern climate, is his relative, the scarlet tanager. I occasionally meet him in the deep hemlocks, and know no stronger contrast in nature. I almost fear he will kindle the dry limb on which he alights. He is quite a solitary bird, and in this section seems to prefer the high, remote woods, even going quite to the mountain's top. Indeed, the event of my last visit to the mountain was meeting one of these brilliant creatures near the summit, in full song. The breeze carried the notes far and wide. He seemed to enjoy the elevation, and I imagined his song had more scope and freedom than usual. When he had flown far down the mountain-side, the breeze still brought me his finest notes. In plumage he is the most brilliant bird we have. The bluebird is not entirely blue; nor will the indigo-bird bear a close inspection, nor the goldfinch, nor the summer redbird. But the tanager loses nothing by a near view; the deep scarlet of his body and the black of his wings and tail are quite perfect. This is his holiday suit; in the fall he becomes a dull yellowish green,—the color of the female the whole season.

One of the leading songsters in this choir of the old Barkpeeling is the purple finch or linnet. He sits somewhat apart, usually on a dead hemlock, and warbles most exquisitely. He is one of our finest songsters, and stands at the head of the finches, as the hermit at the head of the thrushes. His song approaches an ecstasy, and, with the exception of the winter wren's, is the most rapid and copious strain to be heard in these woods. It is quite destitute of the trills and the liquid, silvery, bubbling notes that characterize the wren's; but there runs through it a round, richly modulated whistle, very sweet and very pleasing. The call of the robin is brought in at a certain point with marked effect, and, throughout, the variety is so great and the strain so rapid that the impression is as of two or three birds

## IN THE HEMLOCKS

singing at the same time. He is not common here, and I only find him in these or similar woods. His color is peculiar, and looks as if it might have been imparted by dipping a brown bird in diluted pokeberry juice. Two or three more dippings would have made the purple complete. The female is the color of the song sparrow, a little larger, with heavier beak, and tail much more forked.

In a little opening quite free from brush and trees, I step down to bathe my hands in the brook, when a small, light slate-colored bird flutters out of the bank, not three feet from my head, as I stoop down, and, as if severely lamed or injured, flutters through the grass and into the nearest bush. As I do not follow, but remain near the nest, she *chips* sharply, which brings the male, and I see it is the speckled Canada warbler. I find no authority in the books for this bird to build upon the ground, yet here is the nest, made chiefly of dry grass, set in a slight excavation in the bank not two feet from the water, and looking a little perilous to anything but ducklings or sandpipers. There are two young birds and one little speckled egg just pipped. But how is this? what mystery is here? One nestling is much larger than the other, monopolizes most of the nest, and lifts its open mouth far above that of its companion, though obviously both are of the same age, not more than a day old. Ah! I see; the old trick of the cow bunting, with a stinging human significance. Taking the interloper by the nape of the neck, I deliberately drop it into the water, but not without a pang, as I see its naked form, convulsed with chills, float downstream. Cruel? So is Nature cruel. I take one life to save two. In less than two days this pot-bellied intruder would have caused the death of the two rightful occupants of the nest; so I step in and turn things into their proper channel again.

It is a singular freak of nature, this instinct which prompts one bird to lay its eggs in the nests of others, and thus shirk the responsibility of rearing its own young. The cow buntings always resort to this cunning trick; and when one reflects upon their numbers, it is evident that these little tragedies are quite frequent. In Europe the parallel case is that of the cuckoo, and occasionally our own cuckoo imposes upon a robin or a thrush in the same manner. The cow bunting seems to have no conscience about the matter, and, so far as I have observed, invariably selects the nest of a bird smaller than itself. Its egg is usually the first to hatch; its young overreaches all the rest when food is brought; it grows with great rapidity, spreads and fills the nest, and the starved and crowded occupants soon perish, when the parent bird removes their dead bodies, giving its whole energy and care to the foster-child.

The warblers and smaller flycatchers are generally the sufferers, though I sometimes see the slate-colored snowbird unconsciously duped in like manner; and the other day, in a tall tree in the woods, I discovered the black-throated green-backed warbler devoting itself to this dusky, overgrown foundling. An old farmer to whom I pointed out the fact was much surprised that such things should happen in his woods without his knowledge.

These birds may be seen prowling through all parts of the woods at this season, watching for an opportunity to steal their egg into some nest. One day while sitting on a log I saw one moving by short flights through the trees and gradually nearing the ground. Its movements were hurried and stealthy. About fifty yards from me it disappeared behind some low brush, and had evidently alighted upon the ground.

After waiting a few moments I cautiously walked in the direction. When about halfway I accidentally made a slight noise, when the bird flew up, and seeing me, hurried off out of the woods. Arrived at the place, I found a simple nest of dry grass and leaves partially concealed under a prostrate branch. I took it to be the nest of a sparrow. There were three eggs in the nest, and one lying about a foot below it as if it had been rolled out, as of course it had. It suggested the thought that perhaps, when the cowbird finds the full complement of eggs in a nest, it throws out one and deposits its own instead. I revisited the nest a few days afterward and found an egg again cast out, but none had been put in its place. The nest had been abandoned by its owner and the eggs were stale.

In all cases where I have found this egg, I have observed both male and female of the cowbird lingering near, the former uttering his peculiar liquid, glassy note from the tops of the trees.

In July, the young which have been reared in the same neighborhood, and which are now of a dull fawn color, begin to collect in small flocks, which grow to be quite large in autumn.

The speckled Canada is a very superior warbler, having a lively, animated strain, reminding you of certain parts of the canary's, though quite broken and incomplete; the bird, the while, hopping amid the branches with increased liveliness, and indulging in fine sibilant chirps, too happy to keep silent.

His manners are quite marked. He has a habit of courtesying when he discovers you which is very pretty. In form he is an elegant bird, somewhat slender, his back of a bluish lead-color becoming nearly black on his crown: the under part of his body, from his throat down, is of a light, delicate yellow, with a belt of black dots across his breast. He has a fine eye, surrounded by a light yellow ring.

The parent birds are much disturbed by my presence, and keep up a loud emphatic chirping, which attracts the attention of their sympathetic neighbors, and one after another they come to see what

## IN THE HEMLOCKS

has happened. The chestnut-sided and the Blackburnian come in company. The black and yellow warbler pauses a moment and hastens away; the Maryland yellow-throat peeps shyly from the lower bushes and utters his "Fip! fip!" in sympathy; the wood pewee comes straight to the tree overhead, and the red-eyed vireo lingers and lingers, eying me with a curious, innocent look, evidently much puzzled. But all disappear again, one by one, apparently without a word of condolence or encouragement to the distressed pair. I have often noticed among birds this show of sympathy,—if indeed it be sympathy, and not merely curiosity, or desire to be forewarned of the approach of a common danger.

An hour afterward I approach the place, find all still, and the mother bird upon the nest. As I draw near she seems to sit closer, her eyes growing large with an inexpressibly wild, beautiful look. She keeps her place till I am within two paces of her, when she flutters away as at first. In the brief interval the remaining egg has hatched, and the two little nestlings lift their heads without being jostled or overreached by any strange bedfellow. A week afterward and they were flown away,—so brief is the infancy of birds. And the wonder is that they escape, even for this short time, the skunks and minks and muskrats that abound here, and that have a decided partiality for such tidbits.

I pass on through the old Barkpeeling, now threading an obscure cow-path or an overgrown wood-road; now clambering over soft and decayed logs, or forcing my way through a network of briers and hazels; now entering a perfect bower of wild cherry, beech, and soft maple; now emerging into a little grassy lane, golden with buttercups or white with daisies, or wading waist-deep in the red raspberry-bushes.

Whir! whir! whir! and a brood of half-grown partridges start up like an explosion, a few paces from me, and, scattering, disappear in the bushes on all sides. Let me sit down here behind the screen of ferns and briers, and hear this wild hen of the woods call together her brood. At what an early age the partridge flies! Nature seems to concentrate her energies on the wing, making the safety of the bird a point to be looked after first; and while the body is covered with down, and no signs of feathers are visible, the wing-quills sprout and unfold, and in an incredibly short time the young make fair headway in flying.

The same rapid development of wing may be observed in chickens and turkeys, but not in water-fowls, nor in birds that are safely housed in the nest till full-fledged. The other day, by a brook, I came suddenly upon a young sandpiper, a most beautiful creature, enveloped in a soft gray down, swift and nimble and apparently a week or two old, but with no signs of plumage either of body or wing. And it needed none, for it escaped me by taking to the water as readily as if it had flown with wings.

Hark! there arises over there in the brush a soft, persuasive cooing, a sound so subtle and wild and unobtrusive that it requires the most alert and watchful ear to hear it. How gentle and solicitous and full of yearning love! It is the voice of the mother hen. Presently a faint timid "Yeap!" which almost eludes the ear, is heard in various directions,—the young responding. As no danger seems near, the cooing of the parent bird is soon a very audible clucking call, and the young move cautiously in the direction. Let me step never so carefully from my hiding-place, and all sounds instantly cease, and I search in vain for either parent or young.

The partridge is one of our most native and characteristic birds. The woods seem good to be in where I find him. He gives a habitable air to the forest, and one feels as if the rightful occupant was really at home. The woods where I do not find him seem to want something, as if suffering from some neglect of Nature. And then he is such a splendid success, so hardy and vigorous. I think he enjoys the cold and the snow. His wings seem to rustle with more fervency in midwinter. If the snow falls very fast, and promises a heavy storm, he will complacently sit down and allow himself to be snowed under. Approaching him at such times, he suddenly bursts out of the snow at your feet, scattering the flakes in all directions, and goes humming away through the woods like a bombshell,—a picture of native spirit and success.

His drum is one of the most welcome and beautiful sounds of spring. Scarcely have the trees expanded their buds, when, in the still April mornings, or toward nightfall, you hear the hum of his devoted wings. He selects not, as you would predict, a dry and resinous log, but a decayed and crumbling one, seeming to give the preference to old oak-logs that are partly blended with the soil. If a log to his taste cannot be found, he sets up his altar on a rock, which becomes resonant beneath his fervent blows. Who has seen the partridge drum? It is the next thing to catching a weasel asleep, though by much caution and tact it may be done. He does not hug the log, but stands very erect, expands his ruff, gives two introductory blows, pauses half a second, and then resumes, striking faster and faster till the sound becomes a continuous, unbroken whir, the whole lasting less than half a minute. The tips of his wings barely brush the log, so that the sound is produced rather by the force of the blows upon the air and upon his own body as in flying. One log will be used for many years, though not by the same drummer. It seems to be a sort of temple and held in great

## IN THE HEMLOCKS

respect. The bird always approaches on foot, and leaves it in the same quiet manner, unless rudely disturbed. He is very cunning, though his wit is not profound. It is difficult to approach him by stealth; you will try many times before succeeding; but seem to pass by him in a great hurry, making all the noise possible, and with plumage furled he stands as immovable as a knot, allowing you a good view, and a good shot if you are a sportsman.

Passing along one of the old Barkpeelers' roads which wander aimlessly about, I am attracted by a singularly brilliant and emphatic warble, proceeding from the low bushes, and quickly suggesting the voice of the Maryland yellow-throat. Presently the singer hops up on a dry twig, and gives me a good view: lead-colored head and neck, becoming nearly black on the breast; clear olive-green back, and yellow belly. From his habit of keeping near the ground, even hopping upon it occasionally, I know him to be a ground warbler; from his dark breast the ornithologist has added the expletive mourning, hence the mourning ground warbler.

Of this bird both Wilson and Audubon confessed their comparative ignorance, neither ever having seen its nest or become acquainted with its haunts and general habits. Its song is quite striking and novel, though its voice at once suggests the class of warblers to which it belongs. It is very shy and wary, flying but a few feet at a time, and studiously concealing itself from your view. I discover but one pair here. The female has food in her beak, but carefully avoids betraying the locality of her nest. The ground warblers all have one notable feature,—very beautiful legs, as white and delicate as if they had always worn silk stockings and satin slippers. High tree warblers have dark brown or black legs and more brilliant plumage, but less musical ability.

The chestnut-sided belongs to the latter class. He is quite common in these woods, as in all the woods about. He is one of the rarest and handsomest of the warblers; his white breast and throat, chestnut sides, and yellow crown show conspicuously. Last year I found the nest of one in an uplying beech wood, in a low bush near the roadside, where cows passed and browsed daily. Things went on smoothly till the cow bunting stole her egg into it, when other mishaps followed, and the nest was soon empty. A characteristic attitude of the male during this season is a slight drooping of the wings, and tail a little elevated, which gives him a very smart, bantam-like appearance. His song is fine and hurried, and not much of itself, but has its place in the general chorus.

A far sweeter strain, falling on the ear with the true sylvan cadence, is that of the black-throated green-backed warbler, whom I meet at various points. He has no superiors among the true *Sylvia*.

His song is very plain and simple, but remarkably pure and tender, and might be indicated by straight lines, thus, —— —— √ ; the first two marks representing two sweet, silvery notes, in the same pitch of voice, and quite unaccented; the latter marks, the concluding notes, wherein the tone and inflection are changed. The throat and breast of the male are a rich black like velvet, his face yellow, and his back a yellowish green.

Beyond the Barkpeeling, where the woods are mingled hemlock, beech, and birch, the languid midsummer note of the black-throated blue-back falls on my ear. "Twea, twea, twea-e-e!" in the upward slide, and with the peculiar *z-ing* of summer insects, but not destitute of a certain plaintive cadence. It is one of the most languid, unhurried sounds in all the woods. I feel like reclining upon the dry leaves at once. Audubon says he has never heard his love-song; but this is all the love-song he has, and he is evidently a very plain hero with his little brown mistress. He assumes few attitudes, and is not a bold and striking gymnast, like many of his kindred. He has a preference for dense woods of beech and maple, moves slowly amid the lower branches and smaller growths, keeping from eight to ten feet from the ground, and repeating now and then his listless, indolent strain. His back and crown are dark blue; his throat and breast, black; his belly, pure white; and he has a white spot on each wing.

Here and there I meet the black and white creeping warbler, whose fine strain reminds me of hair-wire. It is unquestionably the finest bird-song to be heard. Few insect strains will compare with it in this respect; while it has none of the harsh, brassy character of the latter, being very delicate and tender.

That sharp, uninterrupted, but still continued warble, which, before one has learned to discriminate closely, he is apt to confound with the red-eyed vireo's, is that of the solitary warbling vireo,—a bird slightly larger, much rarer, and with a louder, less cheerful and happy strain. I see him hopping along lengthwise of the limbs, and note the orange tinge of his breast and sides and the white circle around his eye.

But the declining sun and the deepening shadows admonish me that this ramble must be brought to a close, even though only the leading characters in this chorus of forty songsters have been described, and only a small portion of the venerable old woods explored. In a secluded swampy corner of the old Barkpeeling, where I find the great purple orchis in bloom, and where the foot of man or beast seems never to have trod, I linger long, contemplating the wonderful display of lichens and mosses that overrun both the smaller and the larger growths. Every bush and branch and sprig is

## IN THE HEMLOCKS

dressed up in the most rich and fantastic of liveries; and, crowning all, the long bearded moss festoons the branches or sways gracefully from the limbs. Every twig looks a century old, though green leaves tip the end of it. A young yellow birch has a venerable, patriarchal look, and seems ill at ease under such premature honors. A decayed hemlock is draped as if by hands for some solemn festival.

Mounting toward the upland again, I pause reverently as the hush and stillness of twilight come upon the woods. It is the sweetest, ripest hour of the day. And as the hermit's evening hymn goes up from the deep solitude below me, I experience that serene exaltation of sentiment of which music, literature, and religion are but the faint types and symbols.

1865.

# V
## BIRDS'-NESTS

## V

## BIRDS'-NESTS

HOW alert and vigilant the birds are, even when absorbed in building their nests! In an open space in the woods I see a pair of cedar-birds collecting moss from the top of a dead tree. Following the direction in which they fly, I soon discover the nest placed in the fork of a small soft maple, which stands amid a thick growth of wild cherry-trees and young beeches. Carefully concealing myself beneath it, without any fear that the workmen will hit me with a chip or let fall a tool, I await the return of the busy pair. Presently I hear the well-known note, and the female sweeps down and settles unsuspectingly into the half-finished structure. Hardly have her wings rested before her eye has penetrated my screen, and with a hurried movement of alarm she darts away. In a moment the male, with a tuft of wool in his beak (for there is a sheep pasture near), joins her, and the two reconnoitre the premises from the surrounding bushes. With their beaks still loaded, they move around with a frightened look, and refuse to approach the nest till I have moved off and lain down behind a log. Then one of them ventures to alight upon the nest, but, still suspecting all is not right, quickly darts away again. Then they both together come, and after much peeping and spying about, and apparently much anxious consultation, cautiously proceed to work. In less than half an hour it would seem that wool enough has been brought to supply the whole family, real and prospective, with socks, if needles and fingers could be found fine enough to knit it up. In less than a week the female has begun to deposit her eggs,—four of them in as many days,— white tinged with purple, with black spots on the larger end. After two weeks of incubation the young are out.

Excepting the American goldfinch, this bird builds later in the spring than any other,—its nest, in our northern climate, seldom being undertaken till July. As with the goldfinch, the reason is, probably, that suitable food for the young cannot be had at an earlier period.

FINDING A BIRD'S-NEST

## BIRDS'-NESTS

Like most of our common species, as the robin, sparrow, bluebird, pewee, wren, etc., this bird sometimes seeks wild, remote localities in which to rear its young; at others, takes up its abode near that of man. I knew a pair of cedar-birds, one season, to build in an apple-tree, the branches of which rubbed against the house. For a day or two before the first straw was laid, I noticed the pair carefully exploring every branch of the tree, the female taking the lead, the male following her with an anxious note and look. It was evident that the wife was to have her choice this time; and, like one who thoroughly knew her mind, she was proceeding to take it. Finally the site was chosen upon a high branch, extending over one low wing of the house. Mutual congratulations and caresses followed, when both birds flew away in quest of building material. That most freely used is a sort of cotton-bearing plant which grows in old wornout fields. The nest is large for the size of the bird, and very soft. It is in every respect a first-class domicile.

On another occasion, while walking or rather sauntering in the woods (for I have discovered that one cannot run and read the book of nature), my attention was arrested by a dull hammering, evidently but a few rods off. I said to myself, "Some one is building a house." From what I had previously seen, I suspected the builder to be a red-headed woodpecker in the top of a dead oak stub near by. Moving cautiously in that direction, I perceived a round hole, about the size of that made by an inch-and-a-half auger, near the top of the decayed trunk, and the white chips of the workman strewing the ground beneath. When but a few paces from the tree, my foot pressed upon a dry twig, which gave forth a very slight snap. Instantly the hammering ceased, and a scarlet head appeared at the door. Though I remained perfectly motionless, forbearing even to wink till my eyes smarted, the bird refused to go on with his work, but flew quietly off to a neighboring tree. What surprised me was, that, amid his busy occupation down in the heart of the old tree, he should have been so alert and watchful as to catch the slightest sound from without.

The woodpeckers all build in about the same manner, excavating the trunk or branch of a decayed tree and depositing the eggs on the fine fragments of wood at the bottom of the cavity. Though the nest is not especially an artistic work,—requiring strength rather than skill,—yet the eggs and the young of few other birds are so completely housed from the elements, or protected from their natural enemies, the jays, crows, hawks, and owls. A tree with a natural cavity is never selected, but one which has been dead just long enough to have become soft and brittle throughout. The bird goes in horizontally for a few inches, making a hole perfectly round and smooth and adapted to his size, then turns downward, gradually enlarging the hole, as he proceeds, to the depth of ten, fifteen, twenty inches, according to the softness of the tree and the urgency of the mother bird to deposit her eggs. While excavating, male and female work alternately. After one has been engaged fifteen or twenty minutes, drilling and carrying out chips, it ascends to an upper limb, utters a loud call or two, when its mate soon appears, and, alighting near it on the branch, the pair chatter and caress a moment, then the fresh one enters the cavity and the other flies away.

A few days since I climbed up to the nest of the downy woodpecker, in the decayed top of a sugar maple. For better protection against driving rains, the hole, which was rather more than an inch in diameter, was made immediately beneath a branch which stretched out almost horizontally from the main stem. It appeared merely a deeper shadow upon the dark and mottled surface of the bark with which the branches were covered, and could not be detected by the eye until one was within a few feet of it. The young chirped vociferously as I approached the nest, thinking it was the old one with food; but the clamor suddenly ceased as I put my hand on that part of the trunk in which they were concealed, the unusual jarring and rustling alarming them into silence. The cavity, which was about fifteen inches deep, was gourd-shaped, and was wrought out with great skill and regularity. The walls were quite smooth and clean and new.

I shall never forget the circumstance of observing a pair of yellow-bellied woodpeckers—the most rare and secluded, and, next to the red-headed, the most beautiful species found in our woods—breeding in an old, truncated beech in the Beaverkill Mountains, an offshoot of the Catskills. We had been traveling, three of us, all day in search of a trout lake, which lay far in among the mountains, had twice lost our course in the trackless forest, and, weary and hungry, had sat down to rest upon a decayed log. The chattering of the young, and the passing to and fro of the parent birds, soon arrested my attention. The entrance to the nest was on the east side of the tree, about twenty-five feet from the ground. At intervals of scarcely a minute, the old birds, one after the other, would alight upon the edge of the hole with a grub or worm in their beaks; then each in turn would make a bow or two, cast an eye quickly around, and by a single movement place itself in the neck of the passage. Here it would pause a moment, as if to determine in which expectant mouth to place the morsel, and then disappear within. In about half a minute, during which time the chattering of the young gradually subsided, the bird would again emerge, but this time bearing in its beak the ordure of one of the helpless family. Flying away very slowly with head lowered and extended, as if anxious to hold the offensive object as far from its plumage as possible, the bird dropped the unsavory morsel in the course of a few yards, and, alighting on a tree, wiped its bill on the bark and moss. This seems to be the order all day,—carrying in and carrying out. I watched the birds for an hour, while my companions were taking their turn in exploring the lay of the land around us, and noted no variation in the programme. It would be curious to know if the young are fed and waited upon in regular order, and how, amid the darkness and the crowded state of the apartment, the matter is so neatly managed. But ornithologists are all silent upon the subject.

This practice of the birds is not so uncommon as it might at first seem. It is indeed almost an invariable rule among all land birds. With woodpeckers and kindred species, and with birds that burrow in the ground, as bank swallows, kingfishers, etc., it is a necessity. The accumulation of the excrement in the nest would prove most fatal to the young.

But even among birds that neither bore nor mine, but which build a shallow nest on the branch of a tree or upon the ground, as the robin, the finches, the buntings, etc., the ordure of the young is removed to a distance by the parent bird. When the robin is seen going away from its brood with a slow, heavy flight, entirely different from its manner a moment before on approaching the nest with a cherry or worm, it is certain to be engaged in this office. One may observe the social sparrow, when feeding its young, pause a moment after the worm has been given and hop around on the brink of the nest observing the movements within.

The instinct of cleanliness no doubt prompts the action in all cases, though the disposition to secrecy or concealment may not be unmixed with it.

The swallows form an exception to the rule, the excrement being voided by the young over the brink of the nest. They form an exception, also, to the rule of secrecy, aiming not so much to conceal the nest as to render it inaccessible.

Other exceptions are the pigeons, hawks, and water-fowls.

But to return. Having a good chance to note the color and markings of the woodpeckers as they passed in and out at the opening of the nest, I saw that Audubon had made a mistake in figuring or describing the female of this species with the red spot upon the head. I have seen a number of pairs of them, and in no instance have I seen the mother bird marked with red.

The male was in full plumage, and I reluctantly shot him for a specimen. Passing by the place again next day, I paused a moment to note how matters stood. I confess it was not without some compunctions that I heard the cries of the young birds, and saw the widowed mother, her cares now doubled, hastening to and fro in the solitary woods. She would occasionally pause expectantly on the trunk of a tree and utter a loud call.

It usually happens, when the male of any species is killed during the breeding season, that the female soon procures another mate. There are, most likely, always a few unmated birds of both sexes within a given range, and through these the broken links may be restored. Audubon or Wilson, I forget which, tells of a pair of fish hawks, or ospreys, that built their nest in an ancient oak. The male was so zealous in the defense of the young that he actually attacked with beak and claw a person who attempted to climb into his nest, putting his face and eyes in great jeopardy. Arming himself with a heavy club, the climber felled the gallant bird to the ground and killed him. In the course of a few days the female had procured another mate. But naturally enough the stepfather showed none of the spirit and pluck in defense of the brood that had been displayed by the original parent. When danger was nigh he was seen afar off, sailing around in placid unconcern.

It is generally known that when either the wild turkey or domestic turkey begins to lay, and afterwards to sit and rear the brood, she secludes herself from the male, who then, very sensibly, herds with others of his sex, and betakes himself to haunts of his own till male and female, old and young, meet again on common ground, late in the fall. But rob the sitting bird of her eggs, or destroy her tender young, and she immediately sets out in quest of a male, who is no laggard when he hears her call. The same is true of ducks and other aquatic fowls. The propagating instinct is strong, and surmounts all ordinary difficulties. No doubt the widowhood I had caused in the case of the woodpeckers was of short duration, and chance brought, or the widow drummed up, some forlorn male, who was not dismayed by the prospect of having a large family of half-grown birds on his hands at the outset.

I have seen a fine cock robin paying assiduous addresses to a female bird as late as the middle of July; and I have no doubt that his intentions were honorable. I watched the pair for half an hour. The hen, I took it, was in the market for the second time that season; but the cock, from his bright, unfaded plumage, looked like a new arrival. The hen resented every advance of the male. In vain he strutted around her and displayed his fine feathers; every now and then she would make at him in a most spiteful manner. He followed her to the ground, poured into her ear a fine, half-suppressed warble, offered her a worm, flew back to the tree again with a great spread of plumage, hopped around her on the branches, chirruped, chattered, flew gallantly at an intruder, and was back in an instant at her side. No use,—she cut him short at every turn.

The *dénouement* I cannot relate, as the artful bird, followed by her ardent suitor, soon flew away beyond my sight. It may not be rash to conclude, however, that she held out no longer than was prudent.

On the whole, there seems to be a system of Women's Rights prevailing among the birds, which, contemplated from the standpoint of the male, is quite admirable. In almost all cases of joint interest, the female bird is the most active. She determines the site of the nest, and is usually the most absorbed in its construction. Generally, she is more vigilant in caring for the young, and manifests the most concern when danger threatens. Hour after hour I have seen the mother of a brood of blue grosbeaks pass from the nearest meadow to the tree that held her nest, with a cricket or grasshopper in her bill, while her better-dressed half was singing serenely on a distant tree or pursuing his pleasure amid the branches.

Yet among the majority of our song-birds the male is most conspicuous both by his color and manners and by his song, and is to that extent a shield to the female. It is thought that the female is humbler clad for her better concealment during incubation. But this is not satisfactory, as in some cases she is relieved from time to time by the male. In the case of the domestic dove, for instance, promptly at midday the cock is found upon the nest. I should say that the dull or neutral tints of the female were a provision of nature for her greater safety at all times, as her life is far more precious to the species than that of the male. The indispensable office of the male reduces itself to little more than a moment of time, while that of his mate extends over days and weeks, if not months.[1]

In migrating northward, the males precede the females by eight or ten days; returning in the fall, the females and young precede the males by about the same time.

After the woodpeckers have abandoned their nests, or rather chambers, which they do after the first season, their cousins, the nuthatches, chickadees, and brown creepers, fall heir to them. These

---

[1] A recent English writer upon this subject presents an array of facts and considerations that do not support this view. He says that, with very few exceptions, it is the rule that, when both sexes are of strikingly gay and conspicuous colors, the nest is such as to conceal the sitting bird; while, whenever there is a striking contrast of colors, the male being gay and conspicuous, the female dull and obscure, the nest is open and the sitting bird exposed to view. The exceptions to this rule among European birds appear to be very few. Among our own birds, the cuckoos and blue jays build open nests, without presenting any noticeable difference in the coloring of the two sexes. The same is true of the pewees, the kingbird, and the sparrows, while the common bluebird, the oriole, and orchard starling afford examples the other way.

birds, especially the creepers and nuthatches, have many of the habits of the *Picidæ*, but lack their powers of bill, and so are unable to excavate a nest for themselves. Their habitation, therefore, is always second-hand. But each species carries in some soft material of various kinds, or, in other words, furnishes the tenement to its liking. The chickadee arranges in the bottom of the cavity a little mat of a light felt-like substance, which looks as if it came from the hatter's, but which is probably the work of numerous worms or caterpillars. On this soft lining the female deposits six speckled eggs.

I recently discovered one of these nests in a most interesting situation. The tree containing it, a variety of the wild cherry, stood upon the brink of the bald summit of a high mountain. Gray, time-worn rocks lay piled loosely about, or overtoppled the just visible byways of the red fox. The trees had a half-scared look, and that indescribable wildness which lurks about the tops of all remote mountains possessed the place. Standing there, I looked down upon the back of the red-tailed hawk as he flew out over the earth beneath me. Following him, my eye also took in farms and settlements and villages and other mountain ranges that grew blue in the distance.

The parent birds attracted my attention by appearing with food in their beaks, and by seeming much put out. Yet so wary were they of revealing the locality of their brood, or even of the precise tree that held them, that I lurked around over an hour without gaining a point on them. Finally a bright and curious boy who accompanied me secreted himself under a low, projecting rock close to the tree in which we supposed the nest to be, while I moved off around the mountain-side. It was not long before the youth had their secret. The tree, which was low and wide-branching, and overrun with lichens, appeared at a cursory glance to contain not one dry or decayed limb. Yet there was one a few feet long, in which, when my eyes were piloted thither, I detected a small round orifice.

As my weight began to shake the branches, the consternation of both old and young was great. The stump of a limb that held the nest was about three inches thick, and at the bottom of the tunnel was excavated quite to the bark. With my thumb I broke in the thin wall, and the young, which were full-fledged, looked out upon the world for the first time. Presently one of them, with a significant chirp, as much as to say, "It is time we were out of this," began to climb up toward the proper entrance. Placing himself in the hole, he looked around without manifesting any surprise at the grand scene that lay spread out before him. He was taking his bearings, and determining how far he could trust the power of his untried wings to take him out of harm's way. After a moment's pause, with a loud chirrup,

IN A SHEEP PASTURE

he launched out and made tolerable headway. The others rapidly followed. Each one, as it started upward, from a sudden impulse, contemptuously saluted the abandoned nest with its excrement.

Though generally regular in their habits and instincts, yet the birds sometimes seem as whimsical and capricious as superior beings. One is not safe, for instance, in making any absolute assertion as to their place or mode of building. Ground-builders often get up into a bush, and tree-builders sometimes get upon the ground or into a tussock of grass. The song sparrow, which is a ground builder, has been known to build in the knothole of a fence rail; and a chimney swallow once got tired of soot and smoke, and fastened its nest on a rafter in a hay barn. A friend tells me of a pair of barn swallows which, taking a fanciful turn, saddled their nest in the loop of a rope that was pendent from a peg in the peak, and liked it so well that they repeated the experiment next year. I have known the social sparrow, or "hairbird," to build under a shed, in a tuft of hay that hung down, through the loose flooring, from the mow above. It usually contents itself with half a dozen stalks of dry grass and a few long hairs from a cow's tail loosely arranged on the branch of an apple-tree. The rough-winged swallow builds in the wall and in old stone-heaps, and I have seen the robin build in similar localities. Others have found its nest in old, abandoned wells. The house wren will build in anything that has an accessible cavity, from an old boot to a bombshell. A pair of them once persisted in building their nest in the top of a certain pump-tree, getting in through the opening above the handle. The pump being in daily use, the nest was destroyed more than a score of times. This jealous little wretch has the wise forethought, when the box in which he builds contains two compartments, to fill up one of them, so as to avoid the risk of troublesome neighbors.

The less skillful builders sometimes depart from their usual habit, and take up with the abandoned nest of some other species. The blue jay now and then lays in an old crow's nest or cuckoo's nest. The crow blackbird, seized with a fit of indolence, drops its eggs in the cavity of a decayed branch. I heard of a cuckoo that dispossessed a robin of its nest; of another that set a blue jay adrift. Large, loose structures, like the nests of the osprey and certain of the herons, have been found with half a dozen nests of the blackbirds set in the outer edges, like so many parasites, or, as Audubon says, like the retainers about the rude court of a feudal baron.

The same birds breeding in a southern climate construct far less elaborate nests than when breeding in a northern climate. Certain species of water-fowl, that abandon their eggs to the sand and the sun in the warmer zones, build a nest and sit in the usual way in

## BIRDS'-NESTS

Labrador. In Georgia, the Baltimore oriole places its nest upon the north side of the tree; in the Middle and Eastern States, it fixes it upon the south or east side, and makes it much thicker and warmer. I have seen one from the South that had some kind of coarse reed or sedge woven into it, giving it an open-work appearance, like a basket.

Very few species use the same material uniformly. I have seen the nest of the robin quite destitute of mud. In one instance it was composed mainly of long black horse-hairs, arranged in a circular manner, with a lining of fine yellow grass; the whole presenting quite a novel appearance. In another case the nest was chiefly constructed of a species of rock moss.

The nest for the second brood during the same season is often a mere makeshift. The haste of the female to deposit her eggs as the season advances seems very great, and the structure is apt to be prematurely finished. I was recently reminded of this fact by happening, about the last of July, to meet with several nests of the wood or bush sparrow in a remote blackberry field. The nests with eggs were far less elaborate and compact than the earlier nests, from which the young had flown.

Day after day, as I go to a certain piece of woods, I observe a male indigo-bird sitting on precisely the same part of a high branch, and singing in his most vivacious style. As I approach he ceases to sing, and, flirting his tail right and left with marked emphasis, chirps sharply. In a low bush near by, I come upon the object of his solicitude,—a thick, compact nest composed largely of dry leaves and fine grass, in which a plain brown bird is sitting upon four pale blue eggs.

The wonder is that a bird will leave the apparent security of the treetops to place its nest in the way of the many dangers that walk and crawl upon the ground. There, far up out of reach, sings the bird; here, not three feet from the ground, are its eggs or helpless young. The truth is, birds are the greatest enemies of birds, and it is with reference to this fact that many of the smaller species build.

Perhaps the greatest proportion of birds breed along highways. I have known the ruffed grouse to come out of a dense wood and make its nest at the root of a tree within ten paces of the road, where, no doubt, hawks and crows, as well as skunks and foxes, would be less likely to find it out. Traversing remote mountain-roads through dense woods, I have repeatedly seen the veery, or Wilson's thrush, sitting upon her nest, so near me that I could almost take her from it by stretching out my hand. Birds of prey show none of this confidence in man, and, when locating their nests, avoid rather than seek his haunts.

In a certain locality in the interior of New York, I know, every season, where I am sure to find a nest or two of the slate-colored snowbird. It is under the brink of a low mossy bank, so near the highway that it could be reached from a passing vehicle with a whip. Every horse or wagon or foot passenger disturbs the sitting bird. She awaits the near approach of the sound of feet or wheels, and then darts quickly across the road, barely clearing the ground, and disappears amid the bushes on the opposite side.

In the trees that line one of the main streets and fashionable drives leading out of Washington city and less than half a mile from the boundary, I have counted the nests of five different species at one time, and that without any very close scrutiny of the foliage, while, in many acres of woodland half a mile off, I searched in vain for a single nest. Among the five, the nest that interested me most was that of the blue grosbeak. Here this bird, which, according to Audubon's observations in Louisiana, is shy and recluse, affecting remote marshes and the borders of large ponds of stagnant water, had placed its nest in the lowest twig of the lowest branch of a large sycamore, immediately over a great thoroughfare, and so near the ground that a person standing in a cart or sitting on a horse could have reached it with his hand. The nest was composed mainly of fragments of newspaper and stalks of grass, and, though so low, was remarkably well concealed by one of the peculiar clusters of twigs and leaves which characterize this tree. The nest contained young when I discovered it, and, though the parent birds were much annoyed by my loitering about beneath the tree, they paid little attention to the stream of vehicles that was constantly passing. It was a wonder to me when the birds could have built it, for they are much shyer when building than at other times. No doubt they worked mostly in the morning, having the early hours all to themselves.

Another pair of blue grosbeaks built in a graveyard within the city limits. The nest was placed in a low bush, and the male continued to sing at intervals till the young were ready to fly. The song of this bird is a rapid, intricate warble, like that of the indigo-bird, though stronger and louder. Indeed, these two birds so much resemble each other in color, form, manner, voice, and general habits that, were it not for the difference in size,—the grosbeak being nearly as large again as the indigo-bird,—it would be a hard matter to tell them apart. The females of both species are clad in the same reddish-brown suits. So are the young the first season.

Of course in the deep, primitive woods, also, are nests; but how rarely we find them! The simple art of the bird consists in choosing common, neutral-tinted material, as moss, dry leaves, twigs, and various odds and ends, and placing the structure on a convenient branch, where it blends in color with its surroundings; but how consummate is this art, and how skillfully is the nest concealed! We occasionally light upon it, but who, unaided by the movements of the bird, could find it out? During the present season I went to the woods nearly every day for a fortnight without making any discoveries of this kind, till one day, paying them a farewell visit, I chanced to come upon several nests. A black and white creeping warbler suddenly became much alarmed as I approached a crumbling old stump in a dense part of the forest. He alighted upon it, chirped sharply, ran up and down its sides, and finally left it with much reluctance. The nest, which contained three young birds nearly fledged, was placed upon the ground, at the foot of the stump, and in such a position that the color of the young harmonized perfectly with the bits of bark, sticks, etc., lying about. My eye rested upon them for the second time before I made them out. They hugged the nest very closely, but as I put down my hand they all scampered off with loud cries for help, which caused the parent birds to place themselves almost within my reach. The nest was merely a little dry grass arranged in a thick bed of dry leaves.

This was amid a thick undergrowth. Moving on into a passage of large stately hemlocks, with only here and there a small beech or maple rising up into the perennial twilight, I paused to make out a note which was entirely new to me. It is still in my ear. Though unmistakably a bird note, it yet suggested the bleating of a tiny lambkin. Presently the birds appeared,—a pair of the solitary vireo. They came flitting from point to point, alighting only for a moment at a time, the male silent, but the female uttering this strange, tender note. It was a rendering into some new sylvan dialect of the human sentiment of maidenly love. It was really pathetic in its sweetness and childlike confidence and joy. I soon discovered that the pair were building a nest upon a low branch a few yards from me. The male flew cautiously to the spot and adjusted something, and the twain moved on, the female calling to her mate at intervals, *love-e*, *love-e*, with a cadence and tenderness in the tone that rang in the ear long afterward. The nest was suspended to the fork of a small branch, as is usual with the vireos, plentifully lined with lichens, and bound and rebound with masses of coarse spider-webs. There was no attempt at concealment except in the neutral tints, which made it look like a natural growth of the dim, gray woods.

Continuing my random walk, I next paused in a low part of the woods, where the larger trees began to give place to a thick second-growth that covered an old Barkpeeling. I was standing by a large maple, when a small bird darted quickly away from it, as if it might have come out of a hole near its base. As the bird paused a few yards from me, and began to chirp uneasily, my curiosity was at once excited. When I saw it was the female mourning ground warbler, and remembered that the nest of this bird had not yet been seen by any naturalist,—that not even Dr. Brewer had ever seen the eggs,—I felt that here was something worth looking for. So I carefully began the search, exploring inch by inch the ground, the base and roots of the tree, and the various shrubby growths about it, till, finding nothing and fearing I might really put my foot in it, I bethought me to withdraw to a distance and after some delay return again, and, thus forewarned, note the exact point from which the bird flew. This I did, and, returning, had little difficulty in discovering the nest. It was placed but a few feet from the maple-tree, in a bunch of ferns, and about six inches from the ground. It was quite a massive nest, composed entirely of the stalks and leaves of dry grass, with an inner lining of fine, dark brown roots. The eggs, three in number, were of light flesh-color, uniformly specked with fine brown specks. The cavity of the nest was so deep that the back of the sitting bird sank below the edge.

In the top of a tall tree, a short distance farther on, I saw the nest of the red-tailed hawk,—a large mass of twigs and dry sticks. The young had flown, but still lingered in the vicinity, and, as I approached, the mother bird flew about over me, squealing in a very angry, savage manner. Tufts of the hair and other indigestible material of the common meadow mouse lay around on the ground beneath the nest.

As I was about leaving the woods, my hat almost brushed the nest of the red-eyed vireo, which hung basket-like on the end of a low, drooping branch of the beech. I should never have seen it had the bird kept her place. It contained three eggs of the bird's own, and one of the cow bunting. The strange egg was only just perceptibly larger than the others, yet three days after, when I looked into the nest again and found all but one egg hatched, the young interloper was at least four times as large as either of the others, and with such a superabundance of bowels as to almost smother his bedfellows beneath them. That the intruder should fare the same as the rightful occupants, and thrive with them, was more than ordinary potluck; but that it alone should thrive, devouring, as it were, all the rest, is one of those freaks of Nature in which she would seem to discourage the homely virtues of prudence and honesty. Weeds and parasites have the odds greatly against them, yet they wage a very successful war nevertheless.

The woods hold not such another gem as the nest of the hummingbird. The finding of one is an event to date from. It is

ONE OF MR. BURROUGHS'S FAVORITE PLACES OF OBSERVATION

the next best thing to finding an eagle's nest. I have met with but two, both by chance. One was placed on the horizontal branch of a chestnut-tree, with a solitary green leaf, forming a complete canopy, about an inch and a half above it. The repeated spiteful dartings of the bird past my ears, as I stood under the tree, caused me to suspect that I was intruding upon some one's privacy; and, following it with my eye, I soon saw the nest, which was in process of construction. Adopting my usual tactics of secreting myself near by, I had the satisfaction of seeing the tiny artist at work. It was the female, unassisted by her mate. At intervals of two or three minutes she would appear with a small tuft of some cottony substance in her beak, dart a few times through and around the tree, and alighting quickly in the nest, arrange the material she had brought, using her breast as a model.

The other nest I discovered in a dense forest on the side of a mountain. The sitting bird was disturbed as I passed beneath her. The whirring of her wings arrested my attention, when, after a short pause, I had the good luck to see, through an opening in the leaves, the bird return to her nest, which appeared like a mere wart or excrescence on a small branch. The hummingbird, unlike all others, does not alight upon the nest, but flies into it. She enters it as quick as a flash, but as light as any feather. Two eggs are the complement. They are perfectly white, and so frail that only a woman's fingers may touch them. Incubation lasts about ten days. In a week the young have flown.

The only nest like the hummingbird's, and comparable to it in neatness and symmetry, is that of the blue-gray gnatcatcher. This is often saddled upon the limb in the same manner, though it is generally more or less pendent; it is deep and soft, composed mostly of some vegetable down covered all over with delicate tree-lichens, and, except that it is much larger, appears almost identical with the nest of the hummingbird.

But the nest of nests, the ideal nest, after we have left the deep woods, is unquestionably that of the Baltimore oriole. It is the only perfectly pensile nest we have. The nest of the orchard oriole is indeed mainly so, but this bird generally builds lower and shallower, more after the manner of the vireos.

The Baltimore oriole loves to attach its nest to the swaying branches of the tallest elms, making no attempt at concealment, but satisfied if the position be high and the branch pendent. This nest would seem to cost more time and skill than any other bird structure. A peculiar flax-like substance seems to be always sought after and always found. The nest when completed assumes the form of a large, suspended gourd. The walls are thin but firm, and proof against the most driving rain. The mouth is hemmed or overhanded with horse-hair, and the sides are usually sewed through and through with the same.

Not particular as to the matter of secrecy, the bird is not particular as to material, so that it be of the nature of strings or threads. A lady friend once told me that, while working by an open window, one of these birds approached during her momentary absence, and, seizing a skein of some kind of thread or yarn, made off with it to its half-finished nest. But the perverse yarn caught fast in the branches, and, in the bird's effort to extricate it, got hopelessly tangled. She tugged away at it all day, but was finally obliged to content herself with a few detached portions. The fluttering strings were an eyesore to her ever after, and, passing and repassing, she would give them a spiteful jerk, as much as to say, "There is that confounded yarn that gave me so much trouble."

From Pennsylvania, Vincent Barnard (to whom I am indebted for other curious facts) sent me this interesting story of an oriole. He says a friend of his curious in such things, on observing the bird beginning to build, hung out near the prospective nest skeins of many-colored zephyr yarn, which the eager artist readily appropriated. He managed it so that the bird used nearly equal quantities of various high, bright colors. The nest was made unusually deep and capacious, and it may be questioned if such a thing of beauty was ever before woven by the cunning of a bird.

Nuttall, by far the most genial of American ornithologists, relates the following:—

"A female (oriole), which I observed attentively, carried off to her nest a piece of lamp-wick ten or twelve feet long. This long string and many other shorter ones were left hanging out for about a week before both the ends were wattled into the sides of the nest. Some other little birds, making use of similar materials, at times twitched these flowing ends, and generally brought out the busy Baltimore from her occupation in great anger.

"I may perhaps claim indulgence for adding a little more of the biography of this particular bird, as a representative also of the instincts of her race. She completed the nest in about a week's time, without any aid from her mate, who indeed appeared but seldom in her company and was now become nearly silent. For fibrous materials she broke, hackled, and gathered the flax of the asclepias and hibiscus stalks, tearing off long strings and flying with them to the scene of her labors. She appeared very eager and hasty in her pursuits, and collected her materials without fear or restraint while three men were working in the neighboring walks and many persons visiting the garden. Her courage and perseverance were indeed truly admirable. If watched too narrowly, she saluted with her usual scolding, *tshrr, tshrr, tshrr,* seeing no reason, probably, why she should be interrupted in her indispensable occupation.

"Though the males were now comparatively silent on the arrival of their busy mates, I could not help observing this female and a second, continually vociferating, apparently in strife. At last she was observed to attack this *second* female very fiercely, who slyly intruded herself at times into the same tree where she was building. These contests were angry and often repeated. To account for this animosity, I now recollected that *two* fine males had been killed in our vicinity, and I therefore concluded the intruder to be left without a mate; yet she had gained the affections of the consort of the busy female, and thus the cause of their jealous quarrel became apparent. Having obtained the confidence of her faithless paramour, the *second* female began preparing to weave a nest in an adjoining elm by tying together certain pendent twigs as a foundation. The male now associated chiefly with the intruder, whom he even assisted in her labor, yet did not wholly forget his first partner, who called on him one evening in a low, affectionate tone, which was answered in the same strain. While they were thus engaged in friendly whispers, suddenly appeared the rival, and a violent *rencontre* ensued, so that one of the females appeared to be greatly agitated, and fluttered with spreading wings as if considerably hurt. The male, though prudently neutral in the contest, showed his culpable partiality by flying off with his paramour, and for the rest of the evening left the tree to his pugnacious consort. Cares of another kind, more imperious and tender, at length reconciled, or at least terminated, these disputes with the jealous females; and by the aid of the neighboring bachelors, who are never wanting among these and other birds, peace was at length completely restored by the restitution of the quiet and happy condition of monogamy."

Let me not forget to mention the nest under the mountain ledge, the nest of the common pewee,—a modest mossy structure, with four pearl-white eggs,—looking out upon some wild scene and overhung by beetling crags. After all has been said about the elaborate, high-hung structures, few nests perhaps awaken more pleasant emotions in the mind of the beholder than this of the pewee,—the gray, silent rocks, with caverns and dens where the fox and the wolf lurk, and just out of their reach, in a little niche, as if it grew there, the mossy tenement!

Nearly every high projecting rock in my range has one of these nests. Following a trout stream up a wild mountain gorge, not long since, I counted five in the distance of a mile, all within easy reach, but safe from the minks and the skunks, and well housed from the storms. In my native town I know a pine and oak clad hill, round-topped, with a bold, precipitous front extending halfway around it. Near the top, and along this front or side, there crops out a ledge of rocks unusually high and cavernous. One immense layer projects many feet, allowing a person or many persons, standing upright, to move freely beneath it. There is a delicious spring of water there, and plenty of wild, cool air. The floor is of loose stone, now trod by sheep and foxes, once by the Indian and the wolf. How I have delighted from boyhood to spend a summer day in this retreat, or take refuge there from a sudden shower! Always the freshness and coolness, and always the delicate mossy nest of the phœbe-bird! The bird keeps her place till you are within a few feet of her, when she flits to a near branch, and, with many oscillations of her tail, observes you anxiously. Since the country has become settled, this pewee has fallen into the strange practice of occasionally placing its nest under a bridge, hay-shed, or other artificial structure, where it is subject to all kinds of interruptions and annoyances. When placed thus, the nest is larger and coarser. I know a hay-loft beneath which a pair has regularly placed its nest for several successive seasons. Arranged along on a single pole, which sags down a few inches from the flooring it was intended to help support, are three of these structures, marking the number of years the birds have nested there. The foundation is of mud with a superstructure of moss, elaborately lined with hair and feathers. Nothing can be more perfect and exquisite than the interior of one of these nests, yet a new one is built every season. Three broods, however, are frequently reared in it.

The pewees, as a class, are the best architects we have. The kingbird builds a nest altogether admirable, using various soft cotton and woolen substances, and sparing neither time nor material to make it substantial and warm. The green-crested pewee builds its nest in many instances wholly of the blossoms of the white oak. The wood pewee builds a neat, compact, socket-shaped nest of moss and lichens on a horizontal branch. There is never a loose end or shred about it. The sitting bird is largely visible above the rim. She moves her head freely about and seems entirely at her ease,—a circumstance which I have never observed in any other species. The nest of the great-crested flycatcher is seldom free from snake skins, three or four being sometimes woven into it.

About the thinnest, shallowest nest, for its situation, that can be found is that of the turtle-dove. A few sticks and straws are carelessly thrown together, hardly sufficient to prevent the eggs from falling through or rolling off. The nest of the passenger pigeon is equally hasty and insufficient, and the squabs often fall to the ground and perish. The other extreme among our common birds is furnished by the ferruginous thrush, which collects together a mass of material that would fill a half-bushel measure; or by the fish hawk, which adds to and repairs its nest year after year, till the whole would make a cart-load.

One of the rarest of nests is that of the eagle, because the eagle is one of the rarest of birds. Indeed, so seldom is the eagle seen that its presence always seems accidental. It appears as if merely pausing on the way, while bound for some distant unknown region. One September, while a youth, I saw the ring-tailed eagle, the young of the golden eagle, an immense, dusky bird, the sight of which filled me with awe. It lingered about the hills for two days. Some young cattle, a two-year-old colt, and half a dozen sheep were at pasture on a high ridge that led up to the mountain, and in plain view of the house. On the second day this dusky monarch was seen flying about above them. Presently he began to hover over them, after the manner of a hawk watching for mice. He then with extended legs let himself slowly down upon them, actually grappling the backs of the young cattle, and frightening the creatures so that they rushed about the field in great consternation; and finally, as he grew bolder and more frequent in his descents, the whole herd broke over the fence and came tearing down to the house "like mad." It did not seem to be an assault with intent to kill, but was perhaps a stratagem resorted to in order to separate the herd and expose the lambs, which hugged the cattle very closely. When he occasionally alighted upon the oaks that stood near, the branch could be seen to sway and bend beneath him. Finally, as a rifleman started out in pursuit of him, he launched into the air, set his wings, and sailed away southward. A few years afterward, in January, another eagle passed through the same locality, alighting in a field near some dead animal, but tarried briefly.

So much by way of identification. The golden eagle is common to the northern parts of both hemispheres, and places its eyrie on high precipitous rocks. A pair built on an inaccessible shelf of rock along the Hudson for eight successive years. A squad of Revolutionary soldiers, also, as related by Audubon, found a nest along this river, and had an adventure with the bird that came near costing one of their number his life. His comrades let him down by a rope to secure the eggs or young, when he was attacked by the female eagle with such fury that he was obliged to defend himself with his knife. In doing so, by a misstroke, he nearly severed the rope that held him, and was drawn up by a single strand from his perilous position.

The bald eagle, also, builds on high rocks, according to Audubon, though Wilson describes the nest of one which he saw near Great

Egg Harbor, in the top of a large yellow pine. It was a vast pile of sticks, sods, sedge, grass, reeds, etc., five or six feet high by four broad, and with little or no concavity. It had been used for many years, and he was told that the eagles made it a sort of home or lodging-place in all seasons.

The eagle in all cases uses one nest, with more or less repair, for several years. Many of our common birds do the same. The birds may be divided, with respect to this and kindred points, into five general classes. First, those that repair or appropriate the last year's nest, as the wren, swallow, bluebird, great-crested flycatcher, owls, eagles, fish hawk, and a few others. Secondly, those that build anew each season, though frequently rearing more than one brood in the same nest. Of these the phœbe-bird is a well-known example. Thirdly, those that build a new nest for each brood, which includes by far the greatest number of species. Fourthly, a limited number that make no nest of their own, but appropriate the abandoned nests of other birds. Finally, those who use no nest at all, but deposit their eggs in the sand, which is the case with a large number of aquatic fowls.

1866.

# VI

THE HEART OF THE SOUTHERN CATSKILLS

## VI

## THE HEART OF THE SOUTHERN CATSKILLS

ON looking at the southern and more distant Catskills from the Hudson River on the east, or on looking at them from the west from some point of vantage in Delaware County, you see, amid the group of mountains, one that looks like the back and shoulders of a gigantic horse. The horse has got his head down grazing; the shoulders are high, and the descent from them down his neck very steep; if he were to lift up his head, one sees that it would be carried far above all other peaks, and that the noble beast might gaze straight to his peers in the Adirondacks or the White Mountains. But the lowered head never comes up; some spell or enchantment keeps it down there amid the mighty herd; and the high round shoulders and the smooth strong back of the steed are alone visible. The peak to which I refer is Slide Mountain, the highest of the Catskills by some two hundred feet, and probably the most inaccessible; certainly the hardest to get a view of, it is hedged about so completely by other peaks,—the greatest mountain of them all, and apparently the least willing to be seen; only at a distance of thirty or forty miles is it seen to stand up above all other peaks. It takes its name from a landslide which occurred many years ago down its steep northern side, or down the neck of the grazing steed. The mane of spruce and balsam fir was stripped away for many hundred feet, leaving a long gray streak visible from afar.

Slide Mountain is the centre and the chief of the southern Catskills. Streams flow from its base, and from the base of its subordinates, to all points of the compass,—the Rondout and the Neversink to the south; the Beaverkill to the west; the Esopus to the north; and several lesser streams to the east. With its summit as the centre, a radius of ten miles would include within the circle described but very little cultivated land; only a few poor, wild farms in some of the numerous valleys. The soil is poor, a mixture of gravel and clay, and is subject to slides. It lies in the valleys in ridges and small hillocks, as if dumped there from a huge cart. The tops of the southern Catskills are all capped with a kind of conglomerate, or "pudden stone,"—a rock of cemented quartz pebbles which underlies the coal measures. This rock disintegrates under the action of the elements, and the sand and gravel which result are carried into the valleys and make up most of the soil. From the northern Catskills, so far as I know them, this rock has been swept clean. Low down in the valleys the old red sandstone crops out, and, as you go west into Delaware County, in many places it alone remains and makes up most of the soil, all the superincumbent rock having been carried away.

Slide Mountain had been a summons and a challenge to me for many years. I had fished every stream that it nourished, and had camped in the wilderness on all sides of it, and whenever I had caught a glimpse of its summit I had promised myself to set foot there before another season should pass. But the seasons came and went, and my feet got no nimbler, and Slide Mountain no lower, until finally, one July, seconded by an energetic friend, we thought to bring Slide to terms by approaching him through the mountains on the east. With a farmer's son for guide we struck in by way of Weaver Hollow, and, after a long and desperate climb, contented ourselves with the Wittenberg, instead of Slide. The view from the Wittenberg is in many respects more striking, as you are perched immediately above a broader and more distant sweep of country, and are only about two hundred feet lower. You are here on the eastern brink of the southern Catskills, and the earth falls away at your feet and curves down through an immense stretch of forest till it joins the plain of Shokan, and thence sweeps away to the Hudson and beyond. Slide is southwest of you, six or seven miles distant, but is visible only when you climb into a treetop. I climbed and saluted him, and promised to call next time.

We passed the night on the Wittenberg, sleeping on the moss, between two decayed logs, with balsam boughs thrust into the ground and meeting and forming a canopy over us. In coming off the mountain in the morning we ran upon a huge porcupine, and I learned for the first time that the tail of a porcupine goes with a spring like a trap. It seems to be a set-lock; and you no sooner touch with the weight of a hair one of the quills than the tail leaps up in a most surprising manner, and the laugh is not on your side. The beast cantered along the path in my front, and I threw myself upon him, shielded by my roll of blankets. He submitted quietly to the indignity, and lay very still under my blankets, with his broad tail pressed close to the ground. This I proceeded to investigate, but had not fairly made a beginning when it went off like a trap, and my hand and wrist were full of quills. This caused me to let

THE WITTENBERG FROM WOODLAND VALLEY

up on the creature, when it lumbered away till it tumbled down a precipice. The quills were quickly removed from my hand, when we gave chase. When we came up to him, he had wedged himself in between the rocks so that he presented only a back bristling with quills, with the tail lying in ambush below. He had chosen his position well, and seemed to defy us. After amusing ourselves by repeatedly springing his tail and receiving the quills in a rotten stick, we made a slip-noose out of a spruce root, and, after much manœuvring, got it over his head and led him forth. In what a peevish, injured tone the creature did complain of our unfair tactics! He protested and protested, and whimpered and scolded like some infirm old man tormented by boys. His game after we led him forth was to keep himself as much as possible in the shape of a ball, but with two sticks and the cord we finally threw him over on his back and exposed his quill-less and vulnerable under side, when he fairly surrendered and seemed to say, "Now you may do with me as you like." His great chisel-like teeth, which are quite as formidable as those of the woodchuck, he does not appear to use at all in his defense, but relies entirely upon his quills, and when those fail him, he is done for.

After amusing ourselves with him awhile longer, we released him and went on our way. The trail to which we had committed ourselves led us down into Woodland Valley, a retreat which so took my eye by its fine trout brook, its superb mountain scenery, and its sweet seclusion, that I marked it for my own, and promised myself a return to it at no distant day. This promise I kept, and pitched my tent there twice during that season. Both occasions were a sort of laying siege to Slide, but we only skirmished with him at a distance; the actual assault was not undertaken. But the following year, reinforced by two other brave climbers, we determined upon the assault, and upon making it from this the most difficult side. The regular way is by Big Ingin Valley, where the climb is comparatively easy, and where it is often made by women. But from Woodland Valley only men may essay the ascent. Larkins is the upper inhabitant, and from our camping-ground near his clearing we set out early one June morning.

One would think nothing could be easier to find than a big mountain, especially when one is encamped upon a stream which he knows springs out of its very loins. But for some reason or other we had got an idea that Slide Mountain was a very slippery customer and must be approached cautiously. We had tried from several points in the valley to get a view of it, but were not quite sure we had seen its very head. When on the Wittenberg, a neighboring peak, the year before, I had caught a brief glimpse of it only by climbing

## THE HEART OF THE SOUTHERN CATSKILLS

a dead tree and craning up for a moment from its topmost branch. It would seem as if the mountain had taken every precaution to shut itself off from a near view. It was a shy mountain, and we were about to stalk it through six or seven miles of primitive woods, and we seemed to have some unreasonable fear that it might elude us. We had been told of parties who had essayed the ascent from this side, and had returned baffled and bewildered. In a tangle of primitive woods, the very bigness of the mountain baffles one. It is all mountain; whichever way you turn—and one turns sometimes in such cases before he knows it—the foot finds a steep and rugged ascent.

The eye is of little service; one must be sure of his bearings and push boldly on and up. One is not unlike a flea upon a great shaggy beast, looking for the animal's head; or even like a much smaller and much less nimble creature,—he may waste his time and steps, and think he has reached the head when he is only upon the rump. Hence I questioned our host, who had several times made the ascent, closely. Larkins laid his old felt hat upon the table, and, placing one hand upon one side of it and the other upon the other, said: "There Slide lies, between the two forks of the stream, just as my hat lies between my two hands. David will go with you to the forks, and then you will push right on up." But Larkins was not right, though he had traversed all those mountains many times over. The peak we were about to set out for did not lie between the forks, but exactly at the head of one of them; the beginnings of the stream are in the very path of the slide, as we afterward found. We broke camp early in the morning, and with our blankets strapped to our backs and rations in our pockets for two days, set out along an ancient and in places an obliterated bark road that followed and crossed and recrossed the stream. The morning was bright and warm, but the wind was fitful and petulant, and I predicted rain. What a forest solitude our obstructed and dilapidated wood-road led us through! five miles of primitive woods before we came to the forks, three miles before we came to the "burnt shanty," a name merely,—no shanty there now for twenty-five years past. The ravages of the barkpeelers were still visible, now in a space thickly strewn with the soft and decayed trunks of hemlock-trees, and overgrown with wild cherry, then in huge mossy logs scattered through the beech and maple woods. Some of these logs were so soft and mossy that one could sit or recline upon them as upon a sofa.

But the prettiest thing was the stream soliloquizing in such musical tones there amid the moss-covered rocks and boulders. How clean it looked, what purity! Civilization corrupts the streams as it corrupts the Indian; only in such remote woods can you now see a brook in all its original freshness and beauty. Only the sea and the mountain forest brook are pure; all between is contaminated more or less by the work of man. An ideal trout brook was this, now hurrying, now loitering, now deepening around a great boulder, now gliding evenly over a pavement of green-gray stone and pebbles; no sediment or stain of any kind, but white and sparkling as snow-water, and nearly as cool. Indeed, the water of all this Catskill region is the best in the world. For the first few days, one feels as if he could almost live on the water alone; he cannot drink enough of it. In this particular it is indeed the good Bible land, "a land of brooks of water, of fountains and depths that spring out of valleys and hills."

Near the forks we caught, or thought we caught, through an opening, a glimpse of Slide. Was it Slide? was it the head, or the rump, or the shoulder of the shaggy monster we were in quest of? At the forks there was a bewildering maze of underbrush and great trees, and the way did not seem at all certain; nor was David, who was then at the end of his reckoning, able to reassure us. But in assaulting a mountain, as in assaulting a fort, boldness is the watchword. We pressed forward, following a line of blazed trees for nearly a mile, then, turning to the left, began the ascent of the mountain. It was steep, hard climbing. We saw numerous marks of both bears and deer; but no birds, save at long intervals the winter wren flitting here and there, and darting under logs and rubbish like a mouse. Occasionally its gushing, lyrical song would break the silence. After we had climbed an hour or two, the clouds began to gather, and presently the rain began to come down. This was discouraging; but we put our backs up against trees and rocks, and waited for the shower to pass.

"They were wet with the showers of the mountain, and embraced the rocks for want of shelter," as they did in Job's time. But the shower was light and brief, and we were soon under way again. Three hours from the forks brought us out on the broad level back of the mountain upon which Slide, considered as an isolated peak, is reared. After a time we entered a dense growth of spruce which covered a slight depression in the table of the mountain. The moss was deep, the ground spongy, the light dim, the air hushed. The transition from the open, leafy woods to this dim, silent, weird grove was very marked. It was like the passage from the street into the temple. Here we paused awhile and ate our lunch, and refreshed ourselves with water gathered from a little well sunk in the moss.

The quiet and repose of this spruce grove proved to be the calm that goes before the storm. As we passed out of it, we came plump

## THE HEART OF THE SOUTHERN CATSKILLS

upon the almost perpendicular battlements of Slide. The mountain rose like a huge, rock-bound fortress from this plain-like expanse. It was ledge upon ledge, precipice upon precipice, up which and over which we made our way slowly and with great labor, now pulling ourselves up by our hands, then cautiously finding niches for our feet and zigzagging right and left from shelf to shelf. This northern side of the mountain was thickly covered with moss and lichens, like the north side of a tree. This made it soft to the foot, and broke many a slip and fall. Everywhere a stunted growth of yellow birch, mountain-ash, and spruce and fir opposed our progress. The ascent at such an angle with a roll of blankets on your back is not unlike climbing a tree: every limb resists your progress and pushes you back; so that when we at last reached the summit, after twelve or fifteen hundred feet of this sort of work, the fight was about all out of the best of us. It was then nearly two o'clock, so that we had been about seven hours in coming seven miles.

Here on the top of the mountain we overtook spring, which had been gone from the valley nearly a month. Red clover was opening in the valley below, and wild strawberries just ripening; on the summit the yellow birch was just hanging out its catkins, and the claytonia, or spring-beauty, was in bloom. The leaf-buds of the trees were just bursting, making a faint mist of green, which, as the eye swept downward, gradually deepened until it became a dense, massive cloud in the valleys. At the foot of the mountain the clintonia, or northern green lily, and the low shadbush were showing their berries, but long before the top was reached they were found in bloom. I had never before stood amid blooming claytonia, a flower of April, and looked down upon a field that held ripening strawberries. Every thousand feet elevation seemed to make about ten days' difference in the vegetation, so that the season was a month or more later on the top of the mountain than at its base. A very pretty flower which we began to meet with well up on the mountain-side was the painted trillium, the petals white, veined with pink.

The low, stunted growth of spruce and fir which clothes the top of Slide has been cut away over a small space on the highest point, laying open the view on nearly all sides. Here we sat down and enjoyed our triumph. We saw the world as the hawk or the balloonist sees it when he is three thousand feet in the air. How soft and flowing all the outlines of the hills and mountains beneath us looked! The forests dropped down and undulated away over them, covering them like a carpet. To the east we looked over the near-by Wittenberg range to the Hudson and beyond; to the south, Peak-o'-Moose, with its sharp crest, and Table Mountain, with its long level top, were the two conspicuous objects; in the west, Mt. Graham and Double Top, about three thousand eight hundred feet each, arrested the eye; while in our front to the north we looked over the top of Panther Mountain to the multitudinous peaks of the northern Catskills. All was mountain and forest on every hand. Civilization seemed to have done little more than to have scratched this rough, shaggy surface of the earth here and there. In any such view, the wild, the aboriginal, the geographical greatly predominate. The works of man dwindle, and the original features of the huge globe come out. Every single object or point is dwarfed; the valley of the Hudson is only a wrinkle in the earth's surface. You discover with a feeling of surprise that the great thing is the earth itself, which stretches away on every hand so far beyond your ken.

The Arabs believe that the mountains steady the earth and hold it together; but they have only to get on the top of a high one to see how insignificant mountains are, and how adequate the earth looks to get along without them. To the imaginative Oriental people, mountains seemed to mean much more than they do to us. They were sacred; they were the abodes of their divinities. They offered their sacrifices upon them. In the Bible, mountains are used as a symbol of that which is great and holy. Jerusalem is spoken of as a holy mountain. The Syrians were beaten by the Children of Israel because, said they, "their gods are gods of the hills; therefore were they stronger than we." It was on Mount Horeb that God appeared to Moses in the burning bush, and on Sinai that He delivered to him the law. Josephus says that the Hebrew shepherds never pasture their flocks on Sinai, believing it to be the abode of Jehovah. The solitude of mountain-tops is peculiarly impressive, and it is certainly easier to believe the Deity appeared in a burning bush there than in the valley below. When the clouds of heaven, too, come down and envelop the top of the mountain,—how such a circumstance must have impressed the old God-fearing Hebrews! Moses knew well how to surround the law with the pomp and circumstance that would inspire the deepest awe and reverence.

But when the clouds came down and enveloped us on Slide Mountain, the grandeur, the solemnity, were gone in a twinkling; the portentous-looking clouds proved to be nothing but base fog that wet us and extinguished the world for us. How tame, and prosy, and humdrum the scene instantly became! But when the fog lifted, and we looked from under it as from under a just-raised lid, and the eye plunged again like an escaped bird into those vast gulfs of space that opened at our feet, the feeling of grandeur and solemnity quickly came back.

# THE HEART OF THE SOUTHERN CATSKILLS

The first want we felt on the top of Slide, after we had got some rest, was a want of water. Several of us cast about, right and left, but no sign of water was found. But water must be had, so we all started off deliberately to hunt it up. We had not gone many hundred yards before we chanced upon an ice-cave beneath some rocks,—vast masses of ice, with crystal pools of water near. This was good luck, indeed, and put a new and a brighter face on the situation.

Slide Mountain enjoys a distinction which no other mountain in the State, so far as is known, does,—it has a thrush peculiar to itself. This thrush was discovered and described by Eugene P. Bicknell, of New York, in 1880, and has been named Bicknell's thrush. A better name would have been Slide Mountain thrush, as the bird so far has been found only on this mountain.[1] I did not see or hear it upon the Wittenberg, which is only a few miles distant, and only two hundred feet lower. In its appearance to the eye among the trees, one would not distinguish it from the gray-cheeked thrush of Baird, or the olive-backed thrush, but its song is totally different. The moment I heard it I said, "There is a new bird, a new thrush," for the quality of all thrush songs is the same. A moment more, and I knew it was Bicknell's thrush. The song is in a minor key, finer, more attenuated, and more under the breath than that of any other thrush. It seemed as if the bird was blowing in a delicate, slender, golden tube, so fine and yet so flute-like and resonant the song appeared. At times it was like a musical whisper of great sweetness and power. The birds were numerous about the summit, but we saw them nowhere else. No other thrush was seen, though a few times during our stay I caught a mere echo of the hermit's song far down the mountain-side. A bird I was not prepared to see or to hear was the black-poll warbler, a bird usually found much farther north, but here it was, amid the balsam firs, uttering its simple, lisping song.

The rocks on the tops of these mountains are quite sure to attract one's attention, even if he have no eye for such things. They are masses of light reddish conglomerate, composed of round wave-worn quartz pebbles. Every pebble has been shaped and polished upon some ancient seacoast, probably the Devonian. The rock disintegrates where it is most exposed to the weather, and forms a loose sandy and pebbly soil. These rocks form the floor of the coal formation, but in the Catskill region only the floor remains; the superstructure has never existed, or has been swept away; hence one would look for a coal mine here over his head in the air, rather than under his feet.

---

[1] Bicknell's thrush turns out to be the more southern form of the gray-cheeked thrush, and is found on the higher mountains of New York and New England.

This rock did not have to climb up here as we did; the mountain stooped and took it upon its back in the bottom of the old seas, and then got lifted up again. This happened so long ago that the memory of the oldest inhabitants of these parts yields no clew to the time.

A pleasant task we had in reflooring and reroofing the log-hut with balsam boughs against the night. Plenty of small balsams grew all about, and we soon had a huge pile of their branches in the old hut. What a transformation, this fresh green carpet and our fragrant bed, like the deep-furred robe of some huge animal, wrought in that dingy interior! Two or three things disturbed our sleep. A cup of strong beef-tea taken for supper disturbed mine; then the porcupines kept up such a grunting and chattering near our heads, just on the other side of the log, that sleep was difficult. In my wakeful mood I was a good deal annoyed by a little rabbit that kept whipping in at our dilapidated door and nibbling at our bread and hardtack. He persisted even after the gray of the morning appeared. Then about four o'clock it began gently to rain. I think I heard the first drop that fell. My companions were all in sound sleep. The rain increased, and gradually the sleepers awoke. It was like the tread of an advancing enemy which every ear had been expecting. The roof over us was of the poorest, and we had no confidence in it. It was made of the thin bark of spruce and balsam, and was full of hollows and depressions. Presently these hollows got full of water, when there was a simultaneous downpour of bigger and lesser rills upon the sleepers beneath. Said sleepers, as one man, sprang up, each taking his blanket with him; but by the time some of the party had got themselves stowed away under the adjacent rock, the rain ceased. It was little more than the dissolving of the nightcap of fog which so often hangs about these heights. With the first appearance of the dawn I had heard the new thrush in the scattered trees near the hut,—a strain as fine as if blown upon a fairy flute, a suppressed musical whisper from out the tops of the dark spruces. Probably never did there go up from the top of a great mountain a smaller song to greet the day, albeit it was of the purest harmony. It seemed to have in a more marked degree the quality of interior reverberation than any other thrush song I had ever heard. Would the altitude or the situation account for its minor key? Loudness would avail little in such a place. Sounds are not far heard on a mountain-top; they are lost in the abyss of vacant air. But amid these low, dense, dark spruces, which make a sort of canopied privacy of every square rod of ground, what could be more in keeping than this delicate musical whisper? It was but the soft hum of the balsams, interpreted and embodied in a bird's voice.

It was the plan of two of our companions to go from Slide over into the head of the Rondout, and thence out to the railroad at the little

## THE HEART OF THE SOUTHERN CATSKILLS

village of Shokan, an unknown way to them, involving nearly an all-day pull the first day through a pathless wilderness. We ascended to the topmost floor of the tower, and from my knowledge of the topography of the country I pointed out to them their course, and where the valley of the Rondout must lie. The vast stretch of woods, when it came into view from under the foot of Slide, seemed from our point of view very uniform. It swept away to the southeast, rising gently toward the ridge that separates Lone Mountain from Peak-o'-Moose, and presented a comparatively easy problem. As a clew to the course, the line where the dark belt or saddle-cloth of spruce, which covered the top of the ridge they were to skirt, ended, and the deciduous woods began, a sharp, well-defined line was pointed out as the course to be followed. It led straight to the top of the broad level-backed ridge which connected two higher peaks, and immediately behind which lay the headwaters of the Rondout. Having studied the map thoroughly, and possessed themselves of the points, they rolled up their blankets about nine o'clock, and were off, my friend and I purposing to spend yet another day and night on Slide. As our friends plunged down into that fearful abyss, we shouted to them the old classic caution, "Be bold, be bold, *be not too* bold." It required courage to make such a leap into the unknown, as I knew those young men were making, and it required prudence. A faint heart or a bewildered head, and serious consequences might have resulted. The theory of a thing is so much easier than the practice! The theory is in the air, the practice is in the woods; the eye, the thought, travel easily where the foot halts and stumbles. However, our friends made the theory and the fact coincide; they kept the dividing line between the spruce and the birches, and passed over the ridge into the valley safely; but they were torn and bruised and wet by the showers, and made the last few miles of their journey on will and pluck alone, their last pound of positive strength having been exhausted in making the descent through the chaos of rocks and logs into the head of the valley. In such emergencies one overdraws his account; he travels on the credit of the strength he expects to gain when he gets his dinner and some sleep. Unless one has made such a trip himself (and I have several times in my life), he can form but a faint idea what it is like,—what a trial it is to the body, and what a trial it is to the mind. You are fighting a battle with an enemy in ambush. How those miles and leagues which your feet must compass lie hidden there in that wilderness; how they seem to multiply themselves; how they are fortified with logs, and rocks, and fallen trees; how they take refuge in deep gullies, and skulk behind unexpected eminences! Your body not only feels the fatigue of the battle, your mind feels the strain of the undertaking;

you may miss your mark; the mountains may outmanœuvre you. All that day, whenever I looked upon that treacherous wilderness, I thought with misgivings of those two friends groping their way there, and would have given much to know how it fared with them. Their concern was probably less than my own, because they were more ignorant of what was before them. Then there was just a slight shadow of a fear in my mind that I might have been in error about some points of the geography I had pointed out to them. But all was well, and the victory was won according to the campaign which I had planned. When we saluted our friends upon their own doorstep a week afterward, the wounds were nearly healed and the rents all mended.

When one is on a mountain-top, he spends most of the time in looking at the show he has been at such pains to see. About every hour we would ascend the rude lookout to take a fresh observation. With a glass I could see my native hills forty miles away to the northwest. I was now upon the back of the horse, yea, upon the highest point of his shoulders, which had so many times attracted my attention as a boy. We could look along his balsam-covered back to his rump, from which the eye glanced away down into the forests of the Neversink, and on the other hand plump down into the gulf where his head was grazing or drinking. During the day there was a grand procession of thunderclouds filing along over the northern Catskills, and letting down veils of rain and enveloping them. From such an elevation one has the same view of the clouds that he does from the prairie or the ocean. They do not seem to rest across and to be upborne by the hills, but they emerge out of the dim west, thin and vague, and grow and stand up as they get nearer and roll by him, on a level but invisible highway, huge chariots of wind and storm.

In the afternoon a thick cloud threatened us, but it proved to be the condensation of vapor that announces a cold wave. There was soon a marked fall in the temperature, and as night drew near it became pretty certain that we were going to have a cold time of it. The wind rose, the vapor above us thickened and came nearer, until it began to drive across the summit in slender wraiths, which curled over the brink and shut out the view. We became very diligent in getting in our night wood, and in gathering more boughs to calk up the openings in the hut. The wood we scraped together was a sorry lot, roots and stumps and branches of decayed spruce, such as we could collect without an axe, and some rags and tags of birch bark. The fire was built in one corner of the shanty, the smoke finding easy egress through large openings on the east side and in the roof over it. We doubled up the bed, making it thicker and more nest-like, and

## THE HEART OF THE SOUTHERN CATSKILLS

as darkness set in, stowed ourselves into it beneath our blankets. The searching wind found out every crevice about our heads and shoulders, and it was icy cold. Yet we fell asleep, and had slept about an hour when my companion sprang up in an unwonted state of excitement for so placid a man. His excitement was occasioned by the sudden discovery that what appeared to be a bar of ice was fast taking the place of his backbone. His teeth chattered, and he was convulsed with ague. I advised him to replenish the fire, and to wrap himself in his blanket and cut the liveliest capers he was capable of in so circumscribed a place. This he promptly did, and the thought of his wild and desperate dance there in the dim light, his tall form, his blanket flapping, his teeth chattering, the porcupines outside marking time with their squeals and grunts, still provokes a smile, though it was a serious enough matter at the time. After a while, the warmth came back to him, but he dared not trust himself again to the boughs; he fought the cold all night as one might fight a besieging foe. By carefully husbanding the fuel, the beleaguering enemy was kept at bay till morning came; but when morning did come, even the huge root he had used as a chair was consumed. Rolled in my blanket beneath a foot or more of balsam boughs, I had got some fairly good sleep, and was most of the time oblivious of the melancholy vigil of my friend. As we had but a few morsels of food left, and had been on rather short rations the day before, hunger was added to his other discomforts. At that time a letter was on the way to him from his wife, which contained this prophetic sentence: "I hope thee is not suffering with cold and hunger on some lone mountain-top."

Mr. Bicknell's thrush struck up again at the first signs of dawn, notwithstanding the cold. I could hear his penetrating and melodious whisper as I lay buried beneath the boughs. Presently I arose and invited my friend to turn in for a brief nap, while I gathered some wood and set the coffee brewing. With a brisk, roaring fire on, I left for the spring to fetch some water, and to make my toilet. The leaves of the mountain goldenrod, which everywhere covered the ground in the opening, were covered with frozen particles of vapor, and the scene, shut in by fog, was chill and dreary enough.

We were now not long in squaring an account with Slide, and making ready to leave. Round pellets of snow began to fall, and we came off the mountain on the 10th of June in a November storm and temperature. Our purpose was to return by the same valley we had come. A well-defined trail led off the summit to the north; to this we committed ourselves. In a few minutes we emerged at the head of the slide that had given the mountain its name. This was the path made by visitors to the scene; when it ended, the track of the avalanche began; no bigger than your hand, apparently, had it been at first, but it rapidly grew, until it became several rods in width. It dropped down from our feet straight as an arrow until it was lost in the fog, and looked perilously steep. The dark forms of the spruce were clinging to the edge of it, as if reaching out to their fellows to save them. We hesitated on the brink, but finally cautiously began the descent. The rock was quite naked and slippery, and only on the margin of the slide were there any boulders to stay the foot, or bushy growths to aid the hand. As we paused, after some minutes, to select our course, one of the finest surprises of the trip awaited us: the fog in our front was swiftly whirled up by the breeze, like the drop-curtain at the theatre, only much more rapidly, and in a twinkling the vast gulf opened before us. It was so sudden as to be almost bewildering. The world opened like a book, and there were the pictures; the spaces were without a film, the forests and mountains looked surprisingly near; in the heart of the northern Catskills a wild valley was seen flooded with sunlight. Then the curtain ran down again, and nothing was left but the gray strip of rock to which we clung, plunging down into the obscurity. Down and down we made our way. Then the fog lifted again. It was Jack and his beanstalk renewed; new wonders, new views, awaited us every few moments, till at last the whole valley below us stood in the clear sunshine. We passed down a precipice, and there was a rill of water, the beginning of the creek that wound through the valley below; farther on, in a deep depression, lay the remains of an old snow-bank; Winter had made his last stand here, and April flowers were springing up almost amid his very bones. We did not find a palace, and a hungry giant, and a princess, at the end of our beanstalk, but we found a humble roof and the hospitable heart of Mrs. Larkins, which answered our purpose better. And we were in the mood, too, to have undertaken an eating-bout with any giant Jack ever discovered.

Of all the retreats I have found amid the Catskills, there is no other that possesses quite so many charms for me as this valley, wherein stands Larkins's humble dwelling; it is so wild, so quiet, and has such superb mountain views. In coming up the valley, you have apparently reached the head of civilization a mile or more lower down; here the rude little houses end, and you turn to the left into the woods. Presently you emerge into a clearing again, and before you rises the rugged and indented crest of Panther Mountain, and near at hand, on a low plateau, rises the humble roof of Larkins,—you get a picture of the Panther and of the homestead at one glance. Above the house hangs a high, bold cliff covered with

LARKINS'S HUMBLE DWELLING

forest, with a broad fringe of blackened and blasted tree-trunks, where the cackling of the great pileated woodpecker may be heard; on the left a dense forest sweeps up to the sharp spruce-covered cone of the Wittenberg, nearly four thousand feet high, while at the head of the valley rises Slide over all. From a meadow just back of Larkins's barn, a view may be had of all these mountains, while the terraced side of Cross Mountain bounds the view immediately to the east. Running from the top of Panther toward Slide one sees a gigantic wall of rock, crowned with a dark line of fir. The forest abruptly ends, and in its stead rises the face of this colossal rocky escarpment, like some barrier built by the mountain gods. Eagles might nest here. It breaks the monotony of the world of woods very impressively.

I delight in sitting on a rock in one of these upper fields, and seeing the sun go down behind Panther. The rapid-flowing brook below me fills all the valley with a soft murmur. There is no breeze, but the great atmospheric tide flows slowly in toward the cooling forest; one can see it by the motes in the air illuminated by the setting sun: presently, as the air cools a little, the tide turns and flows slowly out. The long, winding valley up to the foot of Slide, five miles of primitive woods, how wild and cool it looks, its one voice the murmur of the creek! On the Wittenberg the sunshine lingers long; now it stands up like an island in a sea of shadows, then slowly sinks beneath the wave. The evening call of a robin or a veery at his vespers makes a marked impression on the silence and the solitude.

The following day my friend and I pitched our tent in the woods beside the stream where I had pitched it twice before, and passed several delightful days, with trout in abundance and wild strawberries at intervals. Mrs. Larkins's cream-pot, butter-jar, and bread-box were within easy reach. Near the camp was an unusually large spring, of icy coldness, which served as our refrigerator. Trout or milk immersed in this spring in a tin pail would keep sweet four or five days. One night some creature, probably a lynx or a raccoon, came and lifted the stone from the pail that held the trout and took out a fine string of them, and ate them up on the spot, leaving only the string and one head. In August bears come down to an ancient and now brushy barkpeeling near by for blackberries. But the creature that most infests these backwoods is the porcupine. He is as stupid and indifferent as the skunk; his broad, blunt nose points a witless head. They are great gnawers, and will gnaw your house down if you do not look out. Of a summer evening they will walk coolly into your open door if not prevented. The most annoying animal to the camper-out in this region, and the one he needs to be most on the lookout for, is the cow. Backwoods cows and young cattle seem always to be famished for salt, and they will fairly lick the fisherman's clothes off his back, and his tent and equipage out of existence, if you give them a chance. On one occasion some wood-ranging heifers and steers that had been hovering around our camp for some days made a raid upon it when we were absent. The tent was shut and everything snugged up, but they ran their long tongues under the tent, and, tasting something savory, hooked out John Stuart Mill's "Essays on Religion," which one of us had brought along, thinking to read in the woods. They mouthed the volume around a good deal, but its logic was too tough for them, and they contented themselves with devouring the paper in which it was wrapped. If the cattle had not been surprised at just that point, it is probable the tent would have gone down before their eager curiosity and thirst for salt.

The raid which Larkins's dog made upon our camp was amusing rather than annoying. He was a very friendly and intelligent shepherd dog, probably a collie. Hardly had we sat down to our first lunch in camp before he called on us. But as he was disposed to be too friendly, and to claim too large a share of the lunch, we rather gave him the cold shoulder. He did not come again; but a few evenings afterward, as we sauntered over to the house on some trifling errand, the dog suddenly conceived a bright little project. He seemed to say to himself, on seeing us, "There come both of them now, just as I have been hoping they would; now, while they are away, I will run quickly over and know what they have got that a dog can eat." My companion saw the dog get up on our arrival, and go quickly in the direction of our camp, and he said something in the cur's manner suggested to him the object of his hurried departure. He called my attention to the fact, and we hastened back. On cautiously nearing camp, the dog was seen amid the pails in the shallow water of the creek investigating them. He had uncovered the butter, and was about to taste it, when we shouted, and he made quick steps for home, with a very "kill-sheep" look. When we again met him at the house next day, he could not look us in the face, but sneaked off, utterly crest-fallen. This was a clear case of reasoning on the part of the dog, and afterward a clear case of a sense of guilt from wrong-doing. The dog will probably be a man before any other animal.

# VII
SPECKLED TROUT

# VII

## SPECKLED TROUT

### I

THE legend of the wary trout, hinted at in the last sketch, is to be further illustrated in this and some following chapters. We shall get at more of the meaning of those dark water-lines, and I hope, also, not entirely miss the significance of the gold and silver spots and the glancing iridescent hues. The trout is dark and obscure above, but behind this foil there are wondrous tints that reward the believing eye. Those who seek him in his wild remote haunts are quite sure to get the full force of the sombre and uninviting aspects,—the wet, the cold, the toil, the broken rest, and the huge, savage, uncompromising nature,—but the true angler sees farther than these, and is never thwarted of his legitimate reward by them.

I have been a seeker of trout from my boyhood, and on all the expeditions in which this fish has been the ostensible purpose I have brought home more game than my creel showed. In fact, in my mature years I find I got more of nature into me, more of the woods, the wild, nearer to bird and beast, while threading my native streams for trout, than in almost any other way. It furnished a good excuse to go forth; it pitched one in the right key; it sent one through the fat and marrowy places of field and wood. Then the fisherman has a harmless, preoccupied look; he is a kind of vagrant that nothing fears. He blends himself with the trees and the shadows. All his approaches are gentle and indirect. He times himself to the meandering, soliloquizing stream; its impulse bears him along. At the foot of the waterfall he sits sequestered and hidden in its volume of sound. The birds know he has no designs upon them, and the animals see that his mind is in the creek. His enthusiasm anneals him, and makes him pliable to the scenes and influences he moves among.

Then what acquaintance he makes with the stream! He addresses himself to it as a lover to his mistress; he wooes it and stays with it till he knows its most hidden secrets. It runs through his thoughts not less than through its banks there; he feels the fret and thrust of every bar and boulder. Where it deepens, his purpose deepens; where it is shallow, he is indifferent. He knows how to interpret its every glance and dimple; its beauty haunts him for days.

I am sure I run no risk of overpraising the charm and attractiveness of a well-fed trout stream, every drop of water in it as bright and pure as if the nymphs had brought it all the way from its source in crystal goblets, and as cool as if it had been hatched beneath a glacier. When the heated and soiled and jaded refugee from the city first sees one, he feels as if he would like to turn it into his bosom and let it flow through him a few hours, it suggests such healing freshness and newness. How his roily thoughts would run clear; how the sediment would go downstream! Could he ever have an impure or an unwholesome wish afterward? The next best thing he can do is to tramp along its banks and surrender himself to its influence. If he reads it intently enough, he will, in a measure, be taking it into his mind and heart, and experiencing its salutary ministrations.

Trout streams coursed through every valley my boyhood knew. I crossed them, and was often lured and detained by them, on my way to and from school. We bathed in them during the long summer noons, and felt for the trout under their banks. A holiday was a holiday indeed that brought permission to go fishing over on Rose's Brook, or up Hardscrabble, or in Meeker's Hollow; all-day trips, from morning till night, through meadows and pastures and beechen woods, wherever the shy, limpid stream led. What an appetite it developed! a hunger that was fierce and aboriginal, and that the wild strawberries we plucked as we crossed the hill teased rather than allayed. When but a few hours could be had, gained perhaps by doing some piece of work about the farm or garden in half the allotted time, the little creek that headed in the paternal domain was handy; when half a day was at one's disposal, there were the hemlocks, less than a mile distant, with their loitering, meditative, log-impeded stream and their dusky, fragrant depths. Alert and wide-eyed, one picked his way along, startled now and then by the sudden bursting-up of the partridge, or by the whistling wings of the "dropping snipe," pressing through the brush and the briers, or finding an easy passage over the trunk of a prostrate tree, carefully letting his hook down through some tangle into a still pool, or standing in some high, sombre avenue and watching his line float in and out amid the moss-covered boulders. In my first essayings I used to go to the edge of these hemlocks, seldom dipping into them beyond the first pool where the stream swept under the roots of two large trees. From this point I could look back into the

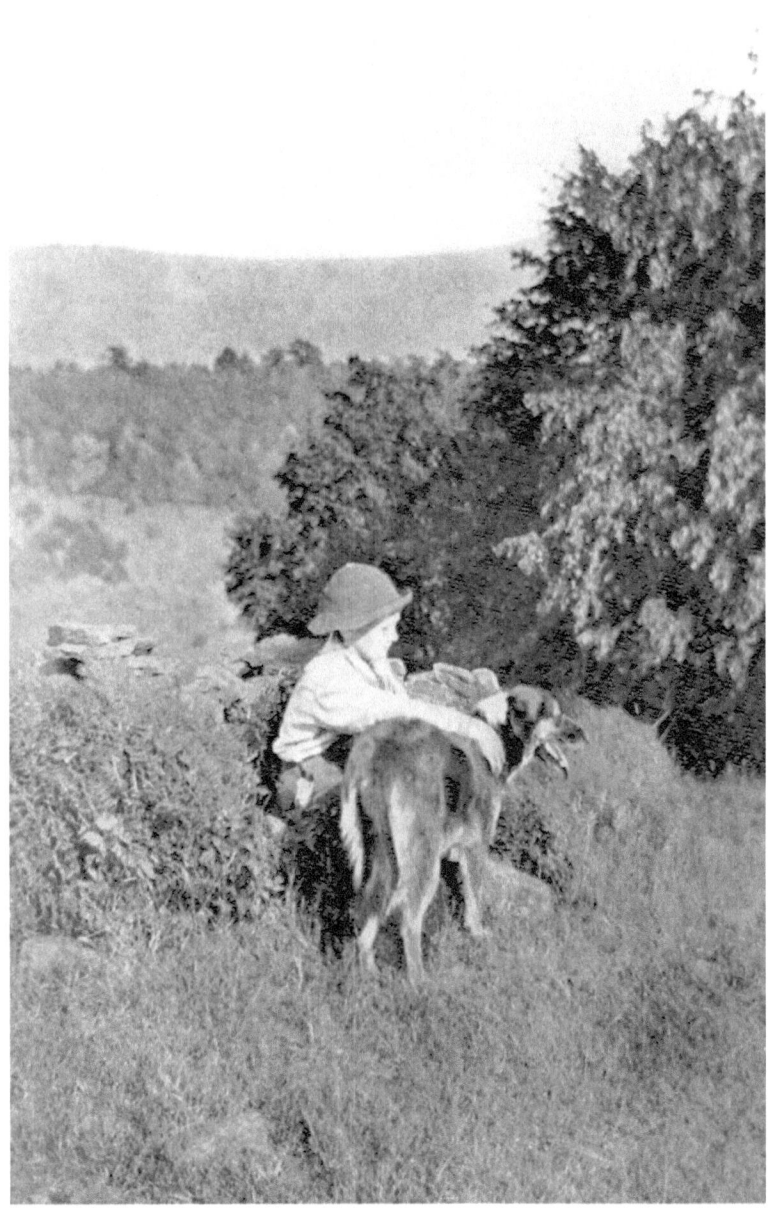

THE FARM BOY

sunlit fields where the cattle were grazing; beyond, all was gloom and mystery; the trout were black, and to my young imagination the silence and the shadows were blacker. But gradually I yielded to the fascination and penetrated the woods farther and farther on each expedition, till the heart of the mystery was fairly plucked out. During the second or third year of my piscatorial experience I went through them, and through the pasture and meadow beyond, and through another strip of hemlocks, to where the little stream joined the main creek of the valley.

In June, when my trout fever ran pretty high, and an auspicious day arrived, I would make a trip to a stream a couple of miles distant, that came down out of a comparatively new settlement. It was a rapid mountain brook presenting many difficult problems to the young angler, but a very enticing stream for all that, with its two saw-mill dams, its pretty cascades, its high, shelving rocks sheltering the mossy nests of the phœbe-bird, and its general wild and forbidding aspects.

But a meadow brook was always a favorite. The trout like meadows; doubtless their food is more abundant there, and, usually, the good hiding-places are more numerous. As soon as you strike a meadow the character of the creek changes: it goes slower and lies deeper; it tarries to enjoy the high, cool banks and to half hide beneath them; it loves the willows, or rather the willows love it and shelter it from the sun; its spring runs are kept cool by the overhanging grass, and the heavy turf that faces its open banks is not cut away by the sharp hoofs of the grazing cattle. Then there are the bobolinks and the starlings and the meadowlarks, always interested spectators of the angler; there are also the marsh marigolds, the buttercups, or the spotted lilies, and the good angler is always an interested spectator of them. In fact, the patches of meadow land that lie in the angler's course are like the happy experiences in his own life, or like the fine passages in the poem he is reading; the pasture oftener contains the shallow and monotonous places. In the small streams the cattle scare the fish, and soil their element and break down their retreats under the banks. Woodland alternates the best with meadow: the creek loves to burrow under the roots of a great tree, to scoop out a pool after leaping over the prostrate trunk of one, and to pause at the foot of a ledge of moss-covered rocks, with ice-cold water dripping down. How straight the current goes for the rock! Note its corrugated, muscular appearance; it strikes and glances off, but accumulates, deepens with well-defined eddies above and to one side; on the edge of these the trout lurk and spring upon their prey.

The angler learns that it is generally some obstacle or hindrance that makes a deep place in the creek, as in a brave life; and his ideal brook is one that lies in deep, well-defined banks, yet makes many a shift from right to left, meets with many rebuffs and adventures, hurled back upon itself by rocks, waylaid by snags and trees, tripped up by precipices, but sooner or later reposing under meadow banks, deepening and eddying beneath bridges, or prosperous and strong in some level stretch of cultivated land with great elms shading it here and there.

But I early learned that from almost any stream in a trout country the true angler could take trout, and that the great secret was this, that, whatever bait you used, worm, grasshopper, grub, or fly, there was one thing you must always put upon your hook, namely, your heart: when you bait your hook with your heart the fish always bite; they will jump clear from the water after it; they will dispute with each other over it; it is a morsel they love above everything else. With such bait I have seen the born angler (my grandfather was one) take a noble string of trout from the most unpromising waters, and on the most unpromising day. He used his hook so coyly and tenderly, he approached the fish with such address and insinuation, he divined the exact spot where they lay: if they were not eager, he humored them and seemed to steal by them; if they were playful and coquettish, he would suit his mood to theirs; if they were frank and sincere, he met them halfway; he was so patient and considerate, so entirely devoted to pleasing the critical trout, and so successful in his efforts,—surely his heart was upon his hook, and it was a tender, unctuous heart, too, as that of every angler is. How nicely he would measure the distance! how dexterously he would avoid an overhanging limb or bush and drop the line exactly in the right spot! Of course there was a pulse of feeling and sympathy to the extremity of that line. If your heart is a stone, however, or an empty husk, there is no use to put it upon your hook; it will not tempt the fish; the bait must be quick and fresh. Indeed, a certain quality of youth is indispensable to the successful angler, a certain unworldliness and readiness to invest yourself in an enterprise that doesn't pay in the current coin. Not only is the angler, like the poet, born and not made, as Walton says, but there is a deal of the poet in him, and he is to be judged no more harshly; he is the victim of his genius: those wild streams, how they haunt him! he will play truant to dull care, and flee to them; their waters impart somewhat of their own perpetual youth to him. My grandfather when he was eighty years old would take down his pole as eagerly as any boy, and step off with wonderful elasticity toward the beloved streams; it used to try my young legs a good deal to follow him, specially on the return trip. And no poet was ever more innocent of worldly success or ambition. For, to paraphrase Tennyson,—

# IN THE CATSKILLS

> "Lusty trout to him were scrip and share,
> And babbling waters more than cent for cent."

He laid up treasures, but they were not in this world. In fact, though the kindest of husbands, I fear he was not what the country people call a "good provider," except in providing trout in their season, though it is doubtful if there was always fat in the house to fry them in. But he could tell you they were worse off than that at Valley Forge, and that trout, or any other fish, were good roasted in the ashes under the coals. He had the Walton requisite of loving quietness and contemplation, and was devout withal. Indeed, in many ways he was akin to those Galilee fishermen who were called to be fishers of men. How he read the Book and pored over it, even at times, I suspect, nodding over it, and laying it down only to take up his rod, over which, unless the trout were very dilatory and the journey very fatiguing, he never nodded!

## II

The Delaware is one of our minor rivers, but it is a stream beloved of the trout. Nearly all its remote branches head in mountain springs, and its collected waters, even when warmed by the summer sun, are as sweet and wholesome as dew swept from the grass. The Hudson wins from it two streams that are fathered by the mountains from whose loins most of its beginnings issue, namely, the Rondout and the Esopus. These swell a more illustrious current than the Delaware, but the Rondout, one of the finest trout streams in the world, makes an uncanny alliance before it reaches its destination, namely, with the malarious Wallkill.

In the same nest of mountains from which they start are born the Neversink and the Beaverkill, streams of wondrous beauty that flow south and west into the Delaware. From my native hills I could catch glimpses of the mountains in whose laps these creeks were cradled, but it was not till after many years, and after dwelling in a country where trout are not found, that I returned to pay my respects to them as an angler.

My first acquaintance with the Neversink was made in company with some friends in 1869. We passed up the valley of the Big Ingin, marveling at its copious ice-cold springs, and its immense sweep of heavy-timbered mountain-sides. Crossing the range at its head, we struck the Neversink quite unexpectedly about the middle of the afternoon, at a point where it was a good-sized trout stream. It proved to be one of those black mountain brooks born of innumerable ice-cold springs, nourished in the shade, and shod, as it were, with thick-matted moss, that every camper-out remembers. The fish are

## SPECKLED TROUT

as black as the stream and very wild. They dart from beneath the fringed rocks, or dive with the hook into the dusky depths,—an integral part of the silence and the shadows. The spell of the moss is over all. The fisherman's tread is noiseless, as he leaps from stone to stone and from ledge to ledge along the bed of the stream. How cool it is! He looks up the dark, silent defile, hears the solitary voice of the water, sees the decayed trunks of fallen trees bridging the stream, and all he has dreamed, when a boy, of the haunts of beasts of prey—the crouching feline tribes, especially if it be near nightfall and the gloom already deepening in the woods—comes freshly to mind, and he presses on, wary and alert, and speaking to his companions in low tones.

After an hour or so the trout became less abundant, and with nearly a hundred of the black sprites in our baskets we turned back. Here and there I saw the abandoned nests of the pigeons, sometimes half a dozen in one tree. In a yellow birch which the floods had uprooted, a number of nests were still in place, little shelves or platforms of twigs loosely arranged, and affording little or no protection to the eggs or the young birds against inclement weather.

Before we had reached our companions the rain set in again and forced us to take shelter under a balsam. When it slackened we moved on and soon came up with Aaron, who had caught his first trout, and, considerably drenched, was making his way toward camp, which one of the party had gone forward to build. After traveling less than a mile, we saw a smoke struggling up through the dripping trees, and in a few moments were all standing round a blazing fire. But the rain now commenced again, and fairly poured down through the trees, rendering the prospect of cooking and eating our supper there in the woods, and of passing the night on the ground without tent or cover of any kind, rather disheartening. We had been told of a bark shanty a couple of miles farther down the creek, and thitherward we speedily took up our line of march. When we were on the point of discontinuing the search, thinking we had been misinformed or had passed it by, we came in sight of a barkpeeling, in the midst of which a small log house lifted its naked rafters toward the now breaking sky. It had neither floor nor roof, and was less inviting on first sight than the open woods. But a board partition was still standing, out of which we built a rude porch on the east side of the house, large enough for us all to sleep under if well packed, and eat under if we stood up. There was plenty of well-seasoned timber lying about, and a fire was soon burning in front of our quarters that made the scene social and picturesque, especially when the frying-pans were brought into requisition, and the coffee, in charge of Aaron, who was an artist in this line, mingled its aroma with the wild-wood air. At dusk a balsam was felled, and the tips of the branches used to make a bed, which was more fragrant than soft; hemlock is better, because its needles are finer and its branches more elastic.

There was a spirt or two of rain during the night, but not enough to find out the leaks in our roof. It took the shower or series of showers of the next day to do that. They commenced about two o'clock in the afternoon. The forenoon had been fine, and we had brought into camp nearly three hundred trout; but before they were half dressed, or the first panfuls fried, the rain set in. First came short, sharp dashes, then a gleam of treacherous sunshine, followed by more and heavier dashes. The wind was in the southwest, and to rain seemed the easiest thing in the world. From fitful dashes to a steady pour the transition was natural. We stood huddled together, stark and grim, under our cover, like hens under a cart. The fire fought bravely for a time, and retaliated with sparks and spiteful tongues of flame; but gradually its spirit was broken, only a heavy body of coal and half-consumed logs in the centre holding out against all odds. The simmering fish were soon floating about in a yellow liquid that did not look in the least appetizing. Point after point gave way in our cover, till standing between the drops was no longer possible. The water coursed down the underside of the boards, and dripped in our necks and formed puddles on our hat-brims. We shifted our guns and traps and viands, till there was no longer any choice of position, when the loaves and the fishes, the salt and the sugar, the pork and the butter, shared the same watery fate. The fire was gasping its last. Little rivulets coursed about it, and bore away the quenched but steaming coals on their bosoms. The spring run in the rear of our camp swelled so rapidly that part of the trout that had been hastily left lying on its banks again found themselves quite at home. For over two hours the floods came down. About four o'clock Orville, who had not yet come from the day's sport, appeared. To say Orville was wet is not much; he was better than that,—he had been washed and rinsed in at least half a dozen waters, and the trout that he bore dangling at the end of a string hardly knew that they had been out of their proper element.

But he brought welcome news. He had been two or three miles down the creek, and had seen a log building,—whether house or stable he did not know, but it had the appearance of having a good roof, which was inducement enough for us instantly to leave our present quarters. Our course lay along an old wood-road, and much of the time we were to our knees in water. The woods were literally flooded everywhere. Every little rill and springlet ran like a mill-tail, while the main stream rushed and roared, foaming, leaping, lashing, its volume increased fifty-fold. The water was not roily, but of a rich coffee-color, from the leachings of the woods. No more trout for the next three days! we thought, as we looked upon the rampant stream.

After we had labored and floundered along for about an hour, the road turned to the left, and in a little stumpy clearing near the creek a gable uprose on our view. It did not prove to be just such a place as poets love to contemplate. It required a greater effort of the imagination than any of us were then capable of to believe it had ever been a favorite resort of wood-nymphs or sylvan deities. It savored rather of the equine and the bovine. The bark-men had kept their teams there, horses on the one side and oxen on the other, and no Hercules had ever done duty in cleansing the stables. But there was a dry loft overhead with some straw, where we might get some sleep, in spite of the rain and the midges; a double layer of boards, standing at a very acute angle, would keep off the former, while the mingled refuse hay and muck beneath would nurse a smoke that would prove a thorough protection against the latter. And then, when Jim, the two-handed, mounting the trunk of a prostrate maple near by, had severed it thrice with easy and familiar stroke, and, rolling the logs in front of the shanty, had kindled a fire, which, getting the better of the dampness, soon cast a bright glow over all, shedding warmth and light even into the dingy stable, I consented to unsling my knapsack and accept the situation. The rain had ceased, and the sun shone out behind the woods. We had trout sufficient for present needs; and after my first meal in an ox-stall, I strolled out on the rude log bridge to watch the angry Neversink rush by. Its waters fell quite as rapidly as they rose, and before sundown it looked as if we might have fishing again on the morrow. We had better sleep that night than either night before, though there were two disturbing causes,—the smoke in the early part of it, and the cold in the latter. The "no-see-ems" left in disgust; and, though disgusted myself, I swallowed the smoke as best I could, and hugged my pallet of straw the closer. But the day dawned bright, and a plunge in the Neversink set me all right again. The creek, to our surprise and gratification, was only a little higher than before the rain, and some of the finest trout we had yet seen we caught that morning near camp.

We tarried yet another day and night at the old stable, but taking our meals outside squatted on the ground, which had now become quite dry. Part of the day I spent strolling about the woods, looking up old acquaintances among the birds, and, as always, half expectant of making some new ones. Curiously enough, the most abundant species were among those I had found rare in most other localities, namely, the small water-wagtail, the mourning ground warbler, and the yellow-bellied woodpecker. The latter seems to be the prevailing woodpecker through the woods of this region.

That night the midges, those motes that sting, held high carnival. We learned afterward, in the settlement below and from the barkpeelers, that it was the worst night ever experienced in that valley. We had done no fishing during the day, but had anticipated some fine sport about sundown. Accordingly Aaron and I started off between six and seven o'clock, one going upstream and the other down. The scene was charming. The sun shot up great spokes of light from behind the woods, and beauty, like a presence, pervaded the atmosphere. But torment, multiplied as the sands of the seashore, lurked in every tangle and thicket. In a thoughtless moment I removed my shoes and socks, and waded in the water to secure a fine trout that had accidentally slipped from my string and was helplessly floating with the current. This caused some delay and gave the gnats time to accumulate. Before I had got one foot half dressed I was enveloped in a black mist that settled upon my hands and neck and face, filling my ears with infinitesimal pipings and covering my flesh with infinitesimal bitings. I thought I should have to flee to the friendly fumes of the old stable, with "one stocking off and one stocking on;" but I got my shoe on at last, though not without many amusing interruptions and digressions.

In a few moments after this adventure I was in rapid retreat toward camp. Just as I reached the path leading from the shanty to the creek, my companion in the same ignoble flight reached it also, his hat broken and rumpled, and his sanguine countenance looking more sanguinary than I had ever before seen it, and his speech, also, in the highest degree inflammatory. His face and forehead were as blotched and swollen as if he had just run his head into a hornets' nest, and his manner as precipitate as if the whole swarm was still at his back.

No smoke or smudge which we ourselves could endure was sufficient in the earlier part of that evening to prevent serious annoyance from the same cause; but later a respite was granted us.

About ten o'clock, as we stood round our camp-fire, we were startled by a brief but striking display of the aurora borealis. My imagination had already been excited by talk of legends and of weird shapes and appearances, and when, on looking up toward the sky, I saw those pale, phantasmal waves of magnetic light chasing each other across the little opening above our heads, and at first sight seeming barely to clear the treetops, I was as vividly impressed as if I had caught a glimpse of a veritable spectre of the Neversink. The sky shook and trembled like a great white curtain.

After we had climbed to our loft and had lain down to sleep, another adventure befell us. This time a new and uninviting customer appeared upon the scene, the *genius loci* of the old stable, namely, the "fretful porcupine." We had seen the marks and work of these animals about the shanty, and had been careful each night to hang our traps, guns, etc., beyond their reach, but of the prickly night-walker himself we feared we should not get a view.

We had lain down some half hour, and I was just on the threshold of sleep, ready, as it were, to pass through the open door into the land of dreams, when I heard outside somewhere that curious sound,—a sound which I had heard every night I spent in these woods, not only on this but on former expeditions, and which I had settled in my mind as proceeding from the porcupine, since I knew the sounds our other common animals were likely to make,—a sound that might be either a gnawing on some hard, dry substance, or a grating of teeth, or a shrill grunting.

Orville heard it also, and, raising up on his elbow, asked, "What is that?"

"What the hunters call a 'porcupig,'" said I.

"Sure?"

"Entirely so."

"Why does he make that noise?"

"It is a way he has of cursing our fire," I replied. "I heard him last night also."

"Where do you suppose he is?" inquired my companion, showing a disposition to look him up.

"Not far off, perhaps fifteen or twenty yards from our fire, where the shadows begin to deepen."

Orville slipped into his trousers, felt for my gun, and in a moment had disappeared down through the scuttle hole. I had no disposition to follow him, but was rather annoyed than otherwise at the disturbance. Getting the direction of the sound, he went picking his way over the rough, uneven ground, and, when he got where the light failed him, poking every doubtful object with the end of his gun. Presently he poked a light grayish object, like a large round stone, which surprised him by moving off. On this hint he fired, making an incurable wound in the "porcupig," which, nevertheless, tried harder than ever to escape. I lay listening, when, close on the heels of the report of the gun, came excited shouts for a revolver. Snatching up my Smith and Wesson, I hastened, shoeless and hatless, to the scene of action, wondering what was up. I found my companion struggling to detain, with the end of the gun, an uncertain object that was trying to crawl off into the darkness. "Look out!" said Orville, as he saw my bare feet, "the quills are lying thick around here."

And so they were; he had blown or beaten them nearly all off the poor creature's back, and was in a fair way completely to disable my gun, the ramrod of which was already broken and splintered clubbing his victim. But a couple of shots from the revolver, sighted by a lighted match, at the head of the animal, quickly settled him.

He proved to be an unusually large Canada porcupine,—an old patriarch, gray and venerable, with spines three inches long, and weighing, I should say, twenty pounds. The build of this animal is much like that of the woodchuck, that is, heavy and pouchy. The nose is blunter than that of the woodchuck, the limbs stronger, and the tail broader and heavier. Indeed, the latter appendage is quite club-like, and the animal can, no doubt, deal a smart blow with it. An old hunter with whom I talked thought it aided them in climbing. They are inveterate gnawers, and spend much of their time in trees gnawing the bark. In winter one will take up its abode in a hemlock, and continue there till the tree is quite denuded. The carcass emitted a peculiar, offensive odor, and, though very fat, was not in the least inviting as game. If it is part of the economy of nature for one animal to prey upon some other beneath it, then the poor devil has indeed a mouthful that makes a meal off the porcupine. Panthers and lynxes have essayed it, but have invariably left off at the first course, and have afterwards been found dead, or nearly so, with their heads puffed up like a pincushion, and the quills protruding on all sides. A dog that understands the business will manœuvre round the porcupine till he gets an opportunity to throw it over on its back, when he fastens on its quilless underbody. Aaron was puzzled to know how long-parted friends could embrace, when it was suggested that the quills could be depressed or elevated at pleasure.

The next morning boded rain; but we had become thoroughly sated with the delights of our present quarters, outside and in, and packed up our traps to leave. Before we had reached the clearing, three miles below, the rain set in, keeping up a lazy, monotonous drizzle till the afternoon.

The clearing was quite a recent one, made mostly by barkpeelers, who followed their calling in the mountains round about in summer, and worked in their shops making shingle in winter. The Biscuit Brook came in here from the west,—a fine, rapid trout stream six or eight miles in length, with plenty of deer in the mountains about its head. On its banks we found the house of an old woodman, to whom we had been directed for information about the section we proposed to traverse.

"Is the way very difficult," we inquired, "across from the Neversink into the head of the Beaverkill?"

## SPECKLED TROUT

"Not to me; I could go it the darkest night ever was. And I can direct you so you can find the way without any trouble. You go down the Neversink about a mile, when you come to Highfall Brook, the first stream that comes down on the right. Follow up it to Jim Reed's shanty, about three miles. Then cross the stream, and on the left bank, pretty well up on the side of the mountain, you will find a wood-road, which was made by a fellow below here who stole some ash logs off the top of the ridge last winter and drew them out on the snow. When the road first begins to tilt over the mountain, strike down to your left, and you can reach the Beaverkill before sundown."

As it was then after two o'clock, and as the distance was six or eight of these terrible hunters' miles, we concluded to take a whole day to it, and wait till next morning. The Beaverkill flowed west, the Neversink south, and I had a mortal dread of getting entangled amid the mountains and valleys that lie in either angle.

Besides, I was glad of another and final opportunity to pay my respects to the finny tribes of the Neversink. At this point it was one of the finest trout streams I had ever beheld. It was so sparkling, its bed so free from sediment or impurities of any kind, that it had a new look, as if it had just come from the hand of its Creator. I tramped along its margin upward of a mile that afternoon, part of the time wading to my knees, and casting my hook, baited only with a trout's fin, to the opposite bank. Trout are real cannibals, and make no bones, and break none either, in lunching on each other. A friend of mine had several in his spring, when one day a large female trout gulped down one of her male friends, nearly one third her own size, and went around for two days with the tail of her liege lord protruding from her mouth! A fish's eye will do for bait, though the anal fin is better. One of the natives here told me that when he wished to catch large trout (and I judged he never fished for any other,—I never do), he used for bait the bullhead, or dart, a little fish an inch and a half or two inches long, that rests on the pebbles near shore and darts quickly, when disturbed, from point to point. "Put that on your hook," said he, "and if there is a big fish in the creek, he is bound to have it." But the darts were not easily found; the big fish, I concluded, had cleaned them all out; and, then, it was easy enough to supply our wants with a fin.

Declining the hospitable offers of the settlers, we spread our blankets that night in a dilapidated shingle-shop on the banks of the Biscuit Brook, first flooring the damp ground with the new shingle that lay piled in one corner. The place had a great-throated chimney with a tremendous expanse of fireplace within, that cried "More!" at every morsel of wood we gave it.

A SETTLER'S HOUSE

## SPECKLED TROUT

But I must hasten over this part of the ground, nor let the delicious flavor of the milk we had that morning for breakfast, and that was so delectable after four days of fish, linger on my tongue; nor yet tarry to set down the talk of that honest, weather-worn passer-by who paused before our door, and every moment on the point of resuming his way, yet stood for an hour and recited his adventures hunting deer and bears on these mountains. Having replenished our stock of bread and salt pork at the house of one of the settlers, midday found us at Reed's shanty,—one of those temporary structures erected by the bark jobber to lodge and board his "hands" near their work. Jim not being at home, we could gain no information from the "women folks" about the way, nor from the men who had just come in to dinner; so we pushed on, as near as we could, according to the instructions we had previously received. Crossing the creek, we forced our way up the side of the mountain, through a perfect *cheval-de-frise* of fallen and peeled hemlocks, and, entering the dense woods above, began to look anxiously about for the wood-road. My companions at first could see no trace of it; but knowing that a casual wood-road cut in winter, when there was likely to be two or three feet of snow on the ground, would present only the slightest indications to the eye in summer, I looked a little closer, and could make out a mark or two here and there. The larger trees had been avoided, and the axe used only on the small saplings and underbrush, which had been lopped off a couple of feet from the ground. By being constantly on the alert, we followed it till near the top of the mountain; but, when looking to see it "tilt" over the other side, it disappeared altogether. Some stumps of the black cherry were found, and a solitary pair of snow-shoes was hanging high and dry on a branch, but no further trace of human hands could we see. While we were resting here a couple of hermit thrushes, one of them with some sad defect in his vocal powers which barred him from uttering more than a few notes of his song, gave voice to the solitude of the place. This was the second instance in which I have observed a song-bird with apparently some organic defect in its instrument. The other case was that of a bobolink, which, hover in mid-air and inflate its throat as it might, could only force out a few incoherent notes. But the bird in each case presented this striking contrast to human examples of the kind, that it was apparently just as proud of itself, and just as well satisfied with its performance, as were its more successful rivals.

After deliberating some time over a pocket compass which I carried, we decided upon our course, and held on to the west. The descent was very gradual. Traces of bear and deer were noted at different points, but not a live animal was seen.

About four o'clock we reached the bank of a stream flowing west. Hail to the Beaverkill! and we pushed on along its banks. The trout were plenty, and rose quickly to the hook; but we held on our way, designing to go into camp about six o'clock. Many inviting places, first on one bank, then on the other, made us linger, till finally we reached a smooth, dry place overshadowed by balsam and hemlock, where the creek bent around a little flat, which was so entirely to our fancy that we unslung our knapsacks at once. While my companions were cutting wood and making other preparations for the night, it fell to my lot, as the most successful angler, to provide the trout for supper and breakfast. How shall I describe that wild, beautiful stream, with features so like those of all other mountain streams? And yet, as I saw it in the deep twilight of those woods on that June afternoon, with its steady, even flow, and its tranquil, many-voiced murmur, it made an impression upon my mind distinct and peculiar, fraught in an eminent degree with the charm of seclusion and remoteness. The solitude was perfect, and I felt that strangeness and insignificance which the civilized man must always feel when opposing himself to such a vast scene of silence and wildness. The trout were quite black, like all wood trout, and took the bait eagerly. I followed the stream till the deepening shadows warned me to turn back. As I neared camp, the fire shone far through the trees, dispelling the gathering gloom, but blinding my eyes to all obstacles at my feet. I was seriously disturbed on arriving to find that one of my companions had cut an ugly gash in his shin with the axe while felling a tree. As we did not carry a fifth wheel, it was not just the time or place to have any of our members crippled, and I had bodings of evil. But, thanks to the healing virtues of the balsam which must have adhered to the blade of the axe, and double thanks to the court-plaster with which Orville had supplied himself before leaving home, the wounded leg, by being favored that night and the next day, gave us little trouble.

That night we had our first fair and square camping out,—that is, sleeping on the ground with no shelter over us but the trees,— and it was in many respects the pleasantest night we spent in the woods. The weather was perfect and the place was perfect, and for the first time we were exempt from the midges and smoke; and then we appreciated the clean new page we had to work on. Nothing is so acceptable to the camper-out as a pure article in the way of woods and waters. Any admixture of human relics mars the spirit of the scene. Yet I am willing to confess that, before we were through those woods, the marks of an axe in a tree were a welcome sight. On resuming our march next day we followed the right bank of the Beaverkill, in order to strike a stream which flowed in from

THE BEAVERKILL

the north, and which was the outlet of Balsam Lake, the objective point of that day's march. The distance to the lake from our camp could not have been over six or seven miles; yet, traveling as we did, without path or guide, climbing up banks, plunging into ravines, making detours around swampy places, and forcing our way through woods choked up with much fallen and decayed timber, it seemed at least twice that distance, and the mid-afternoon sun was shining when we emerged into what is called the "Quaker Clearing," ground that I had been over nine years before, and that lies about two miles south of the lake. From this point we had a well-worn path that led us up a sharp rise of ground, then through level woods till we saw the bright gleam of the water through the trees.

I am always struck, on approaching these little mountain lakes, with the extensive preparation that is made for them in the conformation of the ground. I am thinking of a depression, or natural basin, in the side of the mountain or on its top, the brink of which I shall reach after a little steep climbing; but instead of that, after I have accomplished the ascent, I find a broad sweep of level or gently undulating woodland that brings me after a half hour or so to the lake, which lies in this vast lap like a drop of water in the palm of a man's hand.

Balsam Lake was oval-shaped, scarcely more than half a mile long and a quarter of a mile wide, but presented a charming picture, with a group of dark gray hemlocks filling the valley about its head, and the mountains rising above and beyond. We found a bough house in good repair, also a dug-out and paddle and several floats of logs. In the dug-out I was soon creeping along the shady side of the lake, where the trout were incessantly jumping for a species of black fly, that, sheltered from the slight breeze, were dancing in swarms just above the surface of the water. The gnats were there in swarms also, and did their best toward balancing the accounts by preying upon me while I preyed upon the trout which preyed upon the flies. But by dint of keeping my hands, face, and neck constantly wet, I am convinced that the balance of blood was on my side. The trout jumped most within a foot or two of shore, where the water was only a few inches deep. The shallowness of the water, perhaps, accounted for the inability of the fish to do more than lift their heads above the surface. They came up mouths wide open, and dropped back again in the most impotent manner. Where there is any depth of water, a trout will jump several feet into the air; and where there is a solid, unbroken sheet or column, they will scale falls and dams fifteen feet high.

We had the very cream and flower of our trout-fishing at this lake. For the first time we could use the fly to advantage; and then the contrast between laborious tramping along shore, on the one hand, and sitting in one end of a dug-out and casting your line right and left with no fear of entanglement in brush or branch, while you were gently propelled along, on the other, was of the most pleasing character.

There were two varieties of trout in the lake,—what it seems proper to call silver trout and golden trout; the former were the slimmer, and seemed to keep apart from the latter. Starting from the outlet and working round on the eastern side toward the head, we invariably caught these first. They glanced in the sun like bars of silver. Their sides and bellies were indeed as white as new silver. As we neared the head, and especially as we came near a space occupied by some kind of watergrass that grew in the deeper part of the lake, the other variety would begin to take the hook, their bellies a bright gold color, which became a deep orange on their fins; and as we returned to the place of departure with the bottom of the boat strewn with these bright forms intermingled, it was a sight not soon to be forgotten. It pleased my eye so, that I would fain linger over them, arranging them in rows and studying the various hues and tints. They were of nearly a uniform size, rarely one over ten or under eight inches in length, and it seemed as if the hues of all the precious metals and stones were reflected from their sides. The flesh was deep salmon-color; that of brook trout is generally much lighter. Some hunters and fishers from the valley of the Mill Brook, whom we met here, told us the trout were much larger in the lake, though far less numerous than they used to be. Brook trout do not grow large till they become scarce. It is only in streams that have been long and much fished that I have caught them as much as sixteen inches in length.

The "porcupigs" were numerous about the lake, and not at all shy. One night the heat became so intolerable in our oven-shaped bough house that I was obliged to withdraw from under its cover and lie down a little to one side. Just at daybreak, as I lay rolled in my blanket, something awoke me. Lifting up my head, there was a porcupine with his forepaws on my hips. He was apparently as much surprised as I was; and to my inquiry as to what he at that moment might be looking for, he did not pause to reply, but hitting me a slap with his tail which left three or four quills in my blanket, he scampered off down the hill into the brush.

Being an observer of the birds, of course every curious incident connected with them fell under my notice. Hence, as we stood about our camp-fire one afternoon looking out over the lake, I was the only one to see a little commotion in the water, half hidden by the near branches, as of some tiny swimmer struggling to reach the shore. Rushing to its rescue in the canoe, I found a yellow-rumped warbler, quite exhausted, clinging to a twig that hung down into the water. I brought the drenched and helpless thing to camp, and, putting it into a basket, hung it up to dry. An hour or two afterward I heard it fluttering in its prison, and, cautiously lifting the lid to get a better glimpse of the lucky captive, it darted out and was gone in a twinkling. How came it in the water? That was my wonder, and I can only guess that it was a young bird that had never before flown over a pond of water, and, seeing the clouds and blue sky so perfect down there, thought it was a vast opening or gateway into another summer land, perhaps a short cut to the tropics, and so got itself into trouble. How my eye was delighted also with the redbird that alighted for a moment on a dry branch above the lake, just where a ray of light from the setting sun fell full upon it! A mere crimson point, and yet how it offset that dark, sombre background!

I have thus run over some of the features of an ordinary trouting excursion to the woods. People inexperienced in such matters, sitting in their rooms and thinking of these things, of all the poets have sung and romancers written, are apt to get sadly taken in when they attempt to realize their dreams. They expect to enter a sylvan paradise of trout, cool retreats, laughing brooks, picturesque views, and balsamic couches, instead of which they find hunger, rain, smoke, toil, gnats, mosquitoes, dirt, broken rest, vulgar guides, and salt pork; and they are very apt not to see where the fun comes in. But he who goes in a right spirit will not be disappointed, and will find the taste of this kind of life better, though bitterer, than the writers have described.

# VIII
A BED OF BOUGHS

# VIII

## A BED OF BOUGHS

WHEN Aaron came again to camp and tramp with me, or, as he wrote, "to eat locusts and wild honey with me in the wilderness," it was past the middle of August, and the festival of the season neared its close. We were belated guests, but perhaps all the more eager on that account, especially as the country was suffering from a terrible drought, and the only promise of anything fresh or tonic or cool was in primitive woods and mountain passes.

"Now, my friend," said I, "we can go to Canada, or to the Maine woods, or to the Adirondacks, and thus have a whole loaf and a big loaf of this bread which you know as well as I will have heavy streaks in it, and will not be uniformly sweet; or we can seek nearer woods, and content ourselves with one week instead of four, with the prospect of a keen relish to the last. Four sylvan weeks sound well, but the poetry is mainly confined to the first one. We can take another slice or two of the Catskills, can we not, without being sated with kills and dividing ridges?"

"Anywhere," replied Aaron, "so that we have a good tramp and plenty of primitive woods. No doubt we should find good browsing on Peakamoose, and trout enough in the streams at its base."

So without further ado we made ready, and in due time found ourselves, with our packs on our backs, entering upon a pass in the mountains that led to the valley of the Rondout.

The scenery was wild and desolate in the extreme, the mountains on either hand looking as if they had been swept by a tornado of stone. Stone avalanches hung suspended on their sides, or had shot down into the chasm below. It was a kind of Alpine scenery, where crushed and broken boulders covered the earth instead of snow.

In the depressions in the mountains the rocky fragments seemed to have accumulated, and to have formed what might be called stone glaciers that were creeping slowly down.

Two hours' march brought us into heavy timber where the stone cataclysm had not reached, and before long the soft voice of the

## IN THE CATSKILLS

Rondout was heard in the gulf below us. We paused at a spring run, and I followed it a few yards down its mountain stairway, carpeted with black moss, and had my first glimpse of the unknown stream. I stood upon rocks and looked many feet down into a still, sunlit pool and saw the trout disporting themselves in the transparent water, and I was ready to encamp at once; but my companion, who had not been tempted by the view, insisted upon holding to our original purpose, which was to go farther up the stream. We passed a clearing with three or four houses and a saw-mill. The dam of the latter was filled with such clear water that it seemed very shallow, and not ten or twelve feet deep, as it really was. The fish were as conspicuous as if they had been in a pail.

Two miles farther up we suited ourselves and went into camp.

If there ever was a stream cradled in the rocks, detained lovingly by them, held and fondled in a rocky lap or tossed in rocky arms, that stream is the Rondout. Its course for several miles from its head is over the stratified rock, and into this it has worn a channel that presents most striking and peculiar features. Now it comes silently along on the top of the rock, spread out and flowing over that thick, dark green moss that is found only in the coldest streams; then drawn into a narrow canal only four or five feet wide, through which it shoots, black and rigid, to be presently caught in a deep basin with shelving, overhanging rocks, beneath which the phœbe-bird builds in security, and upon which the fisherman stands and casts his twenty or thirty feet of line without fear of being thwarted by the brush; then into a black, well-like pool, ten or fifteen feet deep, with a smooth, circular wall of rock on one side worn by the water through long ages; or else into a deep, oblong pocket, into which and out of which the water glides without a ripple.

The surface rock is a coarse sandstone superincumbent upon a lighter-colored conglomerate that looks like Shawangunk grits, and when this latter is reached by the water it seems to be rapidly disintegrated by it, thus forming the deep excavations alluded to.

My eyes had never before beheld such beauty in a mountain stream. The water was almost as transparent as the air,—was, indeed, like liquid air; and as it lay in these wells and pits enveloped in shadow, or lit up by a chance ray of the vertical sun, it was a perpetual feast to the eye,—so cool, so deep, so pure; every reach and pool like a vast spring. You lay down and drank or dipped the water up in your cup, and found it just the right degree of refreshing coldness. One is never prepared for the clearness of the water in these streams. It is always a surprise. See them every year for a dozen years, and yet, when you first come upon one, you will utter an exclamation. I saw nothing like it in the Adirondacks, nor in

## A BED OF BOUGHS

Canada. Absolutely without stain or hint of impurity, it seems to magnify like a lens, so that the bed of the stream and the fish in it appear deceptively near. It is rare to find even a trout stream that is not a little "off color," as they say of diamonds, but the waters in the section of which I am writing have the genuine ray; it is the undimmed and untarnished diamond.

If I were a trout, I should ascend every stream till I found the Rondout. It is the ideal brook. What homes these fish have, what retreats under the rocks, what paved or flagged courts and areas, what crystal depths where no net or snare can reach them!—no mud, no sediment, but here and there in the clefts and seams of the rock patches of white gravel,—spawning-beds ready-made.

The finishing touch is given by the moss with which the rock is everywhere carpeted. Even in the narrow grooves or channels where the water runs the swiftest, the green lining is unbroken. It sweeps down under the stream and up again on the other side, like some firmly woven texture. It softens every outline and cushions every stone. At a certain depth in the great basins and wells it of course ceases, and only the smooth-swept flagging of the place-rock is visible.

The trees are kept well back from the margin of the stream by the want of soil, and the large ones unite their branches far above it, thus forming a high winding gallery, along which the fisherman passes and makes his long casts with scarcely an interruption from branch or twig. In a few places he makes no cast, but sees from his rocky perch the water twenty feet below him, and drops his hook into it as into a well.

We made camp at a bend in the creek where there was a large surface of mossy rock uncovered by the shrunken stream,—a clean, free space left for us in the wilderness that was faultless as a kitchen and dining-room, and a marvel of beauty as a lounging-room, or an open court, or what you will. An obsolete wood or bark road conducted us to it, and disappeared up the hill in the woods beyond. A loose boulder lay in the middle, and on the edge next the stream were three or four large natural wash-basins scooped out of the rock, and ever filled ready for use. Our lair we carved out of the thick brush under a large birch on the bank. Here we planted our flag of smoke and feathered our nest with balsam and hemlock boughs and ferns, and laughed at your four walls and pillows of down.

Wherever one encamps in the woods, there is home, and every object and feature about the place take on a new interest and assume a near and friendly relation to one.

We were at the head of the best fishing. There was an old bark-clearing not far off which afforded us a daily dessert of most delicious blackberries,—an important item in the woods,—and then all the features of the place—a sort of cave above ground—were of the right kind.

There was not a mosquito, or gnat, or other pest in the woods, the cool nights having already cut them off. The trout were sufficiently abundant, and afforded us a few hours' sport daily to supply our wants. The only drawback was, that they were out of season, and only palatable to a woodman's keen appetite. What is this about trout spawning in October and November, and in some cases not till March? These trout had all spawned in August, every one of them. The coldness and purity of the water evidently made them that much earlier. The game laws of the State protect the fish after September 1, proceeding upon the theory that its spawning season is later than that,—as it is in many cases, but not in all, as we found out.

The fish are small in these streams, seldom weighing over a few ounces. Occasionally a large one is seen of a pound or pound and a half weight. I remember one such, as black as night, that ran under a black rock. But I remember much more distinctly a still larger one that I caught and lost one eventful day.

I had him on my hook ten minutes, and actually got my thumb in his mouth, and yet he escaped.

It was only the over-eagerness of the sportsman. I imagined I could hold him by the teeth.

The place where I struck him was a deep well-hole, and I was perched upon a log that spanned it ten or twelve feet above the water. The situation was all the more interesting because I saw no possible way to land my fish. I could not lead him ashore, and my frail tackle could not be trusted to lift him sheer from that pit to my precarious perch. What should I do? call for help? but no help was near. I had a revolver in my pocket and might have shot him through and through, but that novel proceeding did not occur to me until it was too late. I would have taken a Sam Patch leap into the water, and have wrestled with my antagonist in his own element, but I knew the slack, thus sure to occur, would probably free him; so I peered down upon the beautiful creature and enjoyed my triumph as far as it went. He was caught very lightly through his upper jaw, and I expected every struggle and somersault would break the hold. Presently I saw a place in the rocks where I thought it possible, with such an incentive, to get down within reach of the water: by careful manœuvring I slipped my pole behind me and got hold of the line, which I cut and wound around my finger; then I made my way toward the end of the log and the place in the rocks, leading my fish along much exhausted on the top of the water. By

## A BED OF BOUGHS

an effort worthy the occasion I got down within reach of the fish, and, as I have already confessed, thrust my thumb into his mouth and pinched his cheek; he made a spring and was free from my hand and the hook at the same time; for a moment he lay panting on the top of the water, then, recovering himself slowly, made his way down through the clear, cruel element beyond all hope of recapture. My blind impulse to follow and try to seize him was very strong, but I kept my hold and peered and peered long after the fish was lost to view, then looked my mortification in the face and laughed a bitter laugh.

"But, hang it! I had all the fun of catching the fish, and only miss the pleasure of eating him, which at this time would not be great."

"The fun, I take it," said my soldier, "is in triumphing, and not in being beaten at the last."

"Well, have it so; but I would not exchange those ten or fifteen minutes with that trout for the tame two hours you have spent in catching that string of thirty. To *see* a big fish after days of small fry is an event; to have a jump from one is a glimpse of the sportsman's paradise; and to hook one, and actually have him under your control for ten minutes,—why, that is paradise itself as long as it lasts."

One day I went down to the house of a settler a mile below, and engaged the good dame to make us a couple of loaves of bread, and in the evening we went down after them. How elastic and exhilarating the walk was through the cool, transparent shadows! The sun was gilding the mountains, and its yellow light seemed to be reflected through all the woods. At one point we looked through and along a valley of deep shadow upon a broad sweep of mountain quite near and densely clothed with woods, flooded from base to summit by the setting sun. It was a wild, memorable scene. What power and effectiveness in Nature, I thought, and how rarely an artist catches her touch! Looking down upon or squarely into a mountain covered with a heavy growth of birch and maple, and shone upon by the sun, is a sight peculiarly agreeable to me. How closely the swelling umbrageous heads of the trees fit together, and how the eye revels in the flowing and easy uniformity, while the mind feels the ruggedness and terrible power beneath!

As we came back, the light yet lingered on the top of Slide Mountain.

"'The last that parleys with the setting sun,'"

said I, quoting Wordsworth.

"That line is almost Shakespearean," said my companion. "It suggests that great hand at least, though it has not the grit and virility of the more primitive bard. What triumph and fresh morning power in Shakespeare's lines that will occur to us at sunrise to-morrow!—

> "'And jocund day
> Stands tiptoe on the misty mountain tops.'

Or in this:—

> "'Full many a glorious morning have I seen
> Flatter the mountain tops wth sovran eye.'

There is savage, perennial beauty there, the quality that Wordsworth and nearly all the modern poets lack."

"But Wordsworth is the poet of the mountains," said I, "and of lonely peaks. True, he does not express the power and aboriginal grace there is in them, nor toy with them and pluck them up by the hair of their heads, as Shakespeare does. There is something in Peakamoose yonder, as we see it from this point, cutting the blue vault with its dark, serrated edge, not in the bard of Grasmere; but he expresses the feeling of loneliness and insignificance that the cultivated man has in the presence of mountains, and the burden of solemn emotion they give rise to. Then there is something much more wild and merciless, much more remote from human interests and ends, in our long, high, wooded ranges than is expressed by the peaks and scarred groups of the lake country of Britain. These mountains we behold and cross are not picturesque,—they are wild and inhuman as the sea. In them you are in a maze, in a weltering world of woods; you can see neither the earth nor the sky, but a confusion of the growth and decay of centuries, and must traverse them by your compass or your science of woodcraft,—a rift through the trees giving one a glimpse of the opposite range or of the valley beneath, and he is more at sea than ever; one does not know his own farm or settlement when framed in these mountain treetops; all look alike unfamiliar."

Not the least of the charm of camping out is your camp-fire at night. What an artist! What pictures are boldly thrown or faintly outlined upon the canvas of the night! Every object, every attitude of your companion is striking and memorable. You see effects and groups every moment that you would give money to be able to carry away with you in enduring form. How the shadows leap, and skulk, and hover about! Light and darkness are in perpetual tilt and warfare, with first the one unhorsed, then the other. The friendly and cheering fire, what acquaintance we make with it! We had almost forgotten there was such an element, we had so long known only its dark offspring, heat. Now we see the wild beauty uncaged and note its manner and temper. How surely it creates its

STOPPING FOR FOOD AT THE HOUSE OF A SETTLER

own draught and sets the currents going, as force and enthusiasm always will! It carves itself a chimney out of the fluid and houseless air. A friend, a ministering angel, in subjection; a fiend, a fury, a monster, ready to devour the world, if ungoverned. By day it burrows in the ashes and sleeps; at night it comes forth and sits upon its throne of rude logs, and rules the camp, a sovereign queen.

Near camp stood a tall, ragged yellow birch, its partially cast-off bark hanging in crisp sheets or dense rolls.

"That tree needs the barber," we said, "and shall have a call from him to-night."

So after dark I touched a match into it, and we saw the flames creep up and wax in fury until the whole tree and its main branches stood wrapped in a sheet of roaring flame. It was a wild and striking spectacle, and must have advertised our camp to every nocturnal creature in the forest.

What does the camper think about when lounging around the fire at night? Not much,—of the sport of the day, of the big fish he lost and might have saved, of the distant settlement, of to-morrow's plans. An owl hoots off in the mountain and he thinks of him; if a wolf were to howl or a panther to scream, he would think of him the rest of the night. As it is, things flicker and hover through his mind, and he hardly knows whether it is the past or the present that possesses him. Certain it is, he feels the hush and solitude of the great forest, and, whether he will or not, all his musings are in some way cast upon that huge background of the night. Unless he is an old camper-out, there will be an undercurrent of dread or half fear. My companion said he could not help but feel all the time that there ought to be a sentinel out there pacing up and down. One seems to require less sleep in the woods, as if the ground and the untempered air rested and refreshed him sooner. The balsam and the hemlock heal his aches very quickly. If one is awakened often during the night, as he invariably is, he does not feel that sediment of sleep in his mind next day that he does when the same interruption occurs at home; the boughs have drawn it all out of him.

And it is wonderful how rarely any of the housed and tender white man's colds or influenzas come through these open doors and windows of the woods. It is our partial isolation from Nature that is dangerous; throw yourself unreservedly upon her and she rarely betrays you.

If one takes anything to the woods to read, he seldom reads it; it does not taste good with such primitive air.

There are very few camp poems that I know of, poems that would be at home with one on such an expedition; there is plenty that is

## A BED OF BOUGHS

weird and spectral, as in Poe, but little that is woody and wild as this scene is. I recall a Canadian poem by the late C. D. Shanly—the only one, I believe, the author ever wrote—that fits well the distended pupil of the mind's eye about the camp-fire at night. It was printed many years ago in the "Atlantic Monthly," and is called "The Walker of the Snow;" it begins thus:—

> "'Speed on, speed on, good master;
> The camp lies far away;
> We must cross the haunted valley
> Before the close of day.'"

"That has a Canadian sound," said Aaron; "give us more of it."

> "'How the snow-blight came upon me
> I will tell you as we go,—
> The blight of the shadow hunter
> Who walks the midnight snow.'

And so on. The intent seems to be to personify the fearful cold that overtakes and benumbs the traveler in the great Canadian forests in winter. This stanza brings out the silence or desolation of the scene very effectively,—a scene without sound or motion:—

> "'Save the wailing of the moose-bird
> With a plaintive note and low;
> And the skating of the red leaf
> Upon the frozen snow.'

"The rest of the poem runs thus:—

> "'And said I, Though dark is falling,
> And far the camp must be,
> Yet my heart it would be lightsome
> If I had but company.

> "'And then I sang and shouted,
> Keeping measure as I sped,
> To the harp-twang of the snow-shoe
> As it sprang beneath my tread.

> "'Nor far into the valley
> Had I dipped upon my way,
> When a dusky figure joined me
> In a capuchin of gray,

> "'Bending upon the snow-shoes
> With a long and limber stride;
> And I hailed the dusky stranger,
> As we traveled side by side.

"'But no token of communion
   Gave he by word or look,
And the fear-chill fell upon me
   At the crossing of the brook.

"'For I saw by the sickly moonlight,
   As I followed, bending low,
That the walking of the stranger
   Left no foot-marks on the snow.

"'Then the fear-chill gathered o'er me,
   Like a shroud around me cast,
As I sank upon the snow-drift
   Where the shadow hunter passed.

"'And the otter-trappers found me,
   Before the break of day,
With my dark hair blanched and whitened
   As the snow in which I lay.

"'But they spoke not as they raised me;
   For they knew that in the night
I had seen the shadow hunter
   And had withered in his sight.

"'Sancta Maria speed us!
   The sun is fallen low:
Before us lies the valley
   Of the Walker of the Snow!'"

"Ah!" exclaimed my companion. "Let us pile on more of those dry birch-logs; I feel both the 'fear-chill' and the 'cold-chill' creeping over me. How far is it to the valley of the Neversink?"

"About three or four hours' march, the man said."

"I hope we have no haunted valleys to cross?"

"None," said I, "but we pass an old log cabin about which there hangs a ghostly superstition. At a certain hour in the night, during the time the bark is loose on the hemlock, a female form is said to steal from it and grope its way into the wilderness. The tradition runs that her lover, who was a bark-peeler and wielded the spud, was killed by his rival, who felled a tree upon him while they were at work. The girl, who helped her mother cook for the 'hands,' was crazed by the shock, and that night stole forth into the woods and was never seen or heard of more. There are old hunters who aver that her cry may still be heard at night at the head of the valley whenever a tree falls in the stillness of the forest."

"Well, I heard a tree fall not ten minutes ago," said Aaron; "a distant, rushing sound with a subdued crash at the end of it, and

## A BED OF BOUGHS

the only answering cry I heard was the shrill voice of the screech owl off yonder against the mountain. But maybe it was not an owl," said he after a moment; "let us help the legend along by believing it was the voice of the lost maiden."

"By the way," continued he, "do you remember the pretty creature we saw seven years ago in the shanty on the West Branch, who was really helping her mother cook for the hands, a slip of a girl twelve or thirteen years old, with eyes as beautiful and bewitching as the waters that flowed by her cabin? I was wrapped in admiration till she spoke; then how the spell was broken! Such a voice! It was like the sound of pots and pans when you expected to hear a lute."

The next day we bade farewell to the Rondout, and set out to cross the mountain to the east branch of the Neversink.

"We shall find tame waters compared with these, I fear,—a shriveled stream brawling along over loose stones, with few pools or deep places."

Our course was along the trail of the bark-men who had pursued the doomed hemlock to the last tree at the head of the valley. As we passed along, a red steer stepped out of the bushes into the road ahead of us, where the sunshine fell full upon him, and, with a half-scared, beautiful look, begged alms of salt. We passed the Haunted Shanty; but both it and the legend about it looked very tame at ten o'clock in the morning. After the road had faded out, we took to the bed of the stream to avoid the gauntlet of the underbrush, skipping up the mountain from boulder to boulder. Up and up we went, with frequent pauses and copious quaffing of the cold water. My soldier declared a "haunted valley" would be a godsend; anything but endless dragging of one's self up such an Alpine stairway. The winter wren, common all through the woods, peeped and scolded at us as we sat blowing near the summit, and the oven-bird, not quite sure as to what manner of creatures we were, hopped down a limb to within a few feet of us and had a good look, then darted off into the woods to tell the news. I also noted the Canada warbler, the chestnut-sided warbler, and the black-throated blue-back,—the latter most abundant of all. Up these mountain brooks, too, goes the belted kingfisher, swooping around through the woods when he spies the fisherman, then wheeling into the open space of the stream and literally making a "blue streak" down under the branches.

At last the stream which had been our guide was lost under the rocks, and before long the top was gained. These mountains are horse-shaped. There is always a broad, smooth back, more or less depressed, which the hunter aims to bestride; rising rapidly from this is pretty sure to be a rough, curving ridge that carries the forest up to some highest peak. We were lucky in hitting the saddle, but we could see a little to the south the sharp, steep neck of the steed sweeping up toward the sky with an erect mane of balsam fir.

These mountains are steed-like in other respects: any timid and vacillating course with them is sure to get you into trouble. One must strike out boldly, and not be disturbed by the curveting and shying; the valley you want lies squarely behind them, but farther off than you think, and if you do not go for it resolutely, you will get bewildered and the mountain will play you a trick.

I may say that Aaron and I kept a tight rein and a good pace till we struck a water-course on the other side, and that we clattered down it with no want of decision till it emptied into a larger stream which we knew must be the East Branch. An abandoned fishpole lay on the stones, marking the farthest point reached by some fisherman. According to our reckoning, we were five or six miles above the settlement, with a good depth of primitive woods all about us.

We kept on down the stream, now and then pausing at a likely place to take some trout for dinner, and with an eye out for a good camping-ground. Many of the trout were full of ripe spawn, and a few had spawned, the season with them being a little later than on the stream we had left, perhaps because the water was less cold. Neither had the creek here any such eventful and startling career. It led, indeed, quite a humdrum sort of life under the roots and fallen treetops and among the loose stones. At rare intervals it beamed upon us from some still reach or dark cover, and won from us our best attention in return.

The day was quite spent before we had pitched our air-woven tent and prepared our dinner, and we gathered boughs for our bed in the gloaming. Breakfast had to be caught in the morning and was not served early, so that it was nine o'clock before we were in motion. A little bird, the red-eyed vireo, warbled most cheerily in the trees above our camp, and, as Aaron said, "gave us a good send-off." We kept down the stream, following the inevitable bark road.

My companion had refused to look at another "dividing ridge" that had neither path nor way, and henceforth I must keep to the open road or travel alone. Two hours' tramp brought us to an old clearing with some rude, tumble-down log buildings that many years before had been occupied by the bark and lumber men. The prospect for trout was so good in the stream hereabouts, and the scene so peaceful and inviting, shone upon by the dreamy August sun, that we concluded to tarry here until the next day. It was a page of pioneer history opened to quite unexpectedly. A dim footpath led us a few yards to a superb spring, in which a trout from the near creek had taken up his abode. We took possession of what had been

## A BED OF BOUGHS

a shingle-shop, attracted by its huge fireplace. We floored it with balsam boughs, hung its walls with our "traps," and sent the smoke curling again from its disused chimney.

The most musical and startling sound we heard in the woods greeted our ears that evening about sundown as we sat on a log in front of our quarters,—the sound of slow, measured pounding in the valley below us. We did not know how near we were to human habitations, and the report of the lumberman's mallet, like the hammering of a great woodpecker, was music to the ear and news to the mind. The air was still and dense, and the silence such as alone broods over these little openings in the primitive woods. My soldier started as if he had heard a signal-gun. The sound, coming so far through the forest, sweeping over those great wind-harps of trees, became wild and legendary, though probably made by a lumberman driving a wedge or working about his mill.

We expected a friendly visit from porcupines that night, as we saw where they had freshly gnawed all about us; hence, when a red squirrel came and looked in upon us very early in the morning and awoke us by his snickering and giggling, my comrade cried out, "There is your porcupig." How the frisking red rogue seemed to enjoy what he had found! He looked in at the door and snickered, then in at the window, then peeked down from between the rafters and cachinnated till his sides must have ached; then struck an attitude upon the chimney, and fairly squealed with mirth and ridicule. In fact, he grew so obstreperous, and so disturbed our repose, that we had to "shoo" him away with one of our boots. He declared most plainly that he had never before seen so preposterous a figure as we cut lying there in the corner of that old shanty.

The morning boded rain, the week to which we had limited ourselves drew near its close, and we concluded to finish our holiday worthily by a good square tramp to the railroad station, twenty-three miles distant, as it proved. Two miles brought us to stumpy fields, and to the house of the upper inhabitant. They told us there was a short cut across the mountain, but my soldier shook his head.

"Better twenty miles of Europe," said he, getting Tennyson a little mixed, "than one of Cathay, or Slide Mountain either."

Drops of the much-needed rain began to come down, and I hesitated in front of the woodshed.

"Sprinkling weather always comes to some bad end," said Aaron, with a reminiscence of an old couplet in his mind, and so it proved, for it did not get beyond a sprinkle, and the sun shone out before noon.

In the next woods I picked up from the middle of the road the tail and one hind leg of one of our native rats, the first I had ever seen except in a museum. An owl or fox had doubtless left it the night before. It was evident the fragments had once formed part of a very elegant and slender creature. The fur that remained (for it was not hair) was tipped with red. My reader doubtless knows that the common rat is an importation, and that there is a native American rat, usually found much farther south than the locality of which I am writing, that lives in the woods,—a sylvan rat, very wild and nocturnal in his habits, and seldom seen even by hunters or woodmen. Its eyes are large and fine, and its form slender. It looks like only a far-off undegenerate cousin of the filthy creature that has come to us from the long-peopled Old World. Some creature ran between my feet and the fire toward morning, the last night we slept in the woods, and I have little doubt it was one of these wood-rats.

The people in these back settlements are almost as shy and furtive as the animals. Even the men look a little scared when you stop them by your questions. The children dart behind their parents when you look at them. As we sat on a bridge resting,—for our packs still weighed fifteen or twenty pounds each,—two women passed us with pails on their arms, going for blackberries. They filed by with their eyes down like two abashed nuns.

In due time we found an old road, to which we had been directed, that led over the mountain to the West Branch. It was a hard pull, sweetened by blackberries and a fine prospect. The snowbird was common along the way, and a solitary wild pigeon shot through the woods in front of us, recalling the nests we had seen on the East Branch,—little scaffoldings of twigs scattered all through the trees.

It was nearly noon when we struck the West Branch, and the sun was scalding hot. We knew that two and three pound trout had been taken there, and yet we wet not a line in its waters. The scene was primitive, and carried one back to the days of his grandfather, stumpy fields, log fences, log houses and barns. A boy twelve or thirteen years old came out of a house ahead of us eating a piece of bread and butter. We soon overtook him and held converse with him. He knew the land well, and what there was in the woods and the waters. He had walked out to the railroad station, fourteen miles distant, to see the cars, and back the same day. I asked him about the flies and mosquitoes, etc. He said they were all gone except the "blunder-heads;" there were some of them left yet.

"What are blunder-heads?" I inquired, sniffing new game.

"The pesky little fly that gets into your eye when you are a-fishing."

Ah, yes! I knew him well. We had got acquainted some days before, and I thanked the boy for the name. It is an insect that hovers before your eye as you thread the streams, and you are

SOME PEOPLE OF THE CATSKILLS

forever vaguely brushing at it under the delusion that it is a little spider suspended from your hat-brim; and just as you want to see clearest, into your eye it goes, head and ears, and is caught between the lids. You miss your cast, but you catch a "blunder-head."

We paused under a bridge at the mouth of Biscuit Brook and ate our lunch, and I can recommend it to be as good a wayside inn as the pedestrian need look for. Better bread and milk than we had there I never expect to find. The milk was indeed so good that Aaron went down to the little log house under the hill a mile farther on and asked for more; and being told they had no cow, he lingered five minutes on the doorstone with his sooty pail in his hand, putting idle questions about the way and distance to the mother while he refreshed himself with the sight of a well-dressed and comely-looking young girl, her daughter.

"I got no milk," said he, hurrying on after me, "but I got something better, only I cannot divide it."

"I know what it is," replied I; "I heard her voice."

"Yes, and it was a good one, too. The sweetest sound I ever heard," he went on, "was a girl's voice after I had been four years in the army, and, by Jove! if I didn't experience something of the same pleasure in hearing this young girl speak after a week in the woods. She had evidently been out in the world and was home on a visit. It was a different look she gave me from that of the natives. This is better than fishing for trout," said he. "You drop in at the next house."

But the next house looked too unpromising.

"There is no milk there," said I, "unless they keep a goat."

"But could we not," said my facetious companion, "go it on that?"

A couple of miles beyond I stopped at a house that enjoyed the distinction of being clapboarded, and had the good fortune to find both the milk and the young lady. A mother and her daughter were again the only occupants save a babe in the cradle, which the young woman quickly took occasion to disclaim.

"It has not opened its dear eyes before since its mother left. Come to aunty," and she put out her hands.

The daughter filled my pail and the mother replenished our stock of bread. They asked me to sit and cool myself, and seemed glad of a stranger to talk with. They had come from an adjoining county five years before, and had carved their little clearing out of the solid woods.

"The men folks," the mother said, "came on ahead and built the house right among the big trees," pointing to the stumps near the door.

## A BED OF BOUGHS

One no sooner sets out with his pack upon his back to tramp through the land than all objects and persons by the way have a new and curious interest to him. The tone of his entire being is not a little elevated, and all his perceptions and susceptibilities quickened. I feel that some such statement is necessary to justify the interest that I felt in this backwoods maiden. A slightly pale face it was, strong and well arched, with a tender, wistful expression not easy to forget.

I had surely seen that face many times before in towns and cities, and in other lands, but I hardly expected to meet it here amid the stumps. What were the agencies that had given it its fine lines and its gracious intelligence amid these simple, primitive scenes? What did my heroine read, or think? or what were her unfulfilled destinies? She wore a sprig of prince's pine in her hair, which gave a touch peculiarly welcome.

"Pretty lonely," she said, in answer to my inquiry; "only an occasional fisherman in summer, and in winter—nobody at all."

And the little new schoolhouse in the woods farther on, with its half-dozen scholars and the girlish face of the teacher seen through the open door,—nothing less than the exhilaration of a journey on foot could have made it seem the interesting object it was. Two of the little girls had been to the spring after a pail of water, and came struggling out of the woods into the road with it as we passed. They set down their pail and regarded us with a half-curious, half-alarmed look.

"What is your teacher's name?" asked one of us.

"Miss Lucinde Josephine—" began the red-haired one, then hesitated, bewildered, when the bright, dark-eyed one cut her short with "Miss Simms," and taking hold of the pail said, "Come on."

"Are there any scholars from above here?" I inquired.

"Yes, Bobbie and Matie," and they hastened toward the door.

We once more stopped under a bridge for refreshments, and took our time, knowing the train would not go on without us. By four o'clock we were across the mountain, having passed from the watershed of the Delaware into that of the Hudson. The next eight miles we had a down grade but a rough road, and during the last half of it we had blisters on the bottoms of our feet. It is one of the rewards of the pedestrian that, however tired he may be, he is always more or less refreshed by his journey. His physical tenement has taken an airing. His respiration has been deepened, his circulation quickened. A good draught has carried off the fumes and the vapors. One's quality is intensified; the color strikes in. At noon that day I was much fatigued; at night I was leg-weary and footsore, but a fresh, hardy feeling had taken possession of me that lasted for weeks.

# MY BOYHOOD

BY

JOHN BURROUGHS

# MY BOYHOOD
## BY
## JOHN BURROUGHS

YOU ask me to give you some account of my life—how it was with me, and now in my seventy-sixth year I find myself in the mood to do so. You know enough about me to know that it will not be an exciting narrative or of any great historical value. It is mainly the life of a country man and a rather obscure man of letters, lived in eventful times indeed, but largely lived apart from the men and events that have given character to the last three quarters of a century. Like tens of thousands of others, I have been a spectator of, rather than a participator in, the activities—political, commercial, sociological, scientific—of the times in which I have lived. My life, like your own, has been along the by-paths rather than along the great public highways. I have known but few great men and have played no part in any great public events—not even in the Civil War which I lived through and in which my duty plainly called me to take part. I am a man who recoils from noise and strife, even from fair competition, and who likes to see his days "linked each to each" by some quiet, congenial occupation.

The first seventeen years of my life were spent on the farm where I was born (1837–1854); the next ten years I was a teacher in rural district schools (1854–1864); then I was for ten years a government clerk in Washington (1864–1873); then in the summer of 1873, while a national bank examiner and bank receiver, I purchased the small fruit farm on the Hudson where you were brought up and where I have since lived, cultivating the land for marketable fruit and the fields and woods for nature literature, as you well know. I have gotten out of my footpaths a few times and traversed some of the great highways of travel—have been twice to Europe, going only as far as Paris (1871 and 1882)—the first time sent to London by the Government with three other men to convey $50,000,000 of bonds to be refunded; the second time going with my family on my own account. I was a member of the Harriman expedition to Alaska in the summer of 1899, going as far as Plover Bay on the extreme N. E. part of Siberia. I was the companion of President Roosevelt on a trip to Yellowstone Park in the spring of 1903. In the winter and spring of 1909 I went to California with two women friends and extended the journey to the Hawaiian Islands, returning home in June. In 1911 I again crossed the continent to California. I have camped and tramped in Maine and in Canada, and have spent part of a winter in Bermuda and in Jamaica. This is an outline of my travels. I have known but few great men. I met Carlyle in the company of Moncure Conway in London in November, 1871. I met Emerson three times—in 1863 at West Point; in 1871 in Baltimore and Washington, where I heard him lecture; and at the Holmes birthday breakfast in Boston in 1879. I knew Walt Whitman intimately from 1863 until his death in 1892. I have met Lowell and Whittier, but not Longfellow or Bryant; I have seen Lincoln, Grant, Sherman, Early, Sumner, Garfield, Cleveland, and other notable men of those days. I heard Tyndall deliver his course of lectures on Light in Washington in 1870 or '71, but missed seeing Huxley during his visit here. I dined with the Rossettis in London in 1871, but was not impressed by them nor they by me. I met Matthew Arnold in New York and heard his lecture on Emerson. My books are, in a way, a record of my life—that part of it that came to flower and fruit in my mind. You could reconstruct my days pretty well from those volumes. A writer who gleans his literary harvest in the fields and woods reaps mainly where he has sown himself. He is a husbandman whose crop springs from the seed of his own heart.

My life has been a fortunate one; I was born under a lucky star. It seems as if both wind and tide had favored me. I have suffered no great losses, or defeats, or illness, or accidents, and have undergone no great struggles or privations; I have had no grouch, I have not wanted the earth. I am pessimistic by night, but by day I am a confirmed optimist, and it is the days that have stamped my life. I have found this planet a good corner of the universe to live in and I am not in a hurry to exchange it for any other. I hope the joy of living may be as keen with you, my dear boy, as it has been with me and that you may have life on as easy terms as I have. With this foreword I will begin the record in more detail.

I have spoken of my good luck. It began in my being born on a farm, of parents in the prime of their days, and in humble circumstances. I deem it good luck too that my birth fell in April, a month in which so many other things find it good to begin life. Father probably tapped the sugar bush about this time or a little earlier; the bluebird and the robin and song sparrow may have

## MY BOYHOOD

arrived that very day. New calves were bleating in the barn and young lambs under the shed. There were earth-stained snow drifts on the hillside, and along the stone walls and through the forests that covered the mountains the coat of snow showed unbroken. The fields were generally bare and the frost was leaving the ground. The stress of winter was over and the warmth of spring began to be felt in the air. I had come into a household of five children, two girls and three boys, the oldest ten years and the youngest two. One had died in infancy, making me the seventh child. Mother was twenty-nine and father thirty-five, a medium-sized, freckled, red-haired man, showing very plainly the Celtic or Welsh strain in his blood, as did mother, who was a Kelly and of Irish extraction on the paternal side. I had come into a family of neither wealth nor poverty as those things were looked upon in those days, but a family dedicated to hard work winter and summer in paying for and improving a large farm, in a country of wide open valleys and long, broad-backed hills and gentle flowing mountain lines; very old geologically, but only one generation from the stump in the history of the settlement. Indeed, the stumps lingered in many of the fields late into my boyhood, and one of my tasks in the dry mid-spring weather was to burn these stumps—an occupation I always enjoyed because the adventure of it made play of the work. The climate was severe in winter, the mercury often dropping to 30° below, though we then had no thermometer to measure it, and the summers, at an altitude of two thousand feet, cool and salubrious. The soil was fairly good, though encumbered with the laminated rock and stones of the Catskill formation, which the old ice sheet had broken and shouldered and transported about. About every five or six acres had loose stones and rock enough to put a rock-bottomed wall around it and still leave enough in and on the soil to worry the ploughman and the mower. All the farms in that section reposing in the valleys and bending up and over the broad-backed hills are checker-boards of stone walls, and the right-angled fields, in their many colors of green and brown and yellow and red, give a striking map-like appearance to the landscape. Good crops of grain, such as rye, oats, buckwheat, and yellow corn, are grown, but grass is the most natural product. It is a grazing country and the dairy cow thrives there, and her products are the chief source of the incomes of the farms.

I had come into a home where all the elements were sweet; the water and the air as good as there is in the world, and where the conditions of life were of a temper to discipline both mind and body. The settlers of my part of the Catskills were largely from Connecticut and Long Island, coming in after or near the close of the Revolution, and with a good mixture of Scotch emigrants.

## MY BOYHOOD

My great-grandfather, Ephraim Burroughs, came, with his family of eight or ten children, from near Danbury, Conn., and settled in the town of Stamford shortly after the Revolution. He died there in 1818. My grandfather, Eden, came into the town of Roxbury, then a part of Ulster County.

I had come into a land flowing with milk, if not with honey. The maple syrup may very well take the place of the honey. The sugar maple was the dominant tree in the woods and the maple sugar the principal sweetening used in the family. Maple, beech, and birch wood kept us warm in winter, and pine and hemlock timber made from trees that grew in the deeper valleys formed the roofs and the walls of the houses. The breath of kine early mingled with my own breath. From my earliest memory the cow was the chief factor on the farm and her products the main source of the family income; around her revolved the haying and the harvesting. It was for her that we toiled from early July until late August, gathering the hay into the barns or into the stacks, mowing and raking it by hand. That was the day of the scythe and the good mower, of the cradle and the good cradler, of the pitchfork and the good pitcher. With the modern agricultural machinery the same crops are gathered now with less than half the outlay of human energy, but the type of farmer seems to have deteriorated in about the same proportion. The third generation of farmers in my native town are much like the third steeping of tea, or the third crop of corn where no fertilizers have been used. The large, picturesque, and original characters who improved the farms and paid for them are about all gone, and their descendants have deserted the farms or are distinctly of an inferior type. The farms keep more stock and yield better crops, owing to the amount of imported grain consumed upon them, but the families have dwindled or gone out entirely, and the social and the neighbourhood spirit is not the same. No more huskings or quiltings, or apple cuts, or raisings or "bees" of any sort. The telephone and the rural free delivery have come and the automobile and the daily newspaper. The roads are better, communication quicker, and the houses and barns more showy, but the men and the women, and especially the children, are not there. The towns and the cities are now coloring and dominating the country which they have depleted of its men, and the rural districts are becoming a faded replica of town life.

The farm work to which I was early called upon to lend a hand, as I have said, revolved around the dairy cow. Her paths were in the fields and woods, her sonorous voice was upon the hills, her fragrant breath was upon every breeze. She was the centre of our industries. To keep her in good condition, well pastured in summer and well

## MY BOYHOOD

housed and fed in winter, and the whole dairy up to its highest point of efficiency—to this end the farmer directed his efforts. It was an exacting occupation. In summer the day began with the milking and ended with the milking; and in winter it began with the foddering and ended with the foddering, and the major part of the work between and during both seasons had for its object, directly or indirectly, the well-being of the herd. Getting the cows and turning away the cows in summer was usually the work of the younger boys; turning them out of the stable and putting them back in winter was usually the work of the older. The foddering them from the stack in the field in winter also fell to the lot of the older members of the family.

In milking we all took a hand when we had reached the age of about ten years, Mother and my sisters usually doing their share. At first we milked the cows in the road in front of the house, setting the pails of milk on the stone work; later we milked them in a yard in the orchard behind the house, and of late years the milking is done in the stable. Mother said that when they first came upon the farm, as she sat milking a cow in the road one evening, she saw a large black animal come out of the woods out where the clover meadow now is, and cross the road and disappear in the woods on the other side. Bears sometimes carried off the farmers' hogs in those days, boldly invading the pens to do so. My father kept about thirty cows of the Durham breed; now the dairy herds are made up of Jerseys or Holsteins. Then the product that went to market was butter, now it is milk. Then the butter was made on the farm by the farmer's wife or the hired girl, now it is made in the creameries by men. My mother made most of the butter for nearly forty years, packing thousands of tubs and firkins of it in that time. The milk was set in tin pans on a rack in the milk house for the cream to rise, and as soon as the milk clabbered it was skimmed.

About three o'clock in the afternoon during the warm weather Mother would begin skimming the milk, carrying it pan by pan to the big cream pan, where with a quick movement of a case knife the cream was separated from the sides of the pan, the pan tilted on the edge of the cream pan and the heavy mantle of cream, in folds or flakes, slid off into the receptacle and the thick milk emptied into pails to be carried to the swill barrel for the hogs. I used to help Mother at times by handing her the pans of milk from the rack and emptying the pails. Then came the washing of the pans at the trough, at which I also often aided her by standing the pans up to dry and sun on the big bench. Rows of drying tin pans were always a noticeable feature about farmhouses in those days, also the churning machine attached to the milk house and the sound of the wheel, propelled by the "old churner"—either a big dog or a wether sheep. Every summer morning by eight o'clock the old sheep or the old dog was brought and tied to his task upon the big wheel. Sheep were usually more unwilling churners than were the dogs. They rarely acquired any sense of duty or obedience as a dog did. This endless walking and getting nowhere very soon called forth vigorous protests. The churner would pull back, brace himself, choke, and stop the machine: one churner threw himself off and was choked to death before he was discovered. I remember when the old hetchel from the day of flax dressing, fastened to a board, did duty behind the old churner, spurring him up with its score or more of sharp teeth when he settled back to stop the machine. "Run and start the old sheep," was a command we heard less often after that. He could not long hold out against the pressure of that phalanx of sharp points upon his broad rear end.

The churn dog was less obdurate and perverse, but he would sometimes hide away as the hour of churning approached and we would have to hustle around to find him. But we had one dog that seemed to take pleasure in the task and would go quickly to the wheel when told to and finish his task without being tied. In the absence of both dog and sheep, I have a few times taken their place on the wheel. In winter and early spring there was less cream to churn and we did it by hand, two of us lifting the dasher together. Heavy work for even big boys, and when the stuff was reluctant and the butter would not come sometimes until the end of an hour, the task tried our mettle. Sometimes it would not gather well after it had come, then some deft handling of the dasher was necessary.

I never tired of seeing Mother lift the great masses of golden butter from the churn with her ladle and pile them up in the big butter bowl, with the drops of buttermilk standing upon them as if they were sweating from the ordeal they had been put through. Then the working and the washing of it to free it from the milk and the final packing into tub or firkin, its fresh odor in the air—what a picture it was! How much of the virtue of the farm went each year into those firkins! Literally the cream of the land. Ah, the alchemy of Life, that in the bee can transform one product of those wild rough fields into honey, and in the cow can transform another product into milk!

The spring butter was packed into fifty-pound tubs to be shipped to market as fast as made. The packing into one-hundred-pound firkins to be held over till November did not begin till the cows were turned out to pasture in May. To have made forty tubs by that time and sold them for eighteen or twenty cents a pound was considered very satisfactory. Then to make forty or fifty firkins

## MY BOYHOOD

during the summer and fall and to get as good a price for it made the farmer's heart glad. When Father first came on the farm, in 1827, butter brought only twelve or fourteen cents per pound, but the price steadily crept up till in my time it sold from seventeen to eighteen and a half. The firkin butter was usually sold to a local butter buyer named Dowie. He usually appeared in early fall, always on horseback, having notified Father in advance. At the breakfast table Father would say, "Dowie is coming to try the butter to-day."

"I hope he will not try that firkin I packed that hot week in July," Mother would say. But very likely that was the one among others he would ask for. His long, half-round steel butter probe or tryer was thrust down the centre of the firkin to the bottom, given a turn or two, and withdrawn, its tapering cavity filled with a sample of every inch of butter in the firkin. Dowie would pass it rapidly to and fro under his nose, maybe sometimes tasting it, then push the tryer back into the hole, then withdrawing it, leaving its core of butter where it found it. If the butter suited him, and it rarely failed to do so, he would make his offer and ride away to the next dairy.

The butter had always to be delivered at a date agreed upon, on the Hudson River at Catskill. This usually took place in November. It was the event of the fall: two loads of butter, of twenty or more firkins each, to be transported fifty miles in a lumber wagon, each round trip taking about four days. The firkins had to be headed up and gotten ready. This job in my time usually fell to Hiram. He would begin the day before Father was to start and have a load headed and placed in the wagon on time, with straw between the firkins so they would not rub. How many times I have heard those loads start off over the frozen ground in the morning before it was light! Sometimes a neighbour's wagon would go slowly jolting by just after or just before Father had started, but on the same errand. Father usually took a bag of oats for his horses and a box of food for himself so as to avoid all needless expenses. The first night would usually find him in Steel's tavern in Greene County, half way to Catskill. The next afternoon would find him at his journey's end and by night unloaded at the steamboat wharf, his groceries and other purchases made, and ready for an early start homeward in the morning. On the fourth night we would be on the lookout for his return. Mother would be sitting, sewing by the light of her tallow dip, with one ear bent toward the road. She usually caught the sound of his wagon first. "There comes your father," she would say, and Hiram or Wilson would quickly get and light the old tin lantern and stand ready on the stonework to receive him and help put out the team. By the time he was in the house his supper would be on the table—a cold pork stew, I remember, used to delight him on such occasions, and a cup of green tea. After supper his pipe, and the story of his trip told, with a list of family purchases, and then to bed. In a few days the second trip would be made. As his boys grew old enough he gave each of them in turn a trip with him to Catskill. It was a great event in the life of each of us. When it came my turn I was probably eleven or twelve years old and the coming event loomed big on my horizon. I was actually to see my first steamboat, the Hudson River, and maybe the steam cars. For several days in advance I hunted the woods for game to stock the provision box so as to keep down the expense. I killed my first partridge and probably a wild pigeon or two and gray squirrels. Perched high on that springboard beside Father, my feet hardly touching the tops of the firkins, at the rate of about two miles an hour over rough roads in chilly November weather, I made my first considerable journey into the world. I crossed the Catskill Mountains and got that surprising panoramic view of the land beyond from the top. At Cairo, where it seems we passed the second night, I disgraced myself in the morning, when Father, after praising me to some bystanders, told me to get up in the wagon and drive the load out in the road. In my earnest effort to do so I ran foul of one side of the big door, and came near smashing things. Father was humiliated and I was dreadfully mortified.

With the wonders of Catskill I was duly impressed, but one of my most vivid remembrances is a passage at arms (verbal) at the steamboat between Father and old Dowie. The latter had questioned the correctness of the weight of the empty firkin which was to be deducted as tare from the total weight. Hot words followed. Father said, "Strip it, strip it." Dowie said, "I will," and in a moment there stood on the scales the naked firkin of butter, sweating drops of salt water. Which won, I do not know. I remember only that peace soon reigned and Dowie continued to buy our butter.

One other incident of that trip still sticks in my mind. I was walking along a street just at dusk, when I saw a drove of cattle coming. The drover, seeing me, called out, "Here, boy, turn those cows up that street!" This was in my line, I was at home with cows, and I turned the drove up in fine style. As the man came along he said, "Well done," and placed six big copper cents in my hand. Never was my palm more unexpectedly and more agreeably tickled. The feel of it is with me yet!

At an earlier date than that of the accident in the old stone school house, my head, and my body too, got some severe bruises. One summer day when I could not have been more than three years old, my sister Jane and I were playing in the big attic chamber and amusing ourselves by lying across the vinegar keg and pushing

## MY BOYHOOD

it about the room with our feet. We came to the top of the steep stairway that ended against the chamber door, a foot or more above the kitchen floor, and I suppose we thought it would be fun to take the stairway on the keg. At the brink of that stairway my memory becomes a blank and when I find myself again I am lying on the bed in the "back-bedroom" and the smell of camphor is rank in the room. How it fared with Jane I do not recall; the injury was probably not serious with either of us, but it is easy to imagine how poor Mother must have been startled when she heard that racket on the stairs and the chamber door suddenly burst open, spilling two of her children, mixed up with the vinegar keg, out on the kitchen floor. Jane was more than two years my senior, and should have known better.

Vivid incidents make a lasting impression. I recall what might have been a very serious accident had not my usual good luck attended me, when I was a few years older. One autumn day I was with my older brothers in the corn lot, where they had gone with the lumber wagon to gather pumpkins. When they had got their load and were ready to start I planted myself on the load above the hind axle and let my legs hang down between the spokes of the big wheel. Luckily one of my brothers saw my perilous position just as the team was about to move and rescued me in time. Doubtless my legs would have been broken and maybe very badly crushed in a moment more. But such good fortune seems to have followed me always. One winter's morning, as I stooped to put on one of my boots beside the kitchen stove at the house of a schoolmate with whom I had passed the night, my face came in close contact with the spout of the boiling tea kettle. The scalding steam barely missed my eye and blistered my brow a finger's breadth above it. With one eye gone, I fancy life would have looked quite different. Another time I was walking along one of the market streets of New York, when a heavy bale of hay, through the carelessness of some workman, dropped from thirty or forty feet above me and struck the pavement at my feet. I heard angry words over the mishap, spoken by someone above me, but I only said to myself, "Lucky again!" I recall a bit of luck of a different kind when I was a treasury clerk in Washington. I had started for the seashore for a week's vacation with a small roll of new greenbacks in my pocket. Shortly after the train had left the station I left my seat and walked through two or three of the forward cars looking for a friend who had agreed to join me. Not finding him, I retraced my steps, and as I was passing along through the car next my own I chanced to see a roll of new bills on the floor near the end of a seat. Instinctively feeling for my own roll of bills and finding it missing, I picked up the money and saw at a glance that it was mine. The passengers near by eyed me in surprise, and I suspect began to feel in their own pockets, but I did not stop to explain and went to my seat startled but happy. I had missed my friend but I might have missed something of more value to me just at that time.

A kind of untoward fate seems inherent in the characters of some persons and makes them the victims of all the ill luck on the road. Such a fate has not been mine. I have met all the good luck on the road. Some kindly influence has sent my best friends my way, or sent me their way. The best thing about me is that I have found a perennial interest in the common universal things which all may have on equal terms, and hence have found plenty to occupy and absorb me wherever I have been. If the earth and the sky are enough for one, why should one sigh for other spheres?

The old farm must have had at least ten miles of stone walls upon it, many of them built new by Father from stones picked up in the fields, and many of them relaid by him, or rather by his boys and hired men. Father was not skilful at any sort of craft work. He was a good ploughman, a good mower and cradler, excellent with a team of oxen drawing rocks, and good at most general farm work, but not an adept at constructing anything. Hiram was the mechanical genius of the family. He was a good wall-layer, and skilful with edged tools. It fell to his lot to make the sleds, the stone-boats, the hay-rigging, the ax helves, the flails, to mend the cradles and rakes, to build the haystacks, and once, I remember, he rebuilt the churning machine. He was slow but he hewed exactly to the line. Before and during my time on the farm Father used to count on building forty or fifty rods of stone wall each year, usually in the spring and early summer. These were the only lines of poetry and prose Father wrote. They are still very legible on the face of the landscape and cannot be easily erased from it. Gathered out of the confusion of nature, built up of fragments of the old Devonian rock and shale, laid with due regard to the wear and tear of time, well-bottomed and well-capped, establishing boundaries and defining possessions, etc., these lines of stone wall afford a good lesson in many things besides wall building. They are good literature and good philosophy. They smack of the soil, they have local color, they are a bit of chaos brought into order. When you deal with nature only the square deal is worth while. How she searches for the vulnerable points in your structure, the weak places in your foundation, the defective material in your building!

The farmer's stone wall, when well built, stands about as long as he does. It begins to reel and look decrepit when he begins to

## MY BOYHOOD

do so. But it can be relaid and he cannot. One day I passed by the roadside to speak with an old man who was rebuilding a wall. "I laid this wall fifty years ago," he said. "When it is laid up again I shall not have the job." He had stood up longer than had his wall.

A stone wall is the friend of all the wild creatures. It is a safe line of communication with all parts of the landscape. What do the chipmunks, red squirrels, and weasels do in a country without stone fences? The woodchucks and the coons and foxes also use them.

It was my duty as a farm boy to help pick up the stone and pry up the rocks. I could put the bait under the lever, even if my weight on top of it did not count for much. The slow, patient, hulky oxen, how they would kink their tails, hump their backs, and throw their weight into the bows when they felt a heavy rock behind them and Father lifted up his voice and laid on the "gad"! It was a good subject for a picture which, I think, no artist has ever painted. How many rocks we turned out of their beds, where they had slept since the great ice sheet tucked them up there, maybe a hundred thousand years ago—how wounded and torn the meadow or pasture looked, bleeding as it were, in a score of places, when the job was finished! But the further surgery of the plough and harrow, followed by the healing touch of the seasons, soon made all whole again.

The work on the farm in those days varied little from year to year. In winter the care of the cattle, the cutting of the wood, and the thrashing of the oats and rye filled the time. From the age of ten or twelve till we were grown up, we went to school only in winter, doing the chores morning and evening, and engaging in general work every other Saturday, which was a holiday. Often my older brothers would have to leave school by three o'clock to get home to put up the cows in my father's absence. Those school days, how they come back to me!—the long walk across lots, through the snow-choked fields and woods, our narrow path so often obliterated by a fresh fall of snow; the cutting winds, the bitter cold, the snow squeaking beneath our frozen cowhide boots, our trousers' legs often tied down with tow strings to keep the snow from pushing them up above our boot tops; the wide-open white landscape with its faint black lines of stone wall when we had passed the woods and began to dip down into West Settlement valley; the Smith boys and Bouton boys and Dart boys, afar off, threading the fields on their way to school, their forms etched on the white hillsides, one of the bigger boys, Ria Bouton, who had many chores to do, morning after morning running the whole distance so as not to be late; the red school house in the distance by the roadside with the dark spot in its centre made by the open door of the entry way; the creek in the valley, often choked with anchor ice, which our path crossed and into which I one morning slumped, reaching the school house with my clothes freezing upon me and the water gurgling in my boots; the boys and girls there, Jay Gould among them, two thirds of them now dead and the living scattered from the Hudson to the Pacific; the teachers now all dead; the studies, the games, the wrestlings, the baseball—all these things and more pass before me as I recall those long-gone days. Two years ago I hunted up one of those schoolmates in California whom I had not seen for over sixty years. She was my senior by seven or eight years, and I had a boy's remembrance of her fresh sweet face, her kindly eyes and gentle manners. I was greeted by a woman of eighty-two, with dimmed sight and dulled hearing, but instantly I recognized some vestiges of the charm and sweetness of my elder schoolmate of so long ago. No cloud was on her mind or memory and for an hour we again lived among the old people and scenes.

What a roomful of pupils, many of them young men and women, there was during those winters, thirty-five or forty each day! In late years there are never more than five or six. The fountains of population are drying up more rapidly than are our streams. Of that generous roomful of young people, many became farmers, a few became business men, three or four became professional men, and only one, so far as I know, took to letters; and he, judged by his environment and antecedents, the last one you would have picked out for such a career. You might have seen in Jay Gould's Jewish look, bright scholarship, and pride of manners some promise of an unusual career; but in the boy of his own age whom he was so fond of wrestling with and of having go home with him at night, but whose visits he would never return, what was there indicative of the future? Surely not much that I can now discover. Jay Gould, who became a sort of Napoleon of finance, early showed a talent for big business and power to deal with men. He had many characteristic traits which came out even in his walk. One day in New York, after more than twenty years since I had known him as a boy, I was walking up Fifth Avenue, when I saw a man on the other side of the street, more than a block away, coming toward me, whose gait arrested my attention as something I had known long before. Who could it be? I thought, and began to ransack my memory for a clue. I had seen that gait before. As the man came opposite me I saw he was Jay Gould. That walk in some subtle way differed from the walk of any other man I had known. It is a curious psychological fact that the two men outside my own family of whom I have oftenest dreamed in my sleep are Emerson and Jay Gould; one to whom I owe so much, the other to whom I owe nothing; one whose name I revere, the other whose name I associate, as does the world, with the dark

## MY BOYHOOD

way of speculative finance. The new expounders of the philosophy of dreams would probably tell me that I had a secret admiration for Jay Gould. If I have, it slumbers deeply in my sub-conscious self and awakens only when my conscious self sleeps.

But I set out to talk of the work on the farm. The threshing was mostly done in winter with the hickory flail, one shock of fifteen sheaves making a flooring. On the dry cold days the grain shelled easily. After a flooring had been thrashed over at least three times, the straw was bound up again in sheaves, the floor completely raked over and the grain banked up against the side of the bay. When the pile became so large it was in the way, it was cleaned up, that is, run through the fanning mill, one of us shoveling in the grain, another turning the mill, and a third measuring the grain and putting it into bags, or into the bins of the granary. One winter when I was a small boy Jonathan Scudder threshed for us in the barn on the hill. He was in love with my sister Olly Ann and wanted to make a good impression on the "old folks." Every night at supper Father would say to him, "Well, Jonathan, how many shock today?" and they grew more and more, until one day he reached the limit of fourteen and he was highly complimented on his day's work. It made an impression on Father, but it did not soften the heart of Olly Ann. The sound of the flail and the fanning mill is heard in the farmers' barns no more. The power threshing machine that travels from farm to farm now does the job in a single day—a few hours of pandemonium, with now and then a hand or an arm crushed in place of the days of leisurely swinging of the hickory flail.

The first considerable work in spring was sugar-making, always a happy time for me. Usually the last half of March, when rills from the melting snow began to come through the fields, the veins of the sugar maples began to thrill with the spring warmth. There was a general awakening about the farm at this time: the cackling of the hens, the bleating of young lambs and calves, and the wistful lowing of the cows. Earlier in the month the "sap spiles" had been overhauled, resharpened, and new ones made, usually from bass wood. In my time the sap gouge was used instead of the auger and the manner of tapping was crude and wasteful. A slanting gash three or four inches long and a half inch or more deep was cut, and an inch below the lower end of this the gouge was driven in to make the place for the spile, a piece of wood two inches wide, shaped to the gouge, and a foot or more in length. It gave the tree a double and unnecessary wound. The bigger the gash the more the sap, seemed to be the theory, as if the tree was a barrel filled with liquid, whereas a small wound made by a half-inch bit does the work just as well and is far less injurious to the tree.

## MY BOYHOOD

When there came a bright morning, wind northwest and warm enough to begin to thaw by eight o'clock, the sugar-making utensils—pans, kettles, spiles, hogsheads—were loaded upon the sled and taken to the woods, and by ten o'clock the trees began to feel the cruel ax and gouge once more. It usually fell to my part to carry the pans and spiles for one of the tappers, Hiram or Father, and to arrange the pans on a level foundation of sticks or stones, in position. Father often used to haggle the tree a good deal in tapping. "By Fagus," he would say, "how awkward I am!" The rapid tinkle of those first drops of sap in the tin pan, how well I remember it! Probably the note of the first song sparrow or first bluebird, or the spring call of the nuthatch, sounded in unison. Usually only patches of snow lingered here and there in the woods and the earth-stained remnants of old drifts on the sides of the hills and along the stone walls. Those lucid warm March days in the naked maple woods under the blue sky, with the first drops of sap ringing in the pans, had a charm that does not fade from my mind. After the trees were all tapped, two hundred and fifty of them, the big kettles were again set up in the old stone-arch, and the hogsheads in which to store the sap placed in position. By four o'clock many of the pans—milk pans from the dairy—would be full, and the gathering with neck yoke and pails began. When I was fourteen or fifteen I took a hand in this part of the work. It used to tax my strength to carry the two twelve-quart pails full through the rough places and up the steep banks in the woods and then lift them up and alternately empty them into the hogsheads without displacing the neck yoke. But I could do it. Now all this work is done by the aid of a team and a pipe fastened on a sled. Before I was old enough to gather sap it fell to me to go to the barns and put in hay for the cows and help stable them. The next morning the boiling of the sap would begin, with Hiram in charge. The big deep iron kettles were slow evaporators compared with the broad shallow sheet-iron pans now in use. Profundity cannot keep up with shallowness in sugar-making, the more superficial your evaporator, within limits, the more rapid your progress. It took the farmers nearly a hundred years to find this out, or at least to act upon it.

At the end of a couple of days of hard boiling Hiram would "syrup off," having reduced two hundred pails of sap to five or six of syrup. The syruping-off often occurred after dark. When the liquid dropped from a dipper which was dipped into it and, held up in the cool air, formed into stiff thin masses, it had reached the stage of syrup. How we minded our steps over the rough path, in the semi-darkness of the old tin lantern, in carrying those precious pails of syrup to the

## MY BOYHOOD

house, where the final process of "sugaring off" was to be completed by Mother and Jane!

The sap runs came at intervals of several days. Two or three days would usually end one run. A change in the weather to below freezing would stop the flow, and a change to much warmer would check it. The fountains of sap are let loose by frosty sunshine. Frost in the ground, or on it in the shape of snow and the air full of sunshine are the most favorable conditions. A certain chill and crispness, something crystalline, in the air are necessary. A touch of enervating warmth from the south or a frigidity from the north and the trees feel it through their thick bark coats very quickly. Between the temperatures of thirty-five to fifty degrees they get in their best work. After we have had one run ending in rain and warmth, a fresh fall of snow—"sap snow", the farmers call such—will give us another run. Three or four good runs make a long and successful season. My boyhood days in the spring sugar bush were my most enjoyable on the farm. How I came to know each one of those two hundred and fifty trees—what a distinct sense of individuality seemed to adhere to most of them, as much so as to each cow in a dairy! I knew at which trees I would be pretty sure to find a full pan and at which ones a less amount. One huge tree always gave a cream-pan full—a double measure—while the others were filling an ordinary pan. This was known as "the old cream-pan tree." Its place has long been vacant; about half the others are still standing, but with the decrepitude of age appearing in their tops, a new generation of maples has taken the place of the vanished veterans.

While tending the kettles there beside the old arch in the bright, warm March or April days, with my brother, or while he had gone to dinner, looking down the long valley and off over the curving backs of the distant mountain ranges, what dreams I used to have, what vague longings, and, I may say, what happy anticipations! I am sure I gathered more than sap and sugar in those youthful days amid the maples. When I visit the old home now I have to walk up to the sugar bush and stand around the old "boiling place," trying to transport myself back into the magic atmosphere of that boyhood time. The man has his dreams too, but to his eyes the world is not steeped in romance as it is to the eyes of youth.

One springtime in the sugar season my cousin, Gib Kelly, a boy of my own age, visited me, staying two or three days. (He died last fall.) When he went away I was minding the kettles in the woods, and as I saw him crossing the bare fields in the March sunshine, his steps bent toward the distant mountains, I still remember what a sense of loss came over me, his comradeship had so brightened my enjoyment of the beautiful days. He seemed to take my whole world with him, and on that and the following day I went about my duties in the sap bush in a wistful and pensive mood I had never before felt. I early showed the capacity for comradeship. A boy friend could throw the witchery of romance over everything. Oh, the enchanted days with my youthful mates! And I have not entirely outgrown that early susceptibility. There are persons in the world whose comradeship can still transmute the baser metal of commonplace scenes and experiences into the purest gold of romance for me. It is probably my feminine idiosyncrasies that explain all this. Another unforgettable passion of comradeship in my youth I experienced toward the son of a cousin, a boy four or five years old, or about half my own age. One spring his mother and he were visiting at our house eight or ten days. The child was very winsome and we soon became inseparable companions. He was like a visitor from another sphere. I frequently carried him on my back, and my heart opened to him more and more each day. One day we started to come down a rather steep pair of stairs from the hog-pen chamber; I had stepped down a few steps and reached out to take little Harry in my arms, as he stood on the floor at the head of the stairs, and carry him down, when in his joy he gave a spring and toppled me over with him in my arms, and we brought up at the bottom with our heads against some solid timbers. It was a severe shake-up but hurt my heart more than it did my head because the boy was badly bruised. The event comes back to me as if it were but yesterday. For weeks after his departure I longed for him day and night and the experience still shines like a star in my boyhood life. I never saw him again until two years ago when, knowing he lived there, a practising physician, I hunted him up in San Francisco. I found him a sedate gray-haired man, with no hint, of course, of the child I had known and loved more than sixty years before. It has been my experience on several occasions to hunt up friends of my youth after the lapse of more than half a century. Last spring I had a letter from a pupil of mine in the first school I ever taught, in 1854 or '55. I had not seen or heard from him in all those years when he recalled himself to my mind. The name I had not forgotten, Roswell Beach, but the face I had. Only two weeks ago, being near his town, it occurred to me to look him up. I did so and was shocked to find him on his deathbed. Too weak to raise his head from his pillow he yet threw his arms around me and spoke my name many times with marked affection. He died a few days later. I was to him what some of my old teachers were to me—stars that never set below my horizon.

My boyish liking for girls was quite different from my liking for boys—there was little or no sense of comradeship in it. When I

## MY BOYHOOD

was eight or nine years old there was one girl in the school toward whom I felt very partial, and I thought she reciprocated till one day I suddenly saw how little she cared for me. The teacher had forbidden us to put our feet upon the seats in front of us. In a spirit of rebellion, I suppose, when the teacher was not looking, I put my brown, soil-stained bare feet upon the forbidden seat. Polly quickly spoke up and said, "Teacher, Johnny Burris put his feet on the seat"—what a blow it was to me for her to tell on me! Like a cruel frost those words nipped the tender buds of my affection and they never sprouted again. Years after, her younger brother married my younger sister, and maybe that unkind cut of our school days kept me from marrying Polly. I had other puppy loves but they all died a natural death.

But let me get back to the farm work.

The gathering of the things in the sugar bush, when the flow of sap had stopped, usually fell to Eden and me. We would carry the pans and spiles together in big piles, where the oxen and sled could reach them. Then when they were taken to the house it was my mother's and sister's task to get them ready for the milk.

The drawing out of the manure and the spring ploughing was the next thing in order on the farm. I took a hand in the former but not in the latter. The spreading of the manure that had been drawn out and placed in heaps in the fields during the winter often fell to me. I remember that I did not bend my back to the work very willingly, especially when the cattle had been bedded with long rye straw, but there were compensations. I could lean on my fork handle and gaze at the spring landscape, I could see the budding trees and listen to the songs of the early birds and maybe catch the note of the first swallow in the air overhead. The farm boy always has the whole of nature at his elbow and he is usually aware of it.

When, armed with my long-handled "knocker," I used to be sent forth in the April meadows to beat up and scatter the fall droppings of the cows—the Juno's cushions as Irving named them—I was in much more congenial employment. Had I known the game of golf in those days I should probably have looked upon this as a fair substitute. To stand the big cushions up on edge and with a real golfer's swing hit them with my mallet and see the pieces fly was more like play than work. Oh, then it was April and I felt the rising tide of spring in my blood, and a bit of free activity like this under the blue sky suited my humor. A boy likes almost any work that affords him an escape from routine and humdrum and has an element of play in it. Turning the grindstone or the fanning mill or carrying together sheaves or picking up potatoes or carrying in wood were duties that were a drag upon my spirits.

The spring ploughing and the sowing of the grain and harrowing fell mainly to Father and my older brothers. The spring work was considered done when the oats were sowed and the corn and potatoes planted: the first in early May, the latter in late May. The buckwheat was not sown until late June. One farmer would ask another, "How many oats are you going to sow, or have you sown?" not how many acres. "Oh, fifteen or twenty bushels," would be the answer.

The working of the roads came in June after the crops were in. All hands, summoned by the "path master," would meet at a given date, at the end of the district down by the old stone school house—men and boys with oxen, horses, scrapers, hoes, crowbars—and begin repairing the highway. It was not strenuous work, but a kind of holiday that we all enjoyed more or less. The road got fixed after a fashion, here and there—a bridge mended, a ditch cleaned out, the loose stones removed, a hole filled up, or a short section "turnpiked"—but the days were eight-hour days and they did not sit heavy upon us. The state does it much better now with road machinery and a few men. Once or twice a year Father used to send me with a hoe to throw the loose stones out of the road.

A pleasanter duty during those years was shooting chipmunks around the corn. These little rodents were so plentiful in my youth that they used to pull up the sprouting corn around the margin of the field near the stone walls. Armed with the old flint-lock musket, sometimes loaded with a handful of hard peas, I used to haunt the edges of the cornfield, watching for the little striped-backed culprits. How remorselessly I used to kill them! In those days there were a dozen where there is barely one now. The woods literally swarmed with them, and when beechnuts and acorns were scarce they were compelled to poach upon the farmer's crops. It was to reduce them and other pests that shooting matches were held. Two men would choose sides as in the spelling matches, seven or eight or more were on a side, and the side that brought in the most trophies at the end of the week won and the losing side had to pay for the supper at the village hotel for the whole crowd. A chipmunk's tail counted one, a red squirrel's three, a gray squirrel's still more. Hawks' heads and owls' heads counted as high as ten, I think. Crows' heads also counted pretty high. One man who had little time to hunt engaged me to help him, offering me so much per dozen units. I remember that I found up in the sap bush a brood of young screech owls just out of the nest and I killed them all. That man is still owing me for those owls. What a lot of motley heads and tails were brought in at the end of the week! I never saw them but wish I had. Repeated shooting matches of this kind, in different parts of the state, so reduced the small wild life, especially the chipmunks, that it has not

## MY BOYHOOD

yet recovered, and probably never will. In those days the farmer's hand was against nearly every wild thing. We used to shoot and trap crows and hen hawks and small hawks as though they were our mortal enemies. Farmers were wont to stand up poles in their meadows and set steel traps on the top of them to catch the hen hawks that came for the meadow mice which were damaging their meadows. The hen hawk is so named because he rarely or never catches a hen or a chicken. He is a mouser. We used to bait the hungry crows in spring with "deacon" legs and shoot them without mercy, and all because they now and then pulled a little corn, forgetting or not knowing of the grubs and worms they pulled and the grasshoppers they ate. But all this is changed and now our sable friends and the high-soaring hawks are seldom molested. The fool with a rifle is very apt to shoot an eagle if the chance comes to him, but he has to be very sly about it.

The buttercups and the daisies would be blooming when we were working the road, and the timothy grass about ready to do so—pointing to the near approach of the great event of the season, the one major task toward which so many other things pointed—"haying;" the gathering of our hundred or more tons of meadow hay. This was always a hard-fought campaign. Our weapons were gotten ready in due time, new scythes and new snaths, new rakes and new forks, the hay riggings repaired or built anew, etc. Shortly after the Fourth of July the first assault upon the legions of timothy would be made in the lodged grass below the barn. Our scythes would turn up great swaths that nearly covered the ground and that put our strength to a severe test. When noon came we would go to the house with shaking knees.

The first day of haying meant nearly a whole day with the scythe, and was the most trying of all. After that a half day mowing, when the weather was good, meant work in curing and hauling each afternoon. From the first day in early July till the end of August we lived for the hayfield. No respite except on rainy days and Sundays, and no change except from one meadow to another. No eight-hour days then, rather twelve and fourteen, including the milking. No horse rakes, no mowing machines or hay tedders or loading or pitching devices then. The scythe, the hand rake, the pitchfork in the calloused hands of men and boys did the work, occasionally the women even taking a turn with the rake or in mowing away. I remember the first wire-toothed horse rake with its two handles, which when the day was hot and the grass heavy nearly killed both man and horse. The holder would throw his weight upon it to make it grip and hold the hay, and then, in a spasm of energy, lift it up and make it drop the hay. From this rude instrument, through various types of wooden and revolving rakes, the modern wheeled rake, with which the raker rides at his ease, has been evolved. At this season the cows were brought to the yard by or before five, breakfast was at six, lunch in the field at ten, dinner at twelve, and supper at five, with milking and hay drawing and heaping up till sundown. Those mid-forenoon lunches of Mother's good rye bread and butter, with crullers or gingerbread, and in August a fresh green cucumber and a sweating jug of water fresh from the spring—sweating, not as we did, because it was hot, but because it was cold, partaken under an ash or a maple tree—how sweet and fragrant the memory of it all is to me!

Till I reached my 'teens it was my task to spread hay and to rake after; later I took my turn with the mowers and pitchers. I never loaded, hence I never pitched over the big beam. How Father watched the weather! The rain that makes the grass ruins the hay. If the morning did not promise a good hay day our scythes would be ground but hung back in their places. When a thunderstorm was gathering in the west and much hay was ready for hauling, how it quickened our steps and our strokes! It was the sound of the guns of the approaching foe. In one hour we would do, or try to do, the work of two. How the wagon would rattle over the road, how the men would mop their faces and how I, while hurrying, would secretly exult that now I would have an hour to finish my crossbow or to work on my pond in the pasture lot!

Those late summer afternoons after the shower—what man who has spent his youth on the farm does not recall them! The high-piled thunder heads of the retreating storm above the eastern mountains, the moist fresh smell of the hay and the fields, the red puddles in the road, the robins singing from the tree tops, the washed and cooler air and the welcomed feeling of relaxation which they brought. It was a good time now to weed the garden, to grind the scythes, and do other odd jobs.

When the haying was finished, usually late in August, in my time, there was usually a let-up for a few days.

I was the seventh child in a family of ten children: Hiram, Olly Ann, Wilson, Curtis, Edmond, and Jane came before me; Eden, Abigail, and Eveline came after me. All were as unlike me in those mental qualities by which I am known to the world as you can well conceive, but all were like me in their more fundamental family traits. We all had the same infirmities of character: we were all tenderfeet—lacking in grit, will power, self-assertion, and the ability to deal with men. We were easily crowded to the wall, easily cheated, always ready to take a back seat, timid, complying, undecided, obstinate but not combative, selfish but not self-asserting, always

## MY BOYHOOD

the easy victims of pushing, coarse-grained, designing men. As with Father, the word came easy but the blow was slow to follow. Only a year or two ago a lightning-rod man made my brother Curtis and his son John have his rods put upon their barn against their wills. They did not want his rods but could not say "No" with enough force. He simply held them up and made them take his rods, willy nilly. Curtis had maps, books, washing machines, etc., forced upon him in the same way. I am able to resist the tree men, book agents, etc., and the lightning-rod man, for a wonder, found me a decided non-conductor; but I can see how my weaker brothers failed. I have settled a lawsuit rather than fight it out when I knew law and justice were on my side. My wife has often said that I never knew when I was imposed upon. I may know it and yet feel that resenting it would cause me more pain than the affront did. Strife and contention kill me, yet come easy to me, and did to all my family. My sense of personal dignity, personal honour, is not a plant of such tender growth that it cannot stand rough winds and nipping frosts. That is a flattering way of saying that we are a very non-chivalrous tribe and would rather run away than fight any time. During the anti-rent war in Delaware County in 1844, Father, who was a "down renter," once fled to a neighbour's house when he saw the posse coming and took refuge under the bed, leaving his feet sticking out. Father never denied it and never seemed a bit humiliated when twitted about it. Grandfather Kelly seems to have used up all our fighting blood in campaigning with Washington, though I more than half suspect that our noncombativeness comes from the paternal side of the family. As a school boy I never had a fight, nor have I ever dealt or received a hostile blow since. And I never saw but one of my brothers fight at school, and he fought the meanest boy in school and punished him well. I can see him now, sitting on the prostrate form of the boy, with his hands clinched in the boy's hair and jamming his face down into the crusty snow till the blood streamed down his face. The nearest I ever came to a fight at school was when, one noontime, we were playing baseball and a boy of my own age and size got angry at me and dared me to lay my hand on him. I did it quickly, but his bite did not follow his bark. I was never whipped at school or at home that I can remember, though I no doubt often deserved it. There was a good deal of loud scolding in our family but very few blows.

Father and Mother had a pretty hard struggle to pay for the farm and to clothe and feed and school us all. We lived off the products of the farm to an extent that people do not think of doing nowadays. Not only was our food largely home grown but our clothes also were home grown and home spun. In my early youth our house linen and our summer shirts and trousers were made from flax that grew on the farm. Those pioneer shirts, how vividly I remember them! They dated from the stump, and bits of the stump in the shape of "shives" were inwoven in their texture and made the wearer of them an unwilling penitent for weeks, or until use and the washboard had subdued them. Peas in your shoes are no worse than "shives" on your shirt. But those tow shirts stood by you. If you lost your hold in climbing a tree and caught on a limb your shirt or your linen trousers would hold you. The stuff from which they were made had a history behind it—pulled up by the roots, rooted on the ground, broken with a crackle, flogged with a swingle, and drawn through a hetchel, and out of all this ordeal came the flax. How clearly I remember Father working with it in the bright, sharp March days, breaking it, then swingling it with a long wooden sword-like tool over the end of an upright board fixed at the base in a heavy block. This was to separate the brittle fragments of the bark from the fibers of the flax. Then in large handfuls he drew it through the hetchel—an instrument with a score or more long sharp iron teeth, set in a board, row behind row. This combed out the tow and other worthless material. It was a mighty good discipline for the flax; it straightened out its fibres and made it as clear and straight as a girl's tresses. Out of the tow we twisted bag strings, flail strings, and other strings. With the worthless portions we made huge bonfires. The flax, Mother would mass upon her distaff and spin into threads. The last I saw of the old crackle, fifty or more years ago, it served as a hen roost under the shed, and the savage old hetchel was doing duty behind the old churner when he sulked and pulled back so as to stop the churning machine. It was hetcheling wool then instead of flax. The flax was spun on a quill which ran by the foot and the quills or spools holding the thread were used in a shuttle when the cloth was woven. The old loom stood in the hog-pen chamber, and there Mother wove her linen, her rag carpets, and her woolen goods. I have "quilled" for her many a time—that is, run the yarn off the reel into spools for use in the shuttle.

Father had a flock of sheep which yielded wool enough for our stockings, mittens, comforts, and underwear, and woolen sheets and comforts for the beds. I have some of those home-made woolen sheets and bed covers now at Slabsides.

Before the sheep were sheared in June they were driven two miles to the creek to be washed. Washing-sheep-day was an event on the farm. It was no small task to get the sheep off the mountain, drive them to the deep pool behind old Jonas More's grist mill, pen them up there, and drag them one by one into the water and make good clean Baptists of them! But sheep are no fighters, they struggle for a moment and then passively submit to the baptism.

## MY BOYHOOD

My older brothers usually did the washing and I the herding. When the shearing was done, a few days later the poor creatures were put through another ordeal, to which after a brief struggle they quickly resigned themselves. Father did the shearing, while I at times held the animal's legs. Father was not an adept hand with the shears and the poor beast usually had to part with many a bit of her hide along with her fleece. It used to make me wince as much as it did the sheep to see the crests of those little wrinkles in her skin clipped off.

I used to wonder how the sheep knew one another and how the lambs knew their mothers when shorn of their fleeces. But they did. The wool was soon sent to the pulling mill and made into rolls, though I have seen it carded and made into rolls at home by hand. How many bundles of rolls tied up into sheets I have seen come home! Then in the long summer afternoons I would hear the hum of the big spinning wheel in the chamber and hear the tread of the girl as she ran it, walking to and fro and drawing out and winding up the yarn. The white rolls, ten inches or more long and the thickness of one's finger, would lie in a pile on the beam of the wheel and one by one would be attached to the spindle and drawn out into yarn of the right size. Each new roll was welded on to the end of the one that went before it so that the yarn did not show the juncture. But now for more than sixty years the music of the spinning wheel has not been heard in the land.

Mother used to pick her geese in the barn where Father used to shear the sheep; and to help gather in the flock was a part of my duty also. The geese would submit to the plucking about as readily as the sheep to the shearing, but they presented a much more ragged and sorry appearance after they had been fleeced than did the sheep. It used to amuse me to see them put their heads together and talk it over and laugh and congratulate each other over the victory they had just won!—they had got out of the hands of the enemy with only the loss of a few feathers which they would not want in the warm weather! The goose is the one inhabitant that cackles as loudly and as cheerfully over a defeat as over a victory. They are so complacent and optimistic that it is a comfort to me to see them about. The very silliness of the goose is a lesson in wisdom. The pride of a plucked gander makes one take courage. I think it quite probable that we learned our habit of hissing our dissent from the goose, and maybe our other habit of trying sometimes to drown an opponent with noise has a like origin. The goose is silly and shallow-pated; yet what dignity and impressiveness in her migrating wild clans driving in ordered ranks across the spring or autumnal skies, linking the Chesapeake Bay and the Canadian Lakes in one flight! The great forces are loosened and winter is behind them in one case, and the tides of spring bear them on in the other. When I hear the trumpet of the wild geese in the sky I know that dramatic events in the seasonal changes are taking place.

I was the only one of the ten children who, as Father said, "took to larnin'," though in seventy-five years of poring over books and periodicals I have not become "learned." But I easily distanced the other children in school. The others barely learned to read and write and cipher a little, Curtis and Wilson barely that, Hiram got into Greenleaf's Grammar and learned to parse, but never to write or speak correctly, and he ciphered nearly through Dayball's Arithmetic. I went through Dayball and then Thompkins and Perkins and got well on into Algebra in the district school. My teacher, however, when I was about thirteen or fourteen, did not seem much impressed by my aptitude, for I recall that he told other scholars, boys and girls of about my own age, to get them each a grammar, but did not tell me. I felt a little slighted but made up my mind I would have a grammar also. Father refusing to buy it for me, I made small cakes of maple sugar in the spring and, peddling them in the village, got money enough to buy the grammar and other books. The teacher was a little taken aback when I produced my book as the others did theirs, but he put me in the class and I kept along with the rest of them, but without any idea that the study had any practical bearing on our daily speaking and writing. That teacher was a superior man, a graduate of the state normal school at Albany, but I failed to impress him with my scholarly aptitudes, which certainly were not remarkable. But long afterward, when he had read some of my earlier magazine articles, he wrote to me, asking if I were indeed his early farm boy pupil. His interest and commendation gave me rare pleasure. I had at last justified that awkward intrusion into his grammar class. Much later in life, after he had migrated to Kansas, while on a visit East he called upon me when I chanced to be in my native town. This gave me a still deeper pleasure. He died in Kansas many years ago and is buried there. I have journeyed through the state many times and always remember that it holds the ashes of my old teacher. It is a satisfaction for me to write his name, James Oliver, in this record.

I was in many respects an odd one in my father's family. I was like a graft from some other tree. And this is always a disadvantage to a man—not to be the logical outcome of what went before him, not to be backed up by his family and inheritance—to be of the nature of a sport. It seems as if I had more intellectual capital than I was entitled to and robbed some of the rest of the family, while I had a full measure of the family weaknesses. I can remember how abashed I used to be as a child when strangers or relatives, visiting us for the first time, after looking the rest of the children over, would ask, pointing to me, "That is not your boy—whose is he?" I have no idea that I looked different from the others, because I can see the family stamp upon my face very plainly until this day. My face resembles Hiram's more than any of the others, and I have a deeper attachment for him than for any of the rest of my brothers. Hiram was a dreamer, too, and he had his own idealism which expressed itself in love of bees, of which he kept many hives at one time, and of fancy stock, sheep, pigs, poultry, and a desire to see other lands. His bees and fancy stock never paid him, but he always expected they would the next year. But they yielded him honey and wool of a certain intangible, satisfying kind. To be the owner of a Cotswold ram or ewe for which he had paid one hundred dollars or more gave him rare satisfaction. One season, in his innocence, he took some of his fancy sheep to the state fair at Syracuse, not knowing that an unknown outsider stood no chance at all on such an occasion.

Hiram always had to have some sort of a plaything. Though no hunter and an indifferent marksman, he had during his life several fancy rifles. Once when he came to Washington to visit me, he brought his rifle with him, carrying the naked weapon in his hand or upon his shoulder. The act was merely the whim of a boy who likes to take his playthings with him. Hiram certainly had not come to "shoot up" the town. In the early '60's he had a fifty-dollar rifle made by a famous rifle maker in Utica. There was some hitch or misunderstanding about it and Hiram made the trip to Utica on foot. I was at home that summer and I recall seeing him start off one June day, wearing a black coat, bent on his fifty-mile walk to see about his pet rifle. Of course nothing came of it. The rifle maker had Hiram's money, and he put him off with fair words; then something happened and the gun never came to Hiram's hand.

Another plaything of his was a kettle drum with which he amused himself in the summer twilight for many seasons. Then he got a bass drum which Curtis learned to play, and a very warlike sound often went up from the peaceful old homestead. When I was married and came driving home one October twilight with my wife, the martial music began as soon as we hove in sight of the house. Early in the Civil War, Hiram seriously talked of enlisting as a drummer, but Father and Mother dissuaded him. I can see what a wretched homesick boy he would have been before one week had passed. For many years he was haunted with a desire to go West, and made himself really believe that the next month or the month after he would go. He kept his valise packed under his bed for more than a year, to be ready when the impulse grew strong enough. One fall it became strong enough to start him and carried him as far as

White Pigeon, Michigan, where it left him stranded. After visiting a cousin who lived there he came back, and henceforth his Western fever assumed only a low, chronic type.

I tell you all these things about Hiram because I am a chip out of the same block and see myself in him. His vain regrets, his ineffectual resolutions, his day-dreams, and his playthings—do I not know them all?—only nature in some way dealt a little more liberally with me and made many of my dreams come true. The dear brother!—he stood next to Father and Mother to me. How many times he broke the path for me through the winter snows on the long way to school! How faithful he was to write to me and to visit me wherever I was, after I left home! How he longed to follow my example and break away from the old place but could never quite screw his courage up to the sticking point! He never read one of my books but he rejoiced in all the good fortune that was mine. Once when I was away at school and fell short of money, Hiram sent me a small sum when Father could not or would not send. In later life he got it paid back manyfold—and what a satisfaction it was to me thus to repay him!

Hiram was always a child, he never grew up, which is true of all of us, more or less, and true of Father also. I was an odd one, but I shared all the family infirmities. In fact, I have always been an odd one amid most of my human relations in life. Place me in a miscellaneous gathering of men and I separate from them, or they from me, like oil from water. I do not mix readily with my fellows. I am not conscious of drawing into my shell, as the saying is, but I am conscious of a certain strain put upon me by those about me. I suppose my shell or my skin is too thin. Burbank experimented with walnuts trying to produce one with a thin shell, till he finally produced one with so thin a shell that the birds ate it up. Well, the birds eat me up for the same reason, if I don't look out. I am social but not gregarious. I do not thrive in clubs, I do not smoke, or tell stories, or drink, or dispute, or keep late hours. I am usually as solitary as a bird of prey, though I trust not for the same reason. I love so much to float on the current of my own thoughts. I mix better with farmers, workers, and country people generally than with professional or business men. Birds of a feather do flock together, and if we do not feel at ease in our company we may be sure we are in the wrong flock. Once while crossing the continent at some station in Minnesota a gray-bearded farmer-like man got on the train and presently began to look eagerly about the Pullman as if to see what kind of company he was in. After a while his eye settled on me at the other end of the car. In a few minutes he came over to me and sat down beside me and began to tell me his story.

## MY BOYHOOD

He had come from Germany as a young man and had lived fifty years on a farm in Minnesota and now he was going back to visit the country of his birth. He had prospered and had left his sons in charge of his farm. What an air he had of a boy out of school! The adventure was warming his blood; he was going home and he wanted someone to whom he could tell the good news. I was probably the only real countryman in the car and he picked me out at once, some quality of rural things hovered about us both and drew us together. I felt that he had paid me an involuntary compliment. How unsophisticated and communicative he was! So much so that I took it upon myself to caution him against the men he was liable to fall in with in New York. I should like to know if he reached the fatherland safely and returned to his Minnesota farm.

When I was a boy six or seven years old a quack phrenologist stopped at our house and Father kept him over night. In the morning he fingered the bumps of all of us to pay for his lodging and breakfast. When he came to my head I remember he grew enthusiastic. "This boy will be a rich man," he said. "His head beats 'em all." And he enlarged on the great wealth I was to accumulate. I forget the rest; but that my bumps were nuggets of gold under the quack's fingers, this I have not forgotten. The prophecy never came true, though more money did come my way than to any of the rest of the family. Three of my brothers, at least, were not successful from a business point of view, and while I myself have failed in every business venture I ever undertook—beginning with that first speculative stroke sometime in the 'forties when, one March morning, I purchased the prospective sap of Curtis's two maple trees for four cents; yet a certain success from a bread-and-butter point of view has been mine. Father took less stock in me than in the other boys—mainly, I suppose, on account of my early proclivity for books; hence it was a deep satisfaction to me, when his other sons had failed him and loaded the old farm with debt, that I could come back and be able to take the burden of the debts upon myself and save the farm from going into strange hands. But it was my good fortune, a kind of constitutional good luck and not any business talent that enabled me to do so. Remembering the prediction of the old quack phrenologist, I used to have my dreams when a boy, especially on one occasion, I remember, when I was tending the sap kettles in the sugar bush on a bright April day, of gaining great wealth and coming home in imposing style and astonishing the natives with my display. How different the reality from the boy's dream! I came back indeed with a couple of thousand dollars in my pocket (on my bank book), sorrowing and oppressed, more like a pilgrim doing penance than like a conqueror returning from his victories. But we kept the old farm, and as you know, it still plays an important part in my life though I passed the title to my brother many years ago. It is my only home, other homes that I have had were mere camping places for a day and night. But the wealth which my bumps indicated turned out to be of a very shadowy and uncommercial kind, yet of a kind that thieves cannot steal or panics disturb.

I remember the first day I went to school, probably near my fifth year. It was at the old stone school house, about one and a half miles from home. I recall vividly the suit Mother made for the occasion out of some striped cotton goods with a pair of little flaps or hound's ears upon my shoulders that tossed about as I ran. I accompanied Olly Ann, my oldest sister. At each one of the four houses we passed on the way I asked, "Who lives there?" I have no recollection of what happened at school those first days, but I remember struggling with the alphabet soon thereafter; the letters were arranged in a column, the vowels first, a, e, i, o, u, and then the consonants. The teacher would call us to her chair three or four times a day, and opening the Colles spelling-book, point to the letters one by one and ask me to name them, drilling them into me in that way. I remember that one of the boys, older than I, Hen Meeker, on one occasion stuck on "e." "I'll bet little Johnny Burris can tell what that letter is. Come up here, Johnny." Up I went and promptly answered, to the humiliation of Hen, "e." "I told you so," said the school marm. How long it took me to learn the alphabet in this arbitrary manner I do not know. But I remember tackling the a, b, abs, and slowly mastering those short columns. I remember also getting down under the desk and tickling the bare ankles of the big girls that sat in the seat in front of me.

The summer days were long and little boys must sit on the hard seats and be quiet and go out only at the regular recess. The seat I sat on was a slab turned flat side up and supported on four legs cut from a sapling. My feet did not touch the floor and I suppose I got very tired. One afternoon the oblivion of sleep came over me and when I came to consciousness again I was in a neighbour's house on a couch and the "smell of camphor pervaded the room." I had fallen off the seat backward and hit my head on the protruding stones of the unplastered wall behind me and cut a hole in it, and I suppose for the moment effectively scattered my childish wits. But Mrs. Reed was a motherly body and consoled me with flowers and sweets and bathed my wounds with camphor and I suppose little Johnny was soon himself again. I have often wondered if a small bony protuberance on the back of my head dated from that collision with the old stone school house.

## MY BOYHOOD

Another early remembrance connected with the old stone school house is that of seeing Hiram, during the summer noons, catch fish in a pail back of old Jonas More's grist mill and put them in the pot holes in the red sandstone rocks, to be kept there till we went home at night. Then he took them in his dinner pail and put them in his pond down in the pasture lot. I suspect that it was this way that chubs were introduced into the West Settlement trout stream. The fish used to swim around and around in the pot holes seeking a way to escape. I would put my finger into the water but jerk it back quickly as the fish came around. I was afraid of them. But before that I was once scared into a panic by a high-soaring hen hawk. I have probably pointed out to you where, one summer day, as I was going along the road out on what we called the big hill, I looked skyward and saw a big hen hawk describing his large circles about me. A sudden fear fell upon me, and I took refuge behind the stone wall. Still earlier in my career I had my first panic farther along on this same road. I suppose I had started off on my first journey to explore the world when, getting well down the Deacon road beside the woods, I looked back and, seeing how far I was from home, was seized with a sudden consternation and turned and ran back as fast as I could go. I have seen a young robin do the same thing when it had wandered out a yard or so on the branch away from its nest.

I mastered only my a-b-c's at the old stone school house. A year or two later we were sent off in the West Settlement district and I went to school at a little unpainted school house with a creek on one side of it and toeing squarely on the highway on the other. This also was about one and a half miles from home, an easy, adventurous journey in the summer with the many allurements of fields, stream, and wood, but in winter often a battle with snow and cold. In winter we went across lots, my elder brothers breaking a path through the fields and woods. How the tracks in the snow—squirrels, hares, skunks, foxes—used to excite my curiosity! And the line of ledges off on the left in the woods where brother Wilson used to set traps for skunks and coons—how they haunted my imagination as I caught dim glimpses of them, trudging along in our narrow path! One mild winter morning, after I had grown to be a boy of twelve or thirteen, my younger brother and I had an adventure with a hare. He sat in his form in the deep snow between the roots of a maple tree that stood beside the path. We were almost upon him before we discovered him. As he did not move I withdrew a few yards to a stone wall and armed myself with a boulder the size of my fist. Returning, I let drive, sure of my game, but I missed by a foot, and the hare bounded away over the wall and out into the open and off for the hemlocks a quarter of a mile away. A rabbit in his form only ten feet away does not so easily become a rabbit in the hand. This desire of the farm boy to slay every wild creature he saw was universal in my time. I trust things have changed in this respect since then.

At the little old school house I had many teachers, Bill Bouton, Bill Allaben, Taylor Grant, Jason Powell, Rossetti Cole, Rebecca Scudder, and others. I got well into Dayball's Arithmetic, Olney's Geography, and read Hall's History of the United States—through the latter getting quite familiar with the Indian wars and the French war and the Revolution. Some books in the district library also attracted me. I think I was the only one of the family that took books from the library. I recall especially "Murphy, the Indian Killer" and the "Life of Washington." The latter took hold of me; I remember one summer Sunday, as I was playing through the house with my older brothers, of stopping to read a certain passage of it aloud, and that it moved me so that I did not know whether I was in the body or out. Many times I read that passage and every time I was submerged, as it were, by a wave of emotion. I mention so trifling a matter only to show how responsive I was to literature at an early age. I should perhaps offset this statement by certain other facts which are by no means so flattering. There was a period in my latter boyhood when comic song-books, mostly of the Negro minstrely sort, satisfied my craving for poetic literature. I used to learn the songs by heart and invent and extemporize tunes for them. To this day I can repeat some of those rank Negro songs.

My taste for books began early, but my taste for good literature was of a much later and of slow growth. My interest in theological and scientific questions antedated my love of literature. During the last half of my 'teens I was greatly interested in phrenology and possessed a copy of Spurgheim's "Phrenology," and of Comb's "Constitution of Man." I also subscribed to Fowler's *Phrenological Journal* and for years accepted the phrenologists' own estimate of the value of their science. And I still see some general truths in it. The size and shape of the brain certainly give clues to the mind within, but its subdivision into many bumps, or numerous small areas, like a garden plot, from each one of which a different crop is produced, is absurd. Certain bodily functions are localized in the brain, but not our mental and emotional traits—veneration, self-esteem, sublimity—these are attributes of the mind as a unit.

As I write these lines I am trying to see wherein I differed from my brothers and from other boys of my acquaintance. I certainly had a livelier interest in things and events about me. When Mr. McClancey proposed to start an academy in the village and came there to feel the pulse of the people and to speak upon the subject I believe I was the only boy in his audience. I was probably ten

## MY BOYHOOD

or twelve years of age. At one point in his address the speaker had occasion to use me to illustrate his point: "About the size of that boy there," he said, pointing to me, and my face flushed with embarrassment. The academy was started and I hoped in a few years to attend it. But the time when Father could see his way to send me there never came. One season when I was fifteen or sixteen, I set my heart on going to school at Harpersfield. A boy whom I knew in the village attended it and I wanted to accompany him. Father talked encouragingly and held it out as a possible reward if I helped hurry the farm work along. This I did, and for the first time taking to field with the team and plough and "summer fallowing" one of the oat-stubble lots. I followed the plough those September days with dreams of Harpersfield Academy hovering about me, but the reality never came. Father concluded, after I had finished my job of ploughing, that he could not afford it. Butter was low and he had too many other ways for using his money. I think it quite possible that my dreams gave me the best there was in Harpersfield anyway—a worthy aspiration is never lost. All these things differentiate me from my brothers.

My interest in theological questions showed itself about the same time. An itinerant lecturer with a smooth, ready tongue came to the village charged with novel ideas about the immortality of the soul, accepting the literal truth of the text "The soul that sinneth, it shall die." I attended the meetings and took notes of the speaker's glib talk. I distinctly remember that it was from his mouth that I first heard the word "encyclopædia." When he cited the "Encyclopædia Britannica" in confirmation of some statement, I had no doubt of its truth, and I resolved sometime to get my hands on that book. I still have those notes and references that I took sixty years ago.

At a much earlier stage of my mental development I had a passion for drawing, but, quite unguided, it resulted only in a waste of paper. I wanted to walk before I could creep, to paint before I could draw, and getting a box of cheap water colors, I indulged my crude artistic instincts. My most ambitious piece was a picture of General Winfield Scott standing beside his horse and some piece of artillery, which I copied from a print. It was of course an awful daub, but in connection with it I heard for the first time a new word,—the word "taste" used in its aesthetic sense. One of the neighbour women was calling at the house, and seeing my picture said to Mother, "What taste that boy has." That application of the word made an impression on me that I have never forgotten.

About this time I heard another new word. We were working on the road, and I with my hoe was working beside an old Quaker farmer, David Corbin, who used to be a school teacher. A large flat stone was turned over, and beneath it in some orderly arrangement were some smaller stones. "Here are some antiquities," said Mr. Corbin, and my vocabulary received another addition. A new word or a new thing was very apt to make its mark upon my mind. I have told elsewhere what a revelation to me was my first glimpse of one of the warblers, the black-throated blue-back, indicating as it did a world of bird life of which I had never dreamed, the bird life in the inner heart of the woods. My brothers and other boys were with me but they did not see the new bird. The first time I saw the veery, or Wilson's thrush, also stands out in my memory. It alighted in the road before us on the edge of the woods. "A brown thrasher," said Bill Chase. It was not the thrasher but it was a new bird to me and the picture of it is in my mind as if made only yesterday. Natural History was a subject unknown to me in my boyhood, and such a thing as nature study in the schools was of course unheard of. Our natural history we got unconsciously in the sport at noon time, or on our way to and from school or in our Sunday excursions to the streams and woods. We learned much about the ways of foxes and woodchucks and coons and skunks and squirrels by hunting them. The partridge too, and the crows, hawks, and owls, and the song birds of the field and orchard, all enter into the farm boy's life. I early became familiar with the songs and habits of all the common birds, and with field mice and the frogs, toads, lizards, and snakes. Also with the wild bees and wasps. One season I made a collection of bumblebee honey, studying the habits of five or six different kinds and rifling their nests. I kept my store of bumble-bee honey in the attic where I had a small box full of the comb and a large phial filled with the honey. How well I came to know the different dispositions of the various kinds—the small red-vested that made its nest in a hole in the ground; the small black-vested, the large black-vested, the yellow-necked, the black-banded, etc., that made their nests in old mice nests in the meadow or in the barn and other places. I used to watch and woo the little piping frogs in the spring marshes when I had driven the cows to pasture at night, till they would sit in my open hand and pipe. I used to creep on my hands and knees through the woods to see the partridge in the act of drumming. I used to watch the mud wasps building their nests in the old attic and noted their complaining cry while in the act of pressing on the mud. I noted the same complaining cry from the bees when working on the flower of the purple-flowering raspberry, what we called "scotch caps." I tried to trap foxes and soon learned how far the fox's cunning surpassed mine. My first lesson in animal psychology I got from old Nat Higby as he came riding by on horseback one winter day, his huge feet almost meeting under the horse, just as a hound was

## MY BOYHOOD

running a fox across our upper mountain lot. "My boy," he said, "that fox may be running as fast as he can, but if you stood behind that big rock beside his course, and as he came along should jump out and shout 'hello,' he would run faster." That was the winter when in fond imagination I saw a stream of silver dollars coming my way from the red foxes I was planning to deprive of their pelts when they needed them most. I have told elsewhere of my trapping experiences and how completely I failed.

I was born at Roxbury, N. Y., April 3, 1837. At least two other American authors of note were born on the third of April—Washington Irving and Edward Everett Hale. The latter once wrote me a birthday letter in which he said, among other things, "I have been looking back over my diaries to see what I was doing the day you were being born. I find I was undergoing an examination in logic at Harvard College." The only other American author born in 1837 is William Dean Howells, who was born in Ohio in March of that year.

I was the son of a farmer, who was the son of a farmer, who was again the son of a farmer. There are no professional or commercial men in my line for several generations, my blood has the flavor of the soil in it; it is rural to the last drop. I can find no city dwellers in the line of my descent in this country. The Burroughs tribe, as far back as I can find any account of them, were mainly countrymen and tillers of the soil. The Rev. George Burroughs, who was hung as a witch at Salem, Mass., in 1694, may have been of the family, though I can find no proof of it. I wanted to believe that he was and in 1898 I made a visit to Salem and to Gallows Hill to see the spot where he, the last victim of the witchcraft craze, ended his life. There is no doubt that the renegade preacher, Stephen Burroughs, who stole a lot of his father's sermons and set up as a preacher and forger on his own account about 1720, was a third or fourth cousin of my father's.

Farmers with a decidedly religious bent contributed the main elements of my personality. I was a countryman dyed in the wool, yea, more than that, born and bred in the bone, and my character is fundamentally reverent and religious. The religion of my fathers underwent in me a kind of metamorphosis and became something which would indeed have appeared like rank atheism to them, but which was nevertheless full of the very essence of true religion—love, reverence, wonder, unworldliness, and devotion to ideal truth—but in no way identified with Church or creed.

I used to feel that my religious temperament was as clearly traceable to the hard Calvinism of my fathers, as the stratified sandstone is traceable to the old granite rock, but that it had undergone a sea change as had the sandstone, or in my case a science-change through the activity of the mind and of the age in which I lived. It was rationalism touched with mysticism and warm with poetic emotion.

My paternal grandfather and great-grandfather came from near Bridgeport in Connecticut about the end of the Revolution and settled in Stamford, Delaware County, New York. Captain Stephen Burroughs of Bridgeport, a mathematician and a man of note in his time, was Father's great uncle. Father used to say that his uncle Stephen could build a ship and sail it around the world. The family name is still common in and about Bridgeport. The first John Burroughs of whom I can find any record came to this country from the West Indies and settled in Stratford, Conn., about 1690. He had ten children, and ten children to a family was the rule down to my own father. One October while on a cruise with a small motor boat on Long Island Sound, stress of weather compelled us to seek shelter in Black Rock harbor, which is a part of Bridgeport. In the morning we went ashore, and as we were walking up a street seeking the trolley line to take us into the city, we saw a large brick building with the legend on it—"The Burroughs Home." I felt like going in and claiming its hospitality—after our rough experience on the Sound its look and its name were especially inviting. Some descendant of Captain Stephen Burroughs was probably its founder.

My great-grandfather, Ephraim, I believe, died in 1818, and was buried in the town of Stamford in a field that is now cultivated. My grandfather, Eden Burroughs, died in Roxbury in 1842, aged 72, and my father, Chauncey A. Burroughs, in 1884 at the age of 81.

My maternal grandfather, Edmund Kelly, was Irish, though born in this country about 1765. It is from his Irish strain that I get many of my Celtic characteristics—my decidedly feminine temperament. I always felt that I was more a Kelly than a Burroughs. Grandfather Kelly was a small man, with a big head and marked Irish features. He entered the Continental army when a mere lad in some menial capacity, but before the end he carried a musket in the ranks. He was with Washington at Valley Forge and had many stories to tell of their hardships. He was upward of seventy-five years old when I first remember him—a little man in a blue coat with brass buttons. He and Granny used to come to our house once or twice a year for a week or two at a time. Their permanent home was with Uncle Martin Kelly in Red Kill, eight miles away. I remember him as a great angler. How many times in the May or June mornings, as soon as he had had his breakfast, have I seen him digging worms and getting ready to go a-fishing up Montgomery Hollow or over in Meeker's Hollow, or over in West Settlement! You could always be sure he would bring home a nice string of trout. Occasionally I was permitted to go with him. How nimbly he would walk, even when

## MY BOYHOOD

he was over eighty, and how skilfully he would take the trout! I was an angler myself before I was ten, but Grandfather would take trout from places in the stream where I would not think it worth while to cast my hook. But I never fished when I went with him, I carried the fish and watched him. The pull home, often two or three miles, tried my young legs, but Grandfather would show very little fatigue, and I know he did not have the ravenous hunger I always had when I went fishing, so much so that I used to think there was in this respect something peculiar about going fishing. One hour along the trout streams would develop more hunger in me than half a day hoeing corn or working on the road—a peculiarly fierce, all-absorbing desire for food, so that a piece of rye bread and butter was the most delicious thing in the world. I remember that one June day my cousin and I, when we were about seven or eight years old, set out for Meeker's Hollow for trout. It was a pull of over two miles and over a pretty hard hill. Our courage held out until we reached the creek, but we were too hungry to fish; we turned homeward and fed upon the wild strawberries in the pastures and meadows we passed through and they kept us alive until we reached home. Oh, that youthful hunger beside the trout stream, was there ever anything else like it in the world!

Grandfather Kelly was a fisherman nearly up to the year of his death at the age of eighty-eight. He had few of the world's goods and he did not want them. His only vice was plug tobacco, his only recreation was angling, and his only reading the Bible. How long and attentively would he pore over the Book!—but I never heard him comment upon it or express any religious opinion or conviction. He believed in witches and hobgoblins: he had seen them and experienced them and used to tell us stories that almost made us afraid of our own shadows. My own youthful horror of darkness, and of dark rooms and recesses and cellars even in the daytime, was due no doubt largely to Grandfather's blood-curdling tales. Yet I may be wrong about this, for I remember a fearful experience I had when I was a child of three or four years. I see myself with some of the other children cowering in a corner of the old kitchen at night with my eyes fixed on the black space of the open door of the bedroom occupied by my father and mother. They were out for the evening and we were waiting for their return. The agony of that waiting I shall never forget. Whether or not the other children shared my fear I do not remember; probably they did, and maybe communicated their fear to me. I could not take my eyes off the entrance to that black cavern, though of what I may have fancied it held that would hurt me I have no idea. It was only the child's inherited fear of the dark, the unknown, the mysterious. Grandfather's stories, no doubt, strengthened that fear. It clung to me all through my boyhood and until my fifteenth or sixteenth year and was peculiarly acute about my twelfth and thirteenth years. The road through the woods at twilight, the barn, the wagon house, the cellar set my imagination on tiptoe. If I had to pass the burying ground up on the hill by the roadside in the dark, I did so very gingerly. I was too scared to run for fear the ghosts of all the dead buried there would be at my heels.

Probably I get my love for the contemplative life and for nature more through my mother than through my father; Mother had the self-consciousness of the Celt, Father not at all, though he had the Celtic temperament: red hair and freckles! The red-haired, freckled, harsh-voiced little man made a great deal of noise about the farm—shouting at the stock, sending the dog after the cows or after the pigs in the garden, or calling his orders to us in the field or shouting back his directions for the work after he had started for the Beaver Dam village. But his bark was always more to be feared than his bite. He would threaten loudly but punish mildly or not at all. But he improved the fields, he cleared the woods, he battled with the rocks and the stones, he paid his debts and he kept his faith. He was not a man of sentiment, though he was a man of feeling. He was easily moved to tears and had strong religious convictions and emotions. These emotions often found vent in his reading his hymn book aloud in a curious undulating sing-song tone. He knew nothing of what we call love of nature and he owed little or nothing to books after his schoolboy days. He usually took two weekly publications—an Albany or a New York newspaper and a religious paper called *The Signs of the Times*, the organ of the Old School Baptist Church, of which he was a member. He never asked me about my own books and I doubt that he ever looked into one of them. How far the current of my thoughts and interests ran from the current of his thoughts and interests! Literature he had never heard of, science and philosophy were an unknown world to him. Religion (hard predestinarianism), politics (democratic), and farming took up all his thoughts and time. He had no desire to travel, he was not a hunter or fisherman, and the shows and vanities of the world disturbed him not. When I grew to crave schooling and books he was disturbed lest I become a Methodist minister—his special aversion. Religion on such easy and wholesale terms as that of his Methodist neighbours made his nostrils dilate with contempt. But literature was an enemy he had never heard of. A writer of books had no place in his category of human occupations; and as for a poet, he would probably have ranked him with the dancing master. Yet late in life, when he saw my picture in a magazine, he is said to have shed tears. Poor Father, his heart was tender, but concerning so much that fills and moves the world, his mind was dark. He was a good farmer, a helpful neighbour, a devoted parent and husband, and he did well the work in the world which fell to his lot to do. The narrowness and bigotry of his class and church and time were his, but probity of character, ready good will, and a fervent religious nature were his also. His heart was much softer than his creed. He might scoff at his neighbour's religion or politics, but he was ever ready to lend him a hand.

The earliest memory I can recall of him dates back to a spring day in my early childhood. The "hired girl" had thrown my straw hat off the stonework into the road. In my grief and helplessness to punish her as I thought she merited, I looked up to the side hill above the house and saw Father striding across the ploughed ground with a bag strung across his breast from which he was sowing grain. His measured strides, the white bag, and his regular swinging arm made a picture on the background of the red soil, all heightened no doubt by my excited state of mind, that stamped itself indelibly upon my memory. He strode across those hills with that bag suspended around his neck, sowing grain, for many years.

Another spring picture of him much later in life, when I was a man grown and home on a visit, comes to mind. I see him following a team of horses hitched to a harrow across a ploughed field, dragging in the oats. To and fro he goes all afternoon, the dust streaming behind him and the ground smoothing as his work progressed. I suppose I had a feeling that I should have taken his place. He always got his crops in in season and gathered in season. His farm was his kingdom and he wanted no other. I can see him going about it, calling the dog, "hollering" at the cattle or the sheep or at the men at work in the fields, making a great deal of unnecessary noise, but always with an eye to his crops and to the best interests of the farm. He was a home body, had no desire to travel, little curiosity about other lands, except, maybe, Bible lands, and felt an honest contempt for city ways and city people. He was as unaffected as a child and would ask a man his politics or a woman her age as soon as ask them the time of day. He had little delicacy of feeling on the conventional side but great tenderness of emotion on the purely human side. His candour was at times appalling, and he often brought a look of shame into Mother's face. He had received a fairly good schooling for those times and had been a school teacher himself in the winter months. Mother was one of his pupils when he taught in Red Kill. I passed the little school house recently and wondered if there was a counterpart of Amy Kelly among the few girls I saw standing about the door, or if there was a red-haired, freckled, country greenhorn at the teacher's desk inside. Father was but once in New York, sometime in the '20's, and never saw the capitol of his country or his state. And I am sure he never sat on a jury or had a lawsuit in my time. He took an interest in politics and was always a Democrat, and during the Civil War, I fear, a "copperhead." His religion saw no evil in slavery. I remember seeing him in some political procession during the Harrison Campaign of 1840. He was with a gang of men standing up in a wagon from the midst of which rose a pole with a coon skin or a stuffed coon upon it. I suppose what I saw was part of a Harrison political procession.

Father "experienced religion" in his early manhood and became a member of the Old School Baptist Church. To become members of that church it was not enough that you wanted to lead a better life and serve God faithfully; you must have had a certain religious experience, have gone through a crisis as Paul did, been convicted of sin in some striking manner, and have descended into the depths of humiliation and despair, and then, when all seemed lost, have heard the voice of forgiveness and acceptance and felt indeed that you were now a child of God. This crucial experience the candidate for church membership was called on to relate before the elders of the church, and if the story rang true, he or she was in due time enrolled in the company of the elect few. No doubt about its being a real experience with most of those people—a storm-and-stress period that lasted for weeks or months before the joy of peace and forgiveness came to their souls. I have heard some of those experiences and have read the record of many more in *The Signs of the Times*, which Father took for more than fifty years. The conversion was radical and lasting, these men led changed lives ever after. With them once a child of God, always a child of God, reformation never miscarried. It was an iron-clad faith and it stood the wear and tear of life well. Father was not ostentatiously religious. Far from it. I have known him to draw in hay on Sunday when a shower threatened, and once I saw him carry a gun when the pigeons were about; but he came back gameless with a guilty look when he saw me, and I think he never wavered in his Old School Baptist faith. There were no religious observances in the family and no religious instruction. Father read his hymn book and his Bible and at times his *Signs*, but never compelled us to read them. His church did not believe in Sunday schools or in any sort of religious training. Their preachers never prepared their sermons but spoke the words that the Spirit put into their mouths. As they were mostly unlettered men the Spirit had many sins of rhetoric and logic to answer for. Their discourses did more credit to their hearts than to their heads. I recall some of their preachers, or Elders, as they were called, very distinctly—Elder Jim Mead, Elder Morrison, Elder

## MY BOYHOOD

Hewett, Elder Fuller, Elder Hubble—all farmers and unlearned in the lore of this world, but earnest men and some of them strong, picturesque characters. Elder Jim Mead usually went barefooted during the summer, and Mother once told me that he often preached barefooted in the school house. Elder Hewett was their strong man during my youth—a narrow and darkened mind tried by the wisdom of the schools, but a man of native force of character and often in his preaching attaining to a strain of true and lofty eloquence. His discourses, if their jumble of Scriptural texts may be called such, were never a call to sinners to repent and be saved—God would attend to that Himself—but a vehement justification from the Scriptures of the Old School Baptist creed, or the doctrine of election and justification by faith, not by works. The Methodists or Arminians, as he called them, were a thorn in his side and he never tired of hurling his Pauline texts at their cheap and easy terms of salvation. Could he have been convinced that he must share Heaven with the Arminians, I believe he would have preferred to take his chance in the other place. Religious intolerance is an ugly thing, but its days in this world are numbered, and the day of the Old School Baptist Society seems numbered. Their church, which was often crowded in my youth, is almost deserted now. This generation is too light and frivolous for such a heroic creed: the sons of the old members are not men enough to stand up under the moral weight of Calvinism and predestination. Absurd as the doctrine seems to us, it went with or begot something in those men and women of an earlier time—a moral fibre and depth of character—to which the later generations are strangers. Of course those men were nearer the stump than we are and had more of the pioneer virtues and hardiness than we have, and struggles and victory or defeat were more a part of their lives than they are of ours, a hard creed with heroic terms of salvation fitted their moods better than it fits ours.

My youthful faith in a jealous and vengeful God, which in some way had been instilled into my mind, was rudely shaken one summer day during a thunderstorm. The idea had somehow got into my head that if in any way we mocked the powers up above or became disrespectful toward them, vengeance would follow, quick and sure. At a loud peal overhead the boy I was playing with deliberately stuck up his scornful lips at the clouds and in other ways expressed his defiance. I fairly cringed in my tracks; I expected to see my companion smitten with a thunderbolt at my side. That I recall the incident so vividly shows what a deep impression it made upon me. But I have long ceased to think that the Ruler of the storms sees or cares whether we make faces at the clouds or not—do your work well and make all the wry faces you please.

## MY BOYHOOD

My native mountain, out of whose loins I sprang, is called the Old Clump. It sits there with bare head but mantled sides, looking southward and holding the home farm of three hundred and fifty acres in its lap. The farm with its checkered fields lies there like a huge apron, reaching up over the smooth sloping thighs on the west and on the east and coming well up on the breast, forming the big rough mountain fields where the sheep and young cattle graze. Those mountain pastures rarely knew the plough, but the broad side-hill fields, four of them, that cover the inside of the western thigh, have been alternately ploughed and grazed since my boyhood and before. They yield good crops of rye, oats, buckwheat, and potatoes, and fair summer grazing. In winter huge snow banks lie there just below the summit of the hill, blotting out the stone fences beneath eight or ten feet of snow. I have known these banks to linger there until the middle of May. I remember carrying a jug of water one hot May day to my brother Curtis who was ploughing the upper and steepest side hill, and whose plough had nearly reached the edge of the huge snow bank. Sometimes the woodchucks feel the call of spring in their dens in the ground beneath them and dig their way out through the coarse, granulated snow, leaving muddy tracks where they go. I have "carried together" both oats and rye in all these fields. One September, during the first year of the Civil War, 1862, we were working in the oats there and Hiram was talking hourly of enlisting in the army as a drummer boy. When the cattle are grazing there, one may often see them from the road over the eastern leg of Old Clump which is lower, silhouetted against the evening sky. The bleating of the sheep in the still summer twilight on the bosom of Old Clump is also a sweet memory. So is the evening song of the vesper sparrow, which one may hear all summer long floating out from these sweet pastoral solitudes. From one of these side-hill fields, Father and his hired man, Rube Dart, were once drawing oats on a sled when the load capsized while Rube had his fork in it on the upper side trying to hold it down, and the fork with Rube clinging to it described a complete circle in the air, Rube landing on his feet below, none the worse for his adventure.

Grandfather's farm, which he and Grandmother carved out of the wilderness in the last years of 1700 and where Father was born in 1802, lies just over the hill on the western knee of Old Clump, and is in the watershed of West Settlement, a much broader and deeper valley of nearly a dozen farms, and to which my home valley is a tributary. The sugar bush lies near the groin of the old mountain, the "beech woods" over the eastern knee, and the Rundle Place, where now is Woodchuck Lodge, is on his skirts that look eastward. Hence, most of the home farm stands apart in a valley by itself.

## MY BOYHOOD

As you approach on the train from the south you may see Old Clump rising up in the north eight or ten miles away, presenting the appearance of a well-defined cone, with the upper portion of the farm showing, and hiding behind it the mountain system of which it is the southern end.

Old Clump figured a good deal in my boyhood life and scarcely less in my life since. The first deer's horn I ever saw we found there one Sunday under a jutting rock as we were on our way to the summit. My excursions to salt and count the sheep often took me there, and my boyhood thirst for the wild and adventurous took me there still oftener. Old Clump used to lift me up into the air three thousand feet and introduce me to his great brotherhood of mountains far and near, and make me acquainted with the full-chested exhilaration that awaits one on mountain tops. Graham, Double Top, Slide Mountain, Peek o' Moose, Table Mountain, Wittenburg, Cornell, and others are visible from the summit. There was as well something so gentle and sweet and primitive about its natural clearings and open glades, about the spring that bubbled up from under a tilted rock just below the summit, about the grassy terraces, its hidden ledges, its scattered, low-branching, moss-covered maples, the cloistered character of its clumps of small beeches, its domestic looking mountain ash, its orchard-like wild black cherries, its garden-like plots of huckleberries, raspberries, and strawberries, the patches of fragrant brakes like dense miniature forests through which one wades as through patches of green midsummer snow, its divine strains of the hermit thrush floating out of the wooded depths below you—all these things drew me as a boy and still draw me as an old man.

From where the road crosses the eastern knee of Old Clump to where it crosses the western knee is over half a mile. Well down in the valley between them the home buildings are situated, and below them the old and very productive meadows, only the upper borders of which have ever known the plough. The little brooklet that drains the valley used to abound in trout, but in sixty years it has dwindled to such an extent and has been so nearly obliterated by grazing cattle that there are no trout until you reach the hemlocks on the threshold of which my fishing excursions of boyhood used to end. The woods were too dark and mysterious for my inflamed imagination—inflamed, I suppose, by Grandfather's spook stories. In this little stream in the pasture I used to build ponds, the ruins of one of which are still visible. In this pond I learned to swim, but none of my brothers would venture in with me. I was the only one in the family who ever mastered the art of swimming and I mastered it by persistent paddling in this pond on Sundays and summer evenings and between my farm duties at other times. All my people were "landlubbers" of the most pronounced type and afraid to get above their knees in the water or to trust themselves to row-boats or other craft. Here again I was an odd one.

I used to make kites and crossbows and darts and puzzle people with the trick of the buncombe blocks. One summer I made a very large kite, larger than any I had ever seen, and attaching a string fully half a mile long sent it up with a meadow mouse tethered to the middle of the frame. I suppose I wanted to give this little creature of the dark and hidden ways of the meadow—so scared of its life from hawks, foxes, and cats, that it rarely shows itself out of its secret tunnels in the meadow bottoms or its retreats under the flat stones in the pastures—a taste of sky and sunshine and a glimpse of the big world in which it lived. He came down winking and blinking but he appeared none the worse for his trip skyward, and I let him go to relate his wonderful adventure to his fellows.

Once I made a miniature sawmill by the roadside on the overflow of water from the house spring that used to cause people passing by to stop and laugh. It had a dam, a flume, an overshot wheel ten inches in diameter, a carriage for the log (a green cucumber), a gate for the tin saw about six inches long, and a superstructure less than two feet high. The water reached the wheel through a piece of old pump log three or four feet long, capped with the body of an old tin dinner horn. Set at quite an angle, the water issued from the half-inch opening in the end of the horn with force enough to make the little wheel hum and send the saw through the cucumber at a rapid rate—only I had to shove the carriage along by hand. Brother Hiram helped me with the installation of this plant. It was my plaything for only one season.

I made a cross-gun that had a barrel (in the end of which you dropped the arrow) and a lock with a trigger, and that was really a spiteful, dangerous weapon. About my fifteenth year I had a real gun, a small, double-barrelled gun made by some ingenious blacksmith, I fancy. But it had fairly good shooting qualities—several times I brought down wild pigeons from the tree tops with it. Rabbits, gray squirrels, partridges, also fell before it. I bought it of a peddler for three dollars, paying on the instalment plan, with money made out of maple sugar.

On the wooded west side of Old Clump we used to hunt rabbits—really the northern hare, brown in summer and white in winter. Their runways made paths among the mountain-maple bushes just below the summit. On the eastern side was a more likely place for gray squirrels, coons, and partridges. Foxes were at home on all sides and Old Clump was a favorite ground of the fox hunters. One

## MY BOYHOOD

day of early Indian summer, as we were digging potatoes on the lower side hill, our attention was attracted by someone calling from the edge of the woods at the upper side of the sheep lot. My brothers rested on their hoe handles a moment and I brushed the soil from my hands and straightened up from my bent attitude of picking up the potatoes. We all listened and looked. Presently we made out the figure of a man up by the edge of the woods and soon decided from his excited voice and gestures that he was calling for help. Finally, we made out that someone was hurt and the oxen and sled were needed to bring him down. It turned out to be a neighbour, Gould Bouton, calling, and Elihu Meeker, his uncle, who was hurt. They were fox hunting and Elihu had fired at the fox from the top of a high rock near the top of Old Clump and in his excitement had in some way slipped from the rock and fallen on the stones fifteen or twenty feet below and sustained serious injury to his side and back. With all possible speed the oxen and sled were got up there and after long waiting they returned to the house with Elihu aboard, groaning and writhing on a heap of straw. The injury had caused him to bleed from his kidneys. In the meantime Doctor Newkirk had been sent for and I remember that I feared Elihu would die before he got there. What a relief I felt when I saw the doctor coming on horseback, in the good old style, running his horse at the top of his speed! "Now," I said, "Elihu will be saved." He had already lost a good deal of blood, but the first thing the doctor did was to take more from him. This was in times when bleeding was about the first thing a doctor did on all occasions. The idea seemed to be that you could sap the strength of the disease by that means without sapping the strength of the man. Well, the old hunter survived the double blood-letting; he was cured of his injury and cured of his fox-hunting fever also.

He was a faithful, hard-working man, a carpenter by trade. He built our "new barn" in 1844 and put a new roof on the old barn. Father got out the timber for the new barn in old Jonas More's hemlocks and hauled it to the sawmill. Lanson Davids worked with him. They had their dinner in the winter woods. One day they had a pork stew and Father said he had never eaten anything in his life that tasted so good. He and Mother were then in the flower of their days and Lanson Davids said to him on this occasion: "Chauncey, you are the biggest hog to eat I ever saw in my life." "I was hungry," said Father.

We had "raisings" in those days, when a new building was put up. The timbers were heavy, often hewn from trees in the woods, set up, pinned together in what were called "bents." In a farmer's barn there were usually four bents, tied together by the "plates" and cross beams. I remember well the early summer day when the new barn was raised. I can see Elihu guiding the corner post of the first bent and when the men were ready calling out: "All together now," "set her up," "heave'o heave, heave'o heave," till the bent was in position.

One June when he was shingling the old barn he engaged me to pick him some wild strawberries. When I came in the afternoon with my four-quart pail nearly full he came down off the roof and gave me a silver quarter, or two shillings, as then called, and I felt very rich.

It is an open country, like an unrolled map, simple in all its lines, with little variety in its scenery, devoid of sharp contrasts and sudden changes and hence lacking in the element of the picturesque which comes from these things. It is a part of the earth's surface that has never been subject to convulsion and upheaval. The stratified rock lies horizontally just as it was laid down in the bottom of the Devonian Seas millions of years ago. The mountains and the valleys are the result of vast ages of gentle erosion, and gentleness and repose are stamped upon every feature of the landscape. The hand of time and the slow but enormous pressure of the great continental ice sheet have rubbed down and smoothed off all sharp angles, giving to the mountains their long sweeping lines, to the hills their broad round backs, and to the valleys their deep, smooth, trough-like contours. The level strata crop out here and there, giving to the hills the effect of heavy eyebrows. But occasionally it is more than that: in the mountains it is often like a cavernous mouth into which one can retreat several yards, where the imaginative farm boy loves to prowl and linger like the half savage that he is and dream of Indians and the wild, adventurous life. There were a few such cavernous ledges in the woods on my father's farm where one could retreat from a sudden shower, but less than a mile away there were two lines of them, one on Pine Hill and one on Chase's Hill, where the foundations of the earth were laid open, presenting a broken and jagged rocky front from ten to thirty or forty feet high, gnawed full of little niches and pockets and cavernous recesses by the never-dulled tooth of geologic time and affording dens and retreats where Indians and wild beasts often took refuge. As a boy how I used to haunt these places, especially on Sunday when young wintergreen and black birch gave us an excuse to go to the woods. What an eternity of time was written in the faces of those rocks! What world-old forces had left their marks there!—in the lines, in the colors, in the huge dislocations and look of impending downfall of many of them, yet with a look of calm and unconquerable age that can be felt only in the presence of such survivals of the primæval. I want no better pastime now, far from my boyhood as I am, than to spend part of a summer or autumn day amid these rocks. One

## MY BOYHOOD

passes from the sunny fields, where the cattle are grazing or the plough is turning the red furrow, into these gray, time-sculptured, monumental ruins, where the foundations of the everlasting hills are crumbling, and yet where the silence and the repose are like that of sidereal space. How relative everything is! The hills and the mountains grow old and pass away in geologic time as invariably as the snow bank in spring, and yet in our little span of life they are the types of the permanent and unchanging.

The phœbe-bird loves to build its mossy nest in these shelving ledges, and once I found that one of our native mice, maybe the jumping mouse, had apparently taken a hint from her and built a nest of thistledown covered with moss on a little shelf three or four feet above the ground. Coons and woodchucks often have their dens in these ledges, and before the country was settled no doubt bears did also. In one place, under a huge ledge that projects twelve or fifteen feet, there is a spring to which cattle come from the near fields to drink. The old earth builders used material of very unequal hardness and durability when they built these hills, their contracts were not well supervised, and the result has been that the more rapid decay of the softer material has undermined the harder layers and led to their downfall. Every fifty or a hundred or two hundred feet in the Catskill formation the old contractors slipped in a layer of soft, slatey, red sandstone which introduces an element of weakness and that we everywhere see the effects of. One effect of this weakness has an element of beauty. I refer to the beautiful waterfalls that are sparsely scattered over this region, made possible, as nearly everywhere else, by the harder strata holding out after the softer ones beneath have eroded away, thus keeping the face of the falls nearly vertical.

The Catskill region is abundantly supplied with springs that yield the best water in the world. My father's farm had a spring in nearly every field, each one with a character of its own. What associations linger about each one of them! How eagerly we found our way to them in the hot haying and harvesting days!—the small, cold, never-changing spring in the barn-hill meadow under the beech tree, upon whose now decayed bowl half-obliterated initials of farm boys and hired men of thirty, fifty, and nearly seventy years ago may still be seen; the spring in the old meadow near the barn where the cattle used to drink in winter and where, with the haymakers, I used to drink so eagerly in summer; the copious spring in the bank at the foot of the old orchard which, in the severe drouths of recent years, holds out when other springs fail; the tiny but perennial spring issuing from under the huge tilted rock in the sumac field where the young cattle and the sheep of the mountain pasture drink and where we have all refreshed ourselves so many times; the spring from under a rocky eyebrow on the big side hill which is now piped to the house and which in my boyhood was brought in pine or hemlock "pump logs," and to which I have been sent so many times to clean the leaves off the tin strainer—what associations have we all of us with that spring! For over eighty years it has supplied the family with water, and not till the severe drouths of later years did it fail.

The old beech tree that stands above it is one of the landmarks of the farm. Once when a boy I saw a flock of wild pigeons disappear in its leafy interior, and then saw Abe Meeker, who worked for Father in 1840, shoot into it from the stone wall, six or seven rods below, and bring down four birds which he could not see when he fired. Three of them fell dead and one fell at his feet behind the stone wall. But I need not call the roll of all the fountains of my youth on the home farm—fountains of youth indeed! and fountain of grateful memories in my later years. I never pass any of them now but my footsteps linger by them and I clean them out if they are clogged and neglected and feel that here is a friend of other days whose face is as bright and youthful as ever.

www.ingramcontent.com/pod-product-compliance
Lightning Source LLC
Chambersburg PA
CBHW021855230426
43671CB00006B/395